DELEUZE'S
DIFFERENCE AND REPETITION

Continuum *Reader's Guides*

Continuum's *Reader's Guides* are clear, concise and accessible introductions to classic works of philosophy. Each book explores the major themes, historical and philosophical context and key passages of a major philosophical text, guiding the reader towards a thorough understanding of often demanding material. Ideal for undergraduate students, the guides provide an essential resource for anyone who needs to get to grips with a philosophical text.

Reader's Guides available from Continuum

Aristotle's Nicomachean Ethics – Christopher Warne
Berkeley's Three Dialogues – Aaron Garrett
Deleuze and Guattari's Capitalism and Schizophrenia – Ian Buchanan
Deleuze's Difference and Repetition – Joe Hughes
Descartes' Meditations – Richard Francks
Hegel's Philosophy of Right – David Rose
Heidegger's Being and Time – William Blattner
Hobbes's Leviathan – Laurie M. Johnson Bagby
Hume's Dialogues Concerning Natural Religion – Andrew Pyle
Hume's Enquiry Concerning Human Understanding – Alan Bailey
    and Dan O'Brien
Kant's Critique of Pure Reason – James Luchte
Kant's Groundwork for the Metaphysics of Morals – Paul Guyer
Kuhn's The Structure of Scientific Revolutions – John Preston
Locke's Essay Concerning Human Understanding – William Uzgalis
Locke's Second Treatise of Government – Paul Kelly
Mill's On Liberty – Geoffrey Scarre
Mill's Utilitarianism – Henry West
Nietzsche's On the Genealogy of Morals – Daniel Conway
Plato's Republic – Luke Purshouse
Rousseau's The Social Contract – Christopher Wraight
Spinoza's Ethics – Thomas J. Cook
Wittgenstein's Tractatus Logico Philosophicus – Roger M. White

DELEUZE'S
DIFFERENCE AND REPETTION

A Reader's Guide

JOE HUGHES

continuum

Continuum International Publishing Group
The Tower Building   80 Maiden Lane
11 York Road   Suite 704
London SE1 7NX   New York NY 10038

www.continuumbooks.com

British Library Cataloguing-in-Publication Data
A catalogue record for this book is available from the British Library.

ISBN: HB: 0-8264-2112-1
        978-0-8264-2112-8
    PB: 0-8264-2696-4
        978-0-8264-2696-3

Library of Congress Cataloging-in-Publication Data
Hughes, Joe.
Deleuze's "Difference and repetition" : a reader's guide / Joe Hughes.
p. cm.
Includes bibliographical references (p.) and index.
ISBN 978-0-8264-2112-8 – ISBN 978-0-8264-2696-3
1. Deleuze, Gilles, 1925–1995. Différence et répétition. I. Title.
B2430.D453D456 2009
194–dc22
2008031156

Typeset by Newgen Imaging Systems Pvt Ltd, Chennai, India
Printed and bound in Great Britain by Cromwell Press Ltd,
Trowbridge, Wiltshire

For Mom, Dad and Sarah.

Temporality, finitude – that is what it is all about.
Fear and Trembling, p. 49

CONTENTS

CONTENTS

ACKNOWLEDGEMENTS

This book is the product of several years work on Deleuze, and it owes so much to so many people that it would be impossible to mention them all here. Without the support of Ian Buchanan and Claire Colebrook in particular this book would have never reached the point that it did. I would also like to thank my family, and above all, Sarah Tukua.

NOTE ON THE CITATIONS

I cite three editions of *Difference and Repetition*, each of which has different page numbers: the 1994 Columbia University Press edition; PUF's 2003 French edition; and the 2004 Continuum Impacts edition. The order in which these texts are referenced is as follows:

(Columbia/PUF/Continuum)

I also occasionally reference the French edition of other texts. In these cases the first page number refers to the English translation, the second to the French: (English/French).

ABBREVIATIONS

WORKS BY DELEUZE

AO	*Anti-Oedipus*
BG	*Bergsonism*
C1	*Cinema 1*
C2	*Cinema 2*
DI	*Desert Islands*
EC	*Essays Critical and Clinical*
EP	*Expressionism in Philosophy*
ES	*Empiricism & Subjectivity*
KP	*Kant's Critical Philosophy*
LS	*The Logic of Sense*
NP	*Nietzsche and Philosophy*
PI	*Pure Immanence*
PS	*Proust and Signs*
TF	*The Fold*

WORKS BY OTHER AUTHORS

APS	Husserl, *Passive and Active Synthesis*
CPR	Kant, *Critique of Pure Reason*
CTM	Husserl, *Cartesian Meditations*
E&J	Husserl, *Experience and Judgment*
KPM	Heidegger, *Kant and the Problem of Metaphysics*
LE	Hyppolite, *Logic and Existence*
MM	Bergson, *Matter and Memory*
PP	Merleau-Ponty, *Phenomenology of Perception*

CHAPTER 1

CONTEXT: KANT MEETS HUSSERL

REPRESENTATION: QUALITY AND EXTENSITY

The first section of the conclusion to *Difference and Repetition* is titled '*Critique of Representation*'. It's a good way to start a conclusion because this short phrase contains within it the entire book. If all you were able to draw from a first reading of *Difference and Repetition* was that it was a 'critique of representation' you would have already understood everything, provided that you knew two things: what the word 'representation' meant and what the word 'critique' meant. This is the hard part. Deleuze is a philosopher who never uses a word without transforming and often reinventing its sense.

The word 'representation' has countless meanings in *Difference and Repetition*. Sometimes representation will be equated with the 'form of identity', sometimes with the form of the 'concept'. Sometimes it will be divided up into to a 'fourfold root'. Deleuze will equate representation with 'knowledge', the 'proposition', the solution to a problem, consciousness, opinion and judgement. The list is quite long, but all of these instances refer back to one thing: the object = representation

What does Deleuze mean by the object? This question structured 'The Method of Dramatization', a 1968 talk which shares much of its content with the last two chapters of *Difference and Repetition*. Deleuze begins by asking 'what is a thing?'

> First I want to ask: what is the characteristic or distinctive trait of a thing in general? Such a trait is twofold: the quality or qualities which it possesses, the extension which it occupies. [. . .] In a word, each thing is at the intersection of a twofold synthesis: a synthesis of qualification or specification, and of partition, composition, or organization.[1]

The object has two dimensions: it possesses a quality and it fills out a spatial extension. What is more, Deleuze is clear throughout his talk that by 'thing in general' he means the thing as it is represented.[2] Deleuze is a philosopher who continually reinvents the tradition, but he is remarkably, almost uncomfortably, traditional here. These are the two dimensions objects have been said to have since at least Aristotle. Every object is composed of primary qualities – spatial form – and every object possesses secondary, more transient, qualities such as colour.

Deleuze will stick to this definition of the object in *Difference and Repetition*. Here he speaks of a 'perceptual world' populated by 'developed qualities and extensities' (281/360/351), and he will say that the 'elements of representation' are none other than 'quality and extensity' (235/303/295). The object in general is a representation at the intersection of quality and extensity, and, conversely, 'representation' is made up of these two 'elements': quality and extensity. These two elements of representation are at the foundation of all of the other forms of representation Deleuze uses in the book. They make up the base form of 'identity'. The object is what will be subsumed in the 'concept'. It is what consciousness 'knows'. It is the object-about-which a judgement is passed.

What about the word 'critique'? To characterize *Difference and Repetition* as a critique of representation is not at all to say that it is a collection of barely comprehensible sentences which generally assert an ambiguous disapproval of representation accompanied by an even more ambiguous valorization of something a little more 'rhizomatic' like 'becoming' or 'difference'. Rather, Deleuze has a very specific understanding of the word critique that he had developed as early as *Nietzsche and Philosophy* (1962). Deleuze says that a critique must be both 'total' and 'positive'. It must be total in the sense that 'nothing can escape it'. It is positive in the sense that while it restricts or undermines one thing, it also reveals or releases another.[3] As a critique of representation *Difference and Repetition* will do both of these things. Representation will be submitted to a critique, and this critique will simultaneously reveal another non-representative dimension of thought (a 'latent subject' that repeats difference). This is not yet Deleuze's full notion of critique however.

In order to complete the notion of critique, or in order for a critique to become a 'radical critique', it also has to show – as Nietzsche did in the *Genealogy of Morals* (or even Hegel in *"radical" critique must also show:*

the *Phenomenology of Spirit*) – the genesis of what has been criticized.[4] Deleuze continually emphasizes this point. A truly radical critique is not one that leaves the hollowed out remains of the object of critique lying in the past. A radical critique demonstrates the genesis of that which it has criticized. It shows how that object came to be so convincing that it managed to supplant the new element that critique unveils. Critique 'is radical and well grounded only when it carries out a genesis of [the dimension revealed by critique] and, *simultaneously*, the genesis of [the dimension undermined by critique]' (206/266/257; original emphasis). As a critique of representation then, *Difference and Repetition* will do three things: (1) it will go beyond representation; (2) it will discover a new positive element (a 'latent subject' which repeats difference); and (3) it will show how *both* difference and representation are produced. At the same time that *Difference and Repetition* rejoices in the annihilation of representation, it is also by necessity a detailed account of its genesis.

KANT'S TWO CRITIQUES

The theme of critique alludes to one of the most important philosophical contexts of *Difference and Repetition*: Kant's critical philosophy. In *Nietzsche and Philosophy* Deleuze somewhat infamously concluded that the formal structure of the *Genealogy of Morals* suggested that Nietzsche 'wanted to rewrite the *Critique of Pure Reason*'.[5] While this may be a stretch for the *Genealogy of Morals* it is certainly true of *Difference and Repetition*. The entire formal structure of *Difference and Repetition* is modelled after the *Critique of Pure Reason*, but only as it is seen from the point of view of the *Critique of Judgment*.

One thing that particularly fascinated Deleuze about Kant was that fact that after writing the first two Critiques which would have already established Kant's reputation as one of the most influential and important philosophers in the history of Western thought, Kant rethought everything in his mid-sixties. According to Deleuze, what caused Kant to rethink his system was the 'standpoint of genesis'. The first two Critiques are built up around 'ready-made' faculties. Kant takes a fact, given in experience, and asks what its conditions are. He finds these conditions in faculties whose existence he takes for granted.[6] In the third Critique, everything changes.

The first two Critiques indeed invoke facts, seek out the conditions for these facts, and find them in ready-made faculties. It follows that the first two critiques point to a genesis which they are incapable of securing on their own. But in the aesthetic *Critique of Judgment*, Kant poses the problem of the genesis of the faculties in their original free agreement. Thus he uncovers the ultimate ground still lacking in the other two Critiques. Kant's Critique in general ceases to be a simple *conditioning* to become a transcendental Education, a transcendental Culture, a transcendental Genesis.[7]

The *Critique of Judgment* grounds the other two Critiques by securing their foundation in a transcendental genesis. The faculties are no longer derived by regressing from facts, nor are they treated as ready-made, but are shown to be produced in a genesis.

Deleuze's final lecture on Kant is developed around a conceptual experiment which follows from this reading of the relation between the two Critiques. In this lecture Deleuze wonders what would happen if we rethought the first Critique from the point of view of the third. What happens to the conceptual structure of *The Critique of Pure Reason* if we submit it to the point of view of genesis?

[I]f we don't stay with the *Critique of Pure Reason*, if we go on to one of Kant's last works, where Kant goes deeper and deeper, which is to say if we effect a confrontation with the ultimate work, the *Critique of Judgment*, and if we see its effect on the *Critique of Pure Reason*, we realize that Kant reveals to us in the *Critique of Judgment* an amazing double adventure.[8]

The *Critique of Judgment*, is the story of an 'amazing double adventure'. This double adventure pertains two movements in the *Critique of Pure Reason*: synthesis and schematism. Synthesis is the process by which the mind moves from sensibility up to the understanding; 'the schematism of the understanding' is the reverse movement, from understanding back to sensibility. When Deleuze effects a confrontation between Kant's two works, these two movements undergo two closely related revisions. In the first adventure Deleuze will say that synthesis and the schematism are put in contact with the sublime. They confront their limits, but also their origins. In the second adventure, synthesis and schematism no longer oscillate between two static and ready-made faculties – sensibility and the understanding. Now they are arranged in a genetic line along which each synthesis confronts a limit which awakens it and which causes it in turn to pass on a violence which awakens the next faculty. There is no sensibility and there is no understanding at the start. There is only a transcendental genesis which travels along a line of 'broken' faculties creating each faculty as it goes.

Deleuze only glosses this double adventure in his final lecture, but *Difference and Repetition* will take this theme as its structural model *Difference and Repetition* rewrites the *Critique of Pure Reason* from the point of view of genesis. I will try to clarify each of these points in the order that they appear below,[9] but one thing this means is that it almost impossible to grasp *Difference and Repetition* without a basic understanding of Kant, and in particular of Deleuze's interpretation of Kant. Thankfully his lectures on Kant are readily available online and are not only eminently readable but themselves constitute one the best general introductions to *Difference and Repetition*.

GENETIC PHENOMENOLOGY

Deleuze structures *Difference and Repetition* along the lines of the general framework of the *Critique of Pure Reason*, but he wasn't writing at the turn of the eighteenth century. *Difference and Repetition* gathers together and systematizes many of Deleuze's earlier works, and it belongs largely to the intellectual atmosphere of early- to mid-twentieth-century France. This period of French thought is extremely complicated, bringing what would seem to be deeply opposed discourses into an amorphous and ever shifting field of exchange. It often mixed a profound knowledge of the history of philosophy with psychoanalysis, Husserl with Heidegger (and this sometimes from the point of view of Bergson), and everything happened under the shadow of Hegel and in relation to a fiery politics inspired largely by re-readings of Marx.

Most of these themes play a dominant role at some point or another in *Difference and Repetition*. But what is so interesting about the text is the degree to which it draws from Husserl and occasionally identifies itself with Husserl's late work. The theme of genesis, which is central to *Difference and Repetition*, is by no means specific to Husserl. Deleuze himself often points out that it dominates the thought of the post-Kantians, and in particular Solomon Maïmon and J. G. Fichte (with Hegel always looming in the background as he so often does in Deleuze's work). *Difference and Repetition* differs from these post-Kantian projects in that what is produced is not absolute knowledge or self-knowing, but the object. This was very much the concern of the late Husserl.

Husserl is like Kant in that he never stopped rethinking things. There is no point in Husserl's writings at which he is not ultimately concerned with the foundation of logic, but towards the end of his life he increasingly brought this foundation deeper and deeper into the world. *Experience and Judgment* presents the clearest picture of this attempt. Husserl begins by stating that his theme is a 'genealogy of logic'. He wants to trace logic back to its foundations and watch it emerge from those foundations. He provides a brief analysis of the act of judgement, and then asks what it presupposes. Judgement is always a judgement about something. What is this 'about-which' or 'substrate' of judgement? Ultimately, judgement refers back to the object. '*Original substrates are* [. . .] *individuals, individual objects*, and every thinkable judgment ultimately refers to individual objects'.[10] Husserl does not stop here, however. He continues his genealogy. The object is given in a 'prepredicative experience' but we cannot simply assume the object as given. Where does this individual object come from? Husserl traces the origins of the object back to a series of kinesthetic, passive and temporal syntheses. These syntheses organize the data of sensation and actually produce the object which is then handed over to judgement. The project of a genealogy of logic ultimately ends with an account of the genesis of the object. Because of this emphasis on the original forming of the object in sensory data given over to bodily and temporal syntheses, Husserl's late work is often referred to as a 'transcendental aesthetic'. This project marked a definite shift in Husserl's thought. Husserl himself described his newer phenomenology as a 'genetic' phenomenology and characterized his earlier, more 'logistic phenomenology'[11] as 'static'. His readers in France, however, tended to characterize the turn towards the object as a turn to a new metaphysical position. It was a rejection of Husserl's earlier idealism and a shift towards empiricism and French existentialism. Paul Ricoeur in particular emphasizes this point.[12] In his 1957 essay 'Existential Phenomenology' Ricoeur writes:

> Yet, in becoming more and more existential the phenomenology of the late Husserl became more and more empirical, for the whole order of the understanding – predicative judgment, affirmation and negation, activity of synthesis and consecution – henceforth proceeds from 'passive synthesis' initiated on the very level of perception. Thereafter it is clear that this progression toward an ever more originary original destroys every claim of constituting the world 'in' consciousness or 'beginning from' consciousness. The idealistic tendency of transcendental phenomenology is thus compensated for by the progressive discovery that one does not constitute the originary but only all that one can derive from it.[13]

For Ricoeur – and Husserl would probably never admit this – the consciousness described in genetic phenomenology approaches an outside. In the regression back from the object to its origins, consciousness eventually reaches something that is not consciousness, and this takes away the pretension of consciousness to be the one sole source of the creation of the world. As Ricoeur puts it, from this point of view consciousness is defined by the way it is derived from the world. Genetic phenomenology is a turn towards empiricism and a rejection of Husserl's idealism. In an earlier essay Ricoeur had characterized this as the decisive act of genetic phenomenology. The 'decisive act' is 'the progressive abandonment, upon contact with new analyses, of the idealism of the *Cartesian Meditations*'.[14]

TRANSCENDENTAL EMPIRICISM

This turn towards the object and its original constitution implies rejection of a second type of idealism as well. In Husserl's static phenomenology, the famous 'phenomenological' or 'transcendental' reduction which asked us to turn our gaze inward without importing prejudices of natural perception was immediately followed by an 'eidetic' reduction. In *Ideas I*, which is the high-point of static phenomenology and the very beginning of the turn to a genetic phenomenology, Husserl outlined these two reductions. The transcendental reduction bracketed the natural attitude, and directed the phenomenologist's gaze to the contents of consciousness as contents of consciousness rather than as 'transcendent' things in the world. This reduction was called 'transcendental' for the simple reason that the consciousness it revealed was called transcendental insofar as it was the origin and source of the world. Thus you could say, as many did, that phenomenology begins with an experience of the transcendental. It is a 'transcendental empiricism'. But it wasn't enough for Husserl to simply turn his gaze inward. He wanted to discover the 'lawful regularity' of those experiences. Thus a second reduction, the eidetic reduction, was immediately instituted which discovered the '*eidos*' behind each representation. Notice the two reductions at work in this passage and in particular how the transcendental reduction slides seamlessly into the eidetic:

> I have a *particular* intuition of redness, or rather several such intuitions. I stick strictly to pure immanence; I am careful to perform the phenomenological reduction. I snip away any further significance of redness, any way in which it may be viewed as something transcendent [. . .]. And now I grasp in pure 'seeing' the meaning of the concept of redness *in general* [. . .]. No longer is it the particular as such which is referred to, nor this or that red thing, but redness in general [. . .]. (*Idea of Phenomenology* 44–5; my emphases)

Husserl first performs the transcendental or phenomenological reduction. This restricts his gaze to the contingent particulars of 'pure immanence' or transcendental consciousness. But he continues to snip away the various aspects of this particular red and, out of nowhere, comes the eidetic reduction which moves from the fact to the concept, from the particular red to the concept of redness in general. Husserl insists on the eidetic reduction in his early work because he wanted phenomenology to be a rigorous science. The transcendental reduction only opened up a pure immanence populated by chance encounters and contingencies. It offered no possibility of lawful regularity nor could it explain sense because, as Hegel pointed out, the fleeting singularities of sense-certainty are at best voices of the alienated concept, if not altogether meaningless.

Paul Ricoeur accompanied his 1950 translation of *Ideas I* with a long introduction and a running commentary.[15] Just after Husserl asserts the necessity of the eidetic reduction, Ricoeur makes this brief note: 'the possibility is excluded of a phenomenological reduction without eidetic reduction, that is, of *a transcendental empirical phenomenology*' (*A Key* 116; my emphasis). The eidetic reduction prevents phenomenology from becoming a transcendental empiricism. With the advent of genetic phenomenology and the attempt to trace the genealogy of the object all the way back to the moment of its original constitution, however, the eidetic reduction would seem to be superfluous. Such a phenomenology would then constitute a transcendental empiricism. Ricoeur will articulate this possibility more clearly in a 1954 essay on Husserl's *Cartesian Meditations*:

> I believe that the key difficulty of Husserlian thought is to be sought in this situation. It is not easy to situate the transcendental reduction, which suspends believing in the independence or the in-itself of the world, in relation to the eidetic reduction, which goes from fact to essence. The transcendental reduction entails the eidetic reduction, beginning from the point where consciousness is treated as the field for a seeing, for an intuited experiencing [of consciousness itself]. *If this entailment is not followed up [by the eidetic reduction], phenomenology, in effect, becomes only a transcendental empiricism.* (*An Analysis* 91; my emphasis)

If Ricoeur presents transcendental empiricism as a problem here, it is because Husserl will still claim as late as the

Cartesian Meditations that phenomenology is a transcendental idealism even though the early parts of that work clearly betray Husserl's recent excursion into empiricism. Does Husserl verge on an idealism, or does he go all the way down to an outside? In fact this very ambiguity colours much of the French reception of Husserl, and in particular the tendency to consider psychoanalysis as the ultimate destination of phenomenology.[16] Is phenomenology an idealism or an empiricism? From the point of view of a genetic phenomenology which goes all the way back to scattered sensations there is no doubt about it. Phenomenology is a transcendental empiricism.

Genetic

It is a transcendental empiricism from two points of view. The first is that it begins with an experience of transcendental or of constituting consciousness. The second is in the sense that as this experience penetrates to the deepest levels of consciousness it eventually reveals an outside of consciousness, what Bergson referred to as 'impersonal perception' or Sartre called an 'impersonal transcendental field'.[17] When Deleuze repeatedly describes his philosophy as a 'transcendental empiricism' in *Difference and Repetition*, he explicitly aligns himself with the general direction of Husserl's late thought. He will in no way take up Husserl's thought in any great detail – in part because it was not readily available – but we can outline some important similarities.

Difference and Repetition is a radical critique of representation. In the first moment of this critique it unveils a new dimension. Like the work of art, philosophy 'leaves the domain of representation in order to become 'experience', transcendental empiricism or science of the sensible' (56/79/68). We abandon representation in order to attain 'experience'. This is the first aspect of Husserl's transcendental empiricism, the move from the object back to a prepredicative experience. This empiricism, however, can still remain an idealism as long as it remains within consciousness. Deleuze thus continues, 'Empiricism truly becomes transcendental [. . .] only when we apprehend directly in the sensible that which can only be sensed' (57/79–80/68). This is the second, and more profound aspect of Husserl empiricism: the regression all the way back to the sensible, to the point at which consciousness reaches its outside and from which it is derived.

by participation

At this point we have reached the origin of Deleuze's system, and from here the second moment of critique – genesis – can begin. Consciousness apprehends directly in the sensible that which can only be sensed. Deleuze will say that this raises sens- [1] ibility to its transcendent exercise. It awakens the faculty, but since this faculty is born of the sublime it can do nothing but pass on the violence which awakened it to the imagination. The [2] imagination too will prove to be powerless, and it will pass the experience on to memory, and memory to thought. [3] [4]

In the third chapter of this book I will try to outline this process in as much detail as possible. From the point of view of the genesis of the faculties, we can see that Deleuze is clearly rewriting the *Critique of Pure Reason*, and that the Kant's 'transcendental idealism' has become a transcendental empiricism insofar as the ready-made faculties are subject to a genesis which has its origin in sensibility. But Deleuze is also telling the story of the genesis of the object. In Husserl the object was traced back to sensation and to the passive syntheses which organized sensation. Deleuze will do the same but within a different conceptual structure than Husserl's. The quality and extensity of the object will find their origin in the Idea, but this Idea will in turn find its origin in three passive syntheses – each synthesis being brought about by a particular faculty. Rewriting the Critique and tracing the genealogy of the object merge in Deleuze's critique of representation.

CHAPTER 2

OVERVIEW OF THEMES

REPRESENTING THE WORLD: THE OTHER-STRUCTURE

In the previous chapter I proposed a concrete definition of representation. By representation, Deleuze means the object considered from the point of view of its two distinctive traits: quality and extensity. This assemblage characterizes an individual object of perception. But only in books on philosophy do we ever confront an individual object, self-contained and independent of its surrounding world. Heidegger and Merleau-Ponty, among others, continually criticized philosophy for choosing such a bad example – the stand-alone object – to illustrate the intuitive or perceptual act. The individual object set off from the world is an abstraction. What is primary and immediate is an object embedded within a context which gives that object its sense, its importance, its relation to other objects, its inseparability from our actions and its potential uses, and so on. As Husserl put it, each object is surrounded by a 'halo' of potentialities (APS 42).

This results in what he called the 'essential contradiction' harboured by every perception. 'External perception is a constant pretension to accomplish something that, by its very nature, it is not in a position to accomplish' (APS 39). Every perception tends towards unity, towards a finished product, but at the same time, that unity is dissolved into a horizon of 'potentialities' or 'virtualities'.

> Proper to every appearing thing of each perceptual phase is a new empty horizon, a new system of determinable indeterminacy, a new system of progressing tendencies with corresponding possibilities of entering into determinately ordered systems of possible appearances [. . .]. (APS 43)

Every appearing thing is embedded within a 'system of determinable indeterminacy'. These determinable indeterminacies are called 'potentialities' or 'virtualities'. Here Husserl draws attention to the fact that these potentialities *structure* the field of transcendental experience or 'pure immanence'.

The halo of potentialities forms a 'determinately ordered system' through which we try to anticipate what will come next in the order of appearances. 'There is a constant process of anticipation, of preunderstanding' (APS 43).[1] In the *Cartesian Mediations* Husserl will say that *'every actuality involves its potentialities*, which are not empty possibilities, but rather possibilities intentionally predelineated in respect of content' (CTM 44; original emphasis). Because this system forms an open but determinate totality (an 'idea in the Kantian sense'), and because it structures the appearance of every object, Husserl will call it the 'idea of the world'.[2]

Husserl obviously was not the first to point out that every determinate perception is surrounded by a halo of potentialities. We see similar accounts in James or in Bergson's *Creative Evolution*.[3] One could even point all the way back to Leibniz whose *petites perceptions* swarm, imperceptibly, around any larger perception and provide its contextual backdrop.[4] If we single out Husserl then, it is because Deleuze directly takes up several important aspects of Husserl's description of this phenomenon when he develops his theory of the 'Other'.

Deleuze briefly introduces the idea of the 'Other' at the end of *Difference and Repetition* but the significance of this concept extends far beyond the number of lines devoted to it. What Deleuze says in these pages is highly derivative of an essay published a year earlier, 'Michel Tournier and the World Without Others' and to fully understand the concept it will be necessary to turn briefly to that essay.

In *Difference and Repetition* Deleuze says two things about the Other. The first sounds deeply Husserlian: 'In every psychic system there is a swarm of possibilities around a reality, but our possibles are always others' (260/334/323). In the Tournier essay he calls these 'possibles' by their Husserlian names: 'potentialities or virtualities' (LS 306). There he describes this first function of the Other as follows:

[A]round each object that I perceive or each idea that I think there is the organization of a marginal world, a mantel or background, where other objects and other ideas may come forth in accordance with laws of transition which regulate the passage from one to another. (LS 304)

Like Husserl's idea of the world, the Other-structure envelops any perceived object in a swarm of potentialities which allow the transition from one object to another. In fact Deleuze even calls this structure by its Husserlian name: 'the structure of the world' (LS 306). The 'Other' Deleuze is talking about is therefore not another ego. What is only a potentiality for me, the back side of a chair, for example, is an actuality for the other person standing behind the chair.[5] What is 'other' are the potentialities of the current reality that swarm around that reality.[6]

The second thing Deleuze says about the Other-structure in *Difference and Repetition* is that it is 'expressive'. 'The other cannot be separated from the expressivity which constitutes it' (260/334/323). Each perceived object is connected to the 'expressivity' which *constitutes* that object. How and by what means is the object constituted? What is this expressivity? That is the question which *Difference and Repetition* as a whole provides an answer to. Ultimately, Deleuze will say that the object is constituted by the Idea, and the Idea by the passive syntheses. This point of view brings to light a second sense of the word 'Other'. It refers back to lower strata of consciousness. From consciousness of the object we move back to the Idea, and from the Idea we move back to an evanescent materiality which is given to our sensibility. All three of these moments, matter, Idea and representation are part of one and the same subject.[7] Even if the Other-structure is what encloses 'individuating factors and pre-individual singularities within the limits of objects and subjects which are then offered to representation as perceivers or perceived', it still testifies to the persistence of these lower strata in representation (281–2/360/352).

Before turning to Deleuze's account of the genesis of the object, however, it is necessary to address his use of language throughout *Difference and Repetition*.

FREE INDIRECT DISCOURSE

Perhaps the most difficult aspect of *Difference and Repetition* is not the complexity of the thought, but the mode of expression.

It is extremely rare that Deleuze ever says anything directly, instead approaching everything through a detour. This is not specific to *Difference and Repetition*. His entire oeuvre, from *Empiricism and Subjectivity* to *Pure Immanence*, is composed in free indirect discourse. In fiction, free indirect discourse is a narrative technique which allows the thoughts of a character to emerge more directly. It gives the reader a sense of unmediated access to the consciousness of the character, and it is usually accomplished through a blurring of the first and third person. As Genette puts it, the character's speech becomes mixed with the narrator's speech.[8] Behold, for example, Stephen Dedalus as he picks his nose on the beach:

> He laid the dry snot picked from his nostril on the rock, carefully.
>
> For the rest, let look who will.
>
> Behind. Perhaps there is someone.
>
> His face turned over his shoulder, rere regardant. Moving through the air high spars of a threemaster, her sails brailed up on the crosstrees, homing, upstream, silently moving, a silent ship. (Joyce 50)

The first sentence is in the third person: 'He laid the dry snot . . .'. But the next three, without warning, enter into Stephen's thoughts. Joyce doesn't say in simple indirect discourse something like 'Stephen wondered whether anyone had seen him pick his nose, but at the very moment he told himself he didn't care, he sensed someone behind him and felt compelled to turn around and look.' Instead Joyce transitions from the third-person narration of the first sentence into the first person *freely* or without any indication. 'For the rest, let look who will. Behind. Perhaps there is someone'. Directly following this, again without any indication, we return to the third person. Joyce's narrator tells us that Stephen, retreating from his confident indifference, looks over his shoulder but sees only a passing ship. The words of the narrator and the thoughts of the character blur together, and it is often difficult to tell, especially in Joyce, where one leaves off and the other begins. In Deleuze's own words, 'The author takes a step towards his characters, but the characters take a step towards the author: double becoming' (C2 222).[9]

This narrative technique becomes particularly important in an author for whom the history of philosophy is a series of stories. Throughout his lectures Deleuze repeatedly says things like, 'Assume that I'm telling you a story'[10] or 'Let's approach this like a story'.[11] 'It matters little whether you've read [Spinoza] or not, for I'm telling a story'.[12] Everything is a story for Deleuze. There is the story of the eternal return, the story of the cogito, of the white wall differing only intensity, of time, of analytic truths, and so on. 'I will do the story of reflective judgment on request'[13] or 'I will try to clarify this story of faculties'.[14] Deleuze will say the same thing of his books. *The Logic of Sense* is a 'logical and psychological novel'. *Difference and Repetition* is a 'detective novel' mixing elements of 'science fiction'.[15] For a number of reasons then his books should be read as novels rather than as philosophical tomes. What is at issue in each is the narration of a story. In the case of *Difference and Repetition* the story is rather bland: it is the story of the genesis of representation. But the important point for now is simply that all of these stories are written in the mode of free indirect discourse.

When Deleuze uses free indirect discourse within the context of a philosophical work the relation stays same. There is still a double becoming or an indiscernible mixture of first and third person, but what counts as first and third person has changed. It is no longer a question of narrator and character. Deleuze's authorial voice now fills the role of narrator while the place of the character is usually filled by another author.[16] His earlier books on figures in the history of thought worked in this way. It is often impossible to tell in *Nietzsche and Philosophy*, for example, whether it is Deleuze or Nietzsche speaking, and it has become a frequent complaint that Deleuze critics rarely wonder who is speaking and simply quote Deleuze on Nietzsche as though it were straightforward Deleuze. Even when a reader as sensitive as Alain Badiou recognizes that everything is indirect, it still doesn't prevent him from constantly equating Deleuze's comments on Foucault to Deleuze's own thoughts on a subject. We could ask this question for all of Deleuze's works: where does Proust start and Deleuze end? What is Deleuzian and what is Bergsonian in *Bergsonism*? It is because he merges the speaking subject with the object of that speech so gracefully that we can never tell where Deleuze is Deleuze and not Hume, Proust or Nietzsche.

In the preface to the English edition of *Difference and Repetition* Deleuze says that there 'is a great difference between writing history of philosophy and writing philosophy' and he suggests that this is the first book in which he 'tried to "do philosophy"' and to speak 'in his own name'.[17] But it is hard to take him seriously for a simple reason (besides the fact that he says the opposite in the last paragraph of the original preface): Deleuze *still* doesn't speak in his own name. The whole of *Difference and Repetition* unfolds within the context of either elaborate metaphors or of interpretative paraphrases of other thinkers which indirectly develop and express what Deleuze would claim to say directly. Throughout *Difference and Repetition* Deleuze employs free indirect discourse in the same way that he did in his earlier works. His exposition of the three syntheses takes place entirely under the cover of Hume, Bergson, Nietzsche, Kant, Freud, Lacan Husserl and physics. Nowhere does he speak directly. When he speaks of Ideas, he does so by talking about mathematics and the dice throws of Nietzsche and Mallarmé. When he speaks of intensity, it is through the vocabulary of nineteenth-century energetics. What parts of his description of eternal return pertain to Nietzsche and what parts to Deleuze? When Deleuze speaks of Kant's rejection of the Cartesian cogito, is he speaking for himself, or Kant?

If *Difference and Repetition* is composed in free indirect discourse, we can already see that the worst thing we could do would be to read it literally, or to treat indirect statements as direct statements. Deleuze doesn't develop a philosophy of biology, of differential calculus, or of contemporary physics. His criticisms of Plato, Descartes and others are not arguments that would benefit greatly from being followed out and justified in a more direct prose. There is no doubt that it is essential to see the degree to which Deleuze engages with other philosophers either critically or apologetically (and in particular with Kant), but we have to keep in mind that ultimately Deleuze is telling a story, and these extended metaphors, minor engagements and short polemics are nothing but indices of a larger structure which is what really animates the book.

HISTORY AND LANGUAGE

Perhaps even more important than the fact that Deleuze makes use of free indirect discourse is the reason *why* he uses it.[18] This decision to write indirectly is one of the most important and fundamental aspects of Deleuze's thought, and it would require a much broader and more detailed presentation than I can provide here. Even so we can point to two reasons for why Deleuze makes use of free indirect discourse. The first concerns the question of historical influence raised by Heidegger. One refrain that occurs throughout Heidegger's work is the claim that history is not something that is exclusively past, but which still exerts an immense and unseen influence on us in the present: 'People still hold the view that what is handed down to us by tradition is what in reality lies behind us – while in fact it comes toward us because we are its captives and destined to it' (*What is Called Thinking* 76). We are the captives of history even as, and especially when, we think we have put it behind us.[19] This notion is behind Heidegger's famous concept of 'destruction' which he elaborated in *Being and Time*:

> Da-sein is not only entangled in the world [. . .]; at the same time Da-sein is also entangled in a tradition which it more or less explicitly grasps. This tradition deprives Da-sein of its own leadership in questioning and choosing. [. . .] The tradition that hereby gains dominance makes what it 'transmits' so little accessible that initially and for the most part it covers it over instead. What has been handed down it hands over to obviousness; it bars access to those original 'wellsprings' out of which the traditional categories and concepts were in part genuinely drawn. (*Being and Time* 18–19)

We are *entangled* in history, and we don't even know it because what we unconditionally accept has been handed down as 'obvious'. These comments have an obvious target: Husserl.

Husserl had claimed that by means of the phenomenological reduction, by means of a turn to transcendental experience itself, he was able to find a radically new beginning for philosophy. In a lecture course given just before the publication of *Being and Time* and containing roughly the first half of that work almost unaltered we see Heidegger taking issue with Husserl on just this point.

> [*E*]*ven phenomenological research stands under the constraints of an old tradition, especially when it comes to the most primordial determination of the theme most proper to it, intentionality.* Contrary to its most proper principle, therefore, phenomenology defines its most proper thematic matter not out of the matters themselves but instead out of a traditional prejudgment of it, albeit one that has become quite self-evident. [. . .] What shows itself in the neglect of the primary questions of being as such is rather the force and weight of the tradition to a degree which cannot be easily overestimated. (*History of the Concept of Time* 129; original emphasis)

The unseen 'force and weight of the tradition' has caused phenomenology to prejudge what is 'most proper' to it: the description of transcendental experience. Husserl doesn't attend to the matter itself, he makes a traditional prejudgement of it.

Heidegger is extending the breadth of the reduction. Whereas Husserl bracketed the natural attitude, Heidegger brackets history. He does so in two forms. First, he wants to avoid importing what he calls 'theoretical' presuppositions. These are presuppositions that, for example, tell us before we even look at consciousness what consciousness is: rationality, numerical unity across different spaces and times, and so forth.[20] But second, and more importantly for the French reception of Heidegger, is the question of philosophical language itself. Heidegger continually draws attention to the way in which a philosophical vocabulary brings with it theoretical presuppositions. We see both theory and language come under scrutiny in this passage:

> Before we summarize the significance of categorical intuition and secure its positive scope for ourselves, we should first correct certain misunderstandings which easily creep into the phenomenological concept of categorical intuition.

This happens all the more readily because this discovery is itself obtained in a traditional horizon of inquiry and interpreted with traditional concepts. (*History* 68)

Both the traditional theoretical horizon as well as the traditional philosophical *concepts* must be bracketed. Only after this double reduction has Heidegger secured to his satisfaction a legitimate access to the *experience* of Being.

This tendency for language to carry with it an entire set of historical and theoretical presuppositions is only one aspect of the need to invent a new philosophical discourse. Claire Colebrook emphasizes a second, more Nietzschean, reason: the very structure of language imposes itself on what we talk about. 'Our subject/predicate structures, or the very form of our logic, lead us to think of a being, substance or ground that *then* bears some predicate'.[21] Before the enquiry even begins, the subject is already determined as something that endures above and beyond its transitory predicates, and as Colebrook points out, one is therefore prevented in advance from affirming the original movement through which the subject itself is effected.[22]

All of these points come across quite clearly in an opposition between 'wakeful consciousness' and the 'corporealizing thought' of the body that Pierre Klossowski draws in *Nietzsche and the Vicious Circle*. Klossowski describes the body as a mobile field of 'intensities' and 'changing excitations'. For various reasons, our wakeful consciousness rarely experiences and lives the intensities of the body. One of these reasons is that consciousness is coextensive with language or what Klossowski calls the 'code of everyday signs'. Language has its own logic and its own set of relations, and it *imposes* its 'own linkages in order to conceal the total discontinuity of our [lived] state'.[23] This poses no problems until we want to study the lower depths of consciousness or 'affirm the *authenticity* of life in an intelligible manner'.[24] We then realize that it is impossible to speak of intensity and becoming precisely because '*we have no language to express what is in becoming*'.[25] Language imposes its own connections onto becoming. Every time we try to talk about it we turn it into a noun, or give it a meaning, or turn it into an intelligible thought. Everyday language 'never allows us to speak of our unintelligible depth except by ascribing to what is neither thought, nor said, nor willed a meaning and an aim that we *think* according to language'.[26] For this reason Maurice Blanchot speaks of the inherent 'falsity of all direct discourse'.[27]

Deleuze will make a point that is very similar to Klossowski's in his cinema books. The phenomenological reduction has to be extended to language. It is not enough to only guard against the tendencies of perception. Language itself turns becoming into bodies.

> Indeed *our perception* and *our language* distinguish bodies (nouns), qualities (adjectives) and actions (verbs). But actions, in precisely this sense, have already replaced movement with the idea of a provisional place towards which it is directed or that of a result that it secures. Quality has replaced movement with the idea of a state which persists whilst waiting for another to replace it. Body has replaced movement with the idea of a subject which would carry it out or of an object which would submit to it, of a vehicle which would carry it. We will see that such images *are* formed in the universe [. . .]. But they depend on new conditions and certainly cannot appear for the moment. *For the moment we only have movements, which are called images in order to distinguish them from everything else that have not yet become.* (C1 59–60; my emphases)

Deleuze's goal is to think matter, or movement,[28] independently of everything that it will later become: bodes, qualities and actions. In order to do so, we not only have to bracket natural perception in which every thing appears as an already constituted body, quality or action, but we have to bracket natural language as well. The very word 'action' carries with it the provisional place towards which action is directed. The very word 'quality' carries with it the idea of a place which will bear that quality. The word 'body' carries with it the place of a subject. Determinate bodies, qualities and actions will all be produced in the end thanks to the work of genesis (and *Cinema 1* and *Cinema 2* are the story of this genesis), but, in order to define the foundation of that genesis, and in order to grasp the movement of production, it is necessary to rigorously exclude any intimation of the destination of genesis whether that intimation comes from prejudices of natural perception or from the prejudices of natural language.

Deleuze will develop all of these points in *Difference and Repetition* in a short passage in which he opposes Nietzsche and Kierkegaard to Hegel. In all three thinkers, the goal was to grasp becoming, movement or genesis. Hegel however still grasps movement from the standpoint of language, of identities and oppositions, and this is in part because he remained content to simply represent movement rather than make us live it.

> Kierkegaard and Nietzsche are among those who bring to philosophy a new means of expression. Furthermore, in all their work, *movement* is at issue. Their objection to Hegel is that he does not go beyond false movement – in other words, the abstract logical movement of 'mediation'. They want to put metaphysics in motion, in action. They want to make it act, and make it carry out immediate acts. It is not enough, therefore, for them to propose a new representation of movement; representation is already mediation. Rather, it is a question of producing within the work a movement capable of affecting the mind outside of all representation; it is a question of making movement itself a work, without interposition; of substituting direct signs for mediate representations; of inventing vibrations, rotations, whirlings, gravitations, dances or leaps which directly touch the mind. (8/16/9; original emphasis)[29]

What is striking about this passage is that the objection to Hegel is not made on the level of concepts alone. It is addressed primarily to the way in which he chose to express those concepts (and of course the entire point of the passage is that the two are inseparable). Whereas Hegel *represents* becoming, Kierkegaard and Nietzsche bring to philosophy a new means of expression which produces becoming in the reader. In reading Nietzsche, one should experience the movement of thought. The writer no longer tries to represent the movement of thought, but to create that movement in the reader. Of course we have to be careful because Deleuze is talking about Kierkegaard and Nietzsche, and not himself, and Deleuze's own style will go beyond this particular stylistic device.

Two things, however, are clear. Direct discourse is discounted from the start. As soon as you *directly* represent thought in language, you have lost it. Deleuze therefore gives to philosophy an enormous aesthetic dimension. Logic is neither the object and concern of philosophy nor is it its inescapable *organaon*. Philosophy must make use of 'all the possibilities of language' – in other words, it must become literature – so that it can create movement.[30] If everything worked as planned Deleuze's reader would confront a meaningless and evanescent materiality (i.e. the text which few would deny is often quite meaningless) and by repeating it eventually extract a meaning and a determinate representation of the object. The reader would live the system and realize at the end of his or her work that that work was exactly what was being described the whole time. The second point, my spoiler warning, is simply that the idea of a reader's guide which attempts to bring the vibrations, rotations and whirlings of *Difference and Repetition* into the dubious clarity of everyday language is in fact a fundamental betrayal of Deleuze's aesthetic project, and that perhaps by avoiding this process of sense making we have already missed the entire point of the book.

CHAPTER 3

READING THE TEXT

Difference and Repetition is a detective novel. It tells the story of what some readers of Deleuze might consider a horrendous crime but which most people might find to be rather boring: the birth of representation. There are three general moments of the story: ① its beginning in an evanescent materiality and the repetition of that materiality in a 'latent subject', ② a middle point at which an 'aleatory point' gives rise to Ideas and ③ the conclusion, in which Ideas link up with intensities to create representations. Further, like a good detective novel, for the most part, everything is fragmented. The reader doesn't get the story in one direct communication, but pores over the series of events and imbues even the most trivial thing with a potential significance in search of an Idea or a sense which will pull everything together and make the whole work resonate. A reader's guide however is not a detective novel, and I have rearranged the order of the chapters so that the general story can appear in greater clarity.

Difference and Repetition consists of five chapters bookended by a substantial introduction and conclusion. The introduction, first chapter and conclusion are all chapters in which Deleuze rhapsodically and unpredictably jumps from one part of the story to another. It isn't until the third chapter that we finally get a clear picture of the entire system as it moves from matter to representation, but even there it is given only in a negative way and in the context of a methodology. Chapters two, four and five, are the three central chapters in which the main moments of the system are developed and elaborated in detail. I have therefore grouped them together and treated chapter three as a transitional moment between the introductory chapters and the more central chapters.

SECTION 1. THE INTRODUCTION: REPETITION AND DIFFERENCE

THE SECRET SUBJECT

The introduction, at a general level, has two functions. As one would expect, it introduces the main themes of the book. However, it does so in a highly allusive and suggestive manner which is tremendously difficult to follow. What makes it even more difficult is that nearly everything Deleuze says in the introduction refers to moments that will be developed later in the book within a larger conceptual structure. As in all of Deleuze's works, it is this structure which gives his concepts their sense. Consequently, the introduction might be the worst place to start reading *Difference and Repetition*. But even if there is no real development of themes, and even if the sense of Deleuze's concepts are unavailable because their systematic context is not yet present, at least one thing is clear: throughout the introduction, Deleuze is slowly and elaborately liberating the word 'repetition' so that he can put it to his own use later in the book. This is the second function of the introduction: to gradually zero in on a technical and original use of the word 'repetition'.

The introduction is organized around a distinction Deleuze draws between repetition and representation. 'Our problem concerns the essence of repetition. It is a question of knowing why repetition cannot be explained by the form of identity in concepts or representations; in what sense it demands a superior 'positive' principle' (19/31/22). Repetition cannot be explained by the form of representation, but demands its own superior principle. What does Deleuze mean by representation such that it might be erroneously taken to 'explain' repetition?

I have already suggested that for Deleuze representation has a specific meaning: it is the assemblage of quality and extensity in a given thing. Another word Deleuze uses for this assemblage is 'generality':

[E]xtensity and quality are the two forms of generality. However, precisely this is sufficient to make them the elements of representation. (235/303/295)

The words 'representation' and 'generality' both refer back to the object from the point of view of its quality and extensity. Thus the first sentence of the book restates the distinction Deleuze wishes to draw in the introduction: 'Repetition is not generality'. Repetition cannot be confused with representation. Fine. But why would we confuse the two in the first place? And is it not odd to describe a 'thing', a representation with a determinate quality and extension, as *general*? A thing would seem to be singular or at least particular.

Deleuze answers all of these questions at the beginning of the introduction: 'Generality presents two major orders: the qualitative order of resemblances and the quantitative order of equivalences' (1/7/1). The individual object is by no means general, but it can be equated with generality insofar it grounds resemblance and equivalence. As long as it has a quality, it can resemble another thing. As long as it has a measurable extensity, it can be equivalent to other things. What's more, these are the very laws of generality: 'resemblance is the law of quality, just as equality is that of extensity' (235/303/295). Only insofar as a thing has a quality can it resemble another thing. Only insofar as it has a quantity can it be equivalent to another thing.

It is from this point of view that we might confuse representation and repetition and erroneously mistake representation for an explanation of repetition. If the laws of representation are resemblance and equivalence, if quality always leads to resemblance and quantity to equivalence, it would seem that representation could indeed explain repetition. Repetition would no longer need a 'superior positive principle' because resemblance and equivalence, explain it perfectly well: what would repetition be if not a resemblance or an equivalence between two instances separated by time? In founding resemblance and equivalence, representation would seem to found repetition as well. In fact Deleuze will not deny that this kind of repetition can be explained from the point of view of generality. The problem is that generality itself needs to be explained. Generality is explained by a deeper form of repetition which does not correspond all that well with our ordinary use of the word 'repetition'.[1]

More important than the distinction between repetition and representation then, is the distinction Deleuze develops between *two types of repetition* which, by simplifying a lot, we could describe as a distinction between our ordinary use of the word and Deleuze's own use of it. Our ordinary use of the word describes a resemblance or an equivalence between two things separated by time. Deleuze's own conception on the other hand founds this everyday 'superficial' notion. While we can readily understand 'repetition' in the first sense, it is much more difficult to understand the sense of this second kind of repetition.

We can begin to understand by noting its founding or constitutive role. Deleuze will repeatedly return to this towards the end of the introduction:

> The two repetitions are not independent. One is the singular subject, the interiority and the heart of the other, the depths of the other. The other is only the external envelope, the abstract effect. (24/37/27)

One repetition is the depths of the other. One is a cause. The other is an effect which envelops its cause. One creates representation. The other is coextensive with repetition and generality. This already says a great deal about Deleuze's technical use of the word repetition. His use refers to a repetition which is *prior to* the represented world and which plays a founding and constitutive role in relation to that world. Deleuzian repetition takes place in the 'entrails of the earth' and gives rise to 'external repetition'. As he puts it, repetition allows us 'to *recapture the order of generality*' (25/38/28; my emphasis). It allows us to recapture representation. Put differently, *representation is produced through repetition. Repetition explains representation.*

In the quotation above, Deleuze described the repetition in depth as the 'singular subject' of the superficial repetition. One of the most important moments in this introduction is his insistence on this point: there is a subject of repetition which inhabits those sub-representative depths in which repetition unfolds. It belongs to this repetitious subject to 'recapture' or produce the order of representation:

> We are right to speak of repetition when we find ourselves confronted by identical elements with exactly the same

concept. However, we must distinguish between these discrete elements, these repeated objects, and a secret subject, the real subject of repetition, which repeats itself through them. Repetition must be understood in the pronominal; we must find the Self of repetition, the singularity within that which repeats. (23/36/26)

Two pages later he will make a very similar point:

> However, we wished to show [. . .] how the manifest repetition of identical elements necessarily refers back to a latent subject which repeats itself through (*à travers*) these elements, forming an 'other' repetition at the heart of the first. (25/37–8/28; translation modified)

In both of these passages we first read of a superficial or manifest repetition: the repetition of identical elements in the world of representation. We then read of a 'secret' or 'latent subject'. This subject is the 'subject of repetition'. It *constitutes* the world of representation by 'repeating'. But these two passages go further. What is particularly interesting about these statements is that they tell us this subject *repeats itself* in its product. In other words, if representation is constituted through a sub-representative repetition carried out by a latent subject, then presumably this subject develops itself as the world of representation comes into being. As representation is produced, the subject of repetition becomes the subject of representation. We should therefore temporarily distinguish between two moments of the subject. The 'secret subject' of repetition is a 'latent' subject. For the time being, let us call the developed form of this subjectivity which lives in the world of representation the 'manifest' or even 'empirical' subject. We will see below that these two terminal points of the subject constitute, respectively, a transcendental sensibility and an empirical sensibility.

CONDUCT AND LAW

It is only in the last half of the introduction that Deleuze develops the theme of a subject of repetition. In the first half, not only are both subjects – latent and manifest – already present, but we also learn some very important characteristics of both the world of representation as it is lived by the manifest subject and the sub-representative world of the latent subject. This discussion takes place under the pretence of distinguishing between repetition and generality. Deleuze does so from three points of view: conduct, law and concepts.

First Deleuze draws a distinction between repetition and representation 'from the point of view of conduct'. Who's conduct? Who else is there but the latent-manifest subject?[2] In relation to generality, the *manifest* subject, coexistent with representation, has one mode of conduct: it can 'exchange or substitute' representations (1/8/1). This exchange takes place according to the law of resemblance or equivalence depending on whether the represented thing is considered from the point of view of its quality or extensity.

In relation to 'singularity' the *latent* subject also has one mode of conduct: it repeats.

> By contrast [to exchange in the manifest subject], we can see that repetition is a necessary and justified conduct only in relation to that which cannot be replaced. Repetition as a conduct concerns non-exchangeable and non-substitutable singularities. (1/8/1)

This is by no means a balanced analogy, and the word 'singularity' seems to come out of nowhere. If repetition and generality are being opposed from the point of view of conduct, and if exchange is what we do in relation to generality, then we would expect to find out how the subject conducts itself in relation to repetition. It turns out however that repetition *is* the conduct. It is what the secret subject does when confronted with singularity. The real opposition is not between repetition and generality, but between particularity and singularity. When one is faced with particular representations (quality + quantity), one *exchanges* according to the laws of resemblance and equivalence. When one is faced with singularities, one repeats. What is there to do with a singularity, Deleuze asks, but to repeat it?

In chapter four, Deleuze will make use of a mathematical notion of singularities in which a singular point is said to extend across a series of ordinary points. In this sense, the word 'singular' means 'notable' or 'distinctive', and further it subsumes a series of other points. This not at all the sense in which the word is used in the passage above. There, the word 'singular' doesn't mean 'notable', nor does it refer to a point which gathers other points. Rather it means 'single' or absolutely individual. It refers to the immediate object of intuition without reference to any other object.

This is an important allusion to Hegel, and in particular to Jean Hyppolite's reading of Hegel, which is worth following out. The *Phenomenology of Spirit* begins with the knowledge of the immediate. According to Hegel, it is tempting to take our direct confrontation with the object as a model of certainty. What could I know better than the object right in front of me? But Hegel asks us to imagine what that confrontation would actually look like if we took it to its limit. Immediate presence means, ultimately, that we would have to imagine a solitary consciousness in direct confrontation with a solitary object. We do not compare the object to other objects because that would involve leaving the object, if only momentarily, for another. We would then no longer be in the immediate presence of the object strictly speaking. Nor can we depend on our other faculties to bring truth to the object, because again, we would no longer be in the presence of the object if we were remembering it or imagining it. 'Neither of these things [other objects or other I's] has anything to do with the truth of sense certainty'.[3] Rather, in sense-certainty a singular consciousness 'intends' its object in the object's singularity and revels in the wealth and richness of its immediate knowledge. 'The singular consciousness knows a pure "This", or the single item'.[4] Subject and object merge 'in an immediate relation as close as possible to unity'.[5]

However, as Jean Hyppolite puts it, for Hegel this is the 'worst of all banalities'. Under these conditions knowledge would be impossible. When 'we posit [the singularity of consciousness and its object], we see it dissolve immediately'. '[S]ensible singularity expresses itself truly through its own annihilation'. And with the annihilation of the singular object, 'the singular "I" also passes away'. '[D]eath is the beginning of the life of spirit'.[6] In order for there to be knowledge then, the *immediate* confrontation of consciousness with its object must already be *'mediated'*.

Hyppolite then emphasizes two points: mediation takes place through a complex dialectic, and, further, mediation or dialectic is a genuine genesis. He gives a remarkably lucid and detailed description of this process in his *Genesis and Structure* which I can only loosely summarize here. In general the genesis from sense certainty to the next moment of consciousness, 'perception', begins with the near unity of a singular consciousness contemplating its object. In the first moment of the dialectic, consciousness treats the object as essence. In the second moment, finding the object to lack essence, consciousness turns from the object to itself and considers itself as essence. Finally, in the third moment, the two points of view are sublimated in a unity of subject and object. This unity is no longer the simple unity of a singular consciousness intending its immediate object. It now contains and expresses the various moments of mediation (and in particular, the various relations between singular and universal which were played out in each moment). This new unity contains its history within itself, and thus expresses the progressive development of the object and consciousness. The object is now called the 'thing' and the subject has become a 'thinking subject', both of which will be further developed in the dialectic of perception.

This context is important for at least two reasons. First, we learn that for Deleuze the secret subject contemplates a singularity. If we read 'singularity' in this Hegelian sense, there is a strong suggestion (which will be confirmed later) that repetition is the behaviour of our sensibility in relation to its immediate contemplation of the object. Repetition is the subject's conduct in relation to the immediate object of intuition. The latent subject, our sensibility, repeats a singularity, the immediate object. This interpretation will be consistently borne out by other moments in Deleuze's text in later chapters. Second, there is contained within this brief allusion a veiled critique of Hegel that will become more developed in later sections of the introduction. In the confrontation with singularity, Deleuzian consciousness repeats. Hegelian consciousness mediates. Repetition replaces mediation, and with it the entire model of genesis which proceeds by opposition.

The second point of view from which generality and repetition are opposed is that of 'law'. This opposition also unfolds along the lines of the two subjects, latent and manifest. Both natural and moral law legislate at the level of representation. Law exercises its constraint over *phenomena* from the point of view of their quality and their quantity: 'law determines only the resemblance of the subjects ruled by it, along with their equivalence to terms which it designates' (2/8/2). Law therefore legislates over the manifest subject and the objects it represents to itself. As we already know, however, repetition takes place below this level in a latent subject. It is not therefore subject to the rule of law, but produces the domain itself which is governed by law: 'in every respect, repetition is a transgression. It puts law into question, it denounces its nominal or general character in favor of a more profound and more artistic reality' (2–3/9/3). If law determines resemblance and equivalence, how could it govern a world in which neither quality nor extensity have yet been produced? The developed world of representation is a world governed by laws. The 'deeper' sub-representative world of repetition is an 'artistic' or aesthetic domain in which there are as yet no laws.

If the hidden target of the last opposition was Hegel, in this opposition it is Kant. Kant famously described the understanding as the legislator of nature:

> Thus, as contradictory as it may sound to say that the understanding is itself the source of the laws of nature, and thus of the formal unity of nature, such an assertion is nevertheless correct and appropriate to the object, namely experience. To be sure, empirical laws, as such, can by no means derive their origin from the pure understanding [. . .]. But all empirical laws are only particular determinations of the pure laws of the understanding [. . .]. (CPR A127)

The understanding legislates over nature. It does not determine empirical laws such as the laws of physics, but, as Deleuze puts it, 'it constitutes the laws to which *all* phenomena are subject from the point of view of their form' (KP 17; my emphasis).[7] The laws to which *all* phenomena are subject are the categories. These constitute the rules which any object, insofar as it is an object, must be in accordance with (CPR A126). Crucially, these are also the rules according to which the imagination both schematizes and carries out its synthesis of recognition. We will return to this in much more detail below, but what is important to recognize here is that the secret subject of repetition is not governed by any laws. It has no relation to the *Kantian* categories, and were we to discover that this subject is nothing other than a synthesis, this synthesis would function outside of and independently of the categories.

The first distinction between repetition and generality tells us that the latent subject confronts singularities and repeats them. The second distinction tells us that this repetition is not rule-governed.

FALSE MOVEMENT

After distinguishing between repetition and generality from the point of view of conduct and law, Deleuze draws a series of comparisons between Nietzsche and Kierkegaard – two other philosophers of repetition – which culminate in their opposition or 'objection' to Hegel. 'Their objection to Hegel is that he does not go beyond "false movement" – in other words, the abstract logical movement of "mediation"' (8/16/9). We will see below what exactly are 'false', 'abstract' and 'logical' about Hegelian mediation. What I want to point out here is simply that for Deleuze the word 'repetition' signifies an alternative to 'mediation'.

Even if Deleuze uses the imagery of the theatre to describe movement, the question of movement doesn't refer to movement through space, from point A to point B or from Copenhagen to Berlin, but to movement in 'thought' or 'spirit' – and this is more often than not the movement from a finite thought to an infinite thought.[8] It refers to the philosophical project which Jean Hyppolite described as the attempt to *'grasp passage itself'* (LE 115; original emphasis). What is the nature of this movement? This is perhaps the central question of *Difference and Repetition*. Is the movement of thought one of recollection as in Plato? Is it *kinesis*, the movement from potentiality to actuality as in Aristotle? Is it the synthetic *a priori* proposition as in Kant? Or is it, as Hyppolite claimed, Hegelian 'mediation' (LE 115)? While all of the first three notions will be brought together in various ways in Deleuze's own definition of 'true movement', his notion of movement is ultimately opposed to Hegel's and to the notion of a dialectical movement which proceeds from thesis to antithesis to synthesis. 'Repetition' is the new word for a revised notion of mediation.

contra Hegel

This comes out most clearly in two notes. In the first, which addresses the Kierkegaardian notion of repetition, Deleuze speaks of a 'real movement which is not mediation but "repetition" and which stands opposed to the abstract, logical, false movement described by Hegel' (306n5/17n1/33n5).[9] In another note, Deleuze quotes Gabriel Tarde employing repetition in the same manner as Kierkegaard:

> 'Repetition is a more powerful and less tiring stylistic procedure than antithesis, and moreover, better suited to renew a subject [. . .].' Tarde regarded repetition as a thoroughly French idea; Kierkegaard, it is true, saw it as a thoroughly Danish concept.[10] They meant that it gives rise to a dialectic quite different to that of Hegel. (308n15/39n1/34n15)

This is precisely what is at issue: 'a dialectic quite different to that of Hegel'. 'Repetition' is Deleuze's word for 'mediation'. Repetition is a mediation which no longer unfolds by negation and sublimation. It constitutes a new dialectic – in the words of Kierkegaard, a 'lyrical dialectic'. We will see below that this new dialectic is opposed to the Hegelian dialectic on one basic point: it is 'asymmetrical'. Difference is not pushed all the way to contradiction, and consequently the synthesis is not a balanced synthesis of a thesis and an antithesis. Like mediation, repetition is a *process*, the movement of thought itself, but it is a process consisting of asymmetrical syntheses which have no goal. This is why it can be so difficult to understand what Deleuze means by the word 'repetition'. It is not meant to refer to an equivalence or resemblance of two instances separated in time. It refers to a synthetic *process* by which thought itself is constituted and recognizes itself. 'Repetition' is the name Deleuze gives to his version of the dialectic.

THE BLOCKED CONCEPT

After opposing repetition and generality from the point of view of conduct and of law, Deleuze opposes the two from the point of view of the concept. Here Deleuze outlines the coordinates of what he describes as a 'vulgarized Leibnizianism'. This section is extremely dense and complicated and manoeuvres not only through a vulgarized Leibnizianism but also through a vulgarized Aristotelianism, Kantianism and Hegelianism, and it is impossible to make sense of the passage without understanding the respective contributions of all of these previous histories and the way in which Deleuze merges them with extraordinary virtuosity.[11] There simply isn't enough space here to extract all of these lines, and further, as interesting as this synthesis is, the general point that Deleuze is trying to make doesn't depend on it. Just as he earlier distinguished repetition and generality from the point of view of conduct and law, in this section Deleuze distinguishes them from the point of view of the concept. As we know already, there will be two types of repetition in relation to the concept, one latent, one manifest. The first kind of repetition *presupposes* the concept. The second kind of repetition *produces* the concept.

Deleuze describes in detail four kinds of concepts and the kinds of repetition that result from them (artificial, nominal, natural and concepts of freedom). To take an example which Deleuze uses in his lectures on Leibniz, I can have a concept of drops of water, and this concept will apply to all drops of water. Each drop of water that I encounter in experience will be a repetition of other drops – it will resemble or be equivalent to them – by virtue of its participation in the general concept 'drop of water'. (Deleuze calls this kind of concept the 'artificial' concept in *Difference and Repetition*.) In this sense, the concept does indeed explain repetition, but only a superficial form of repetition. The real question we should ask, Deleuze suggests, is not whether the concept can ground a superficial repetition, but what grounds the concept? From where does it come?

The concept itself refers ultimately to another, deeper repetition. Each of the four types of concept is found to result from a 'blockage', and there would be no blockage without a 'secret' or 'hidden' repetition. Deleuze explains the situation in this way in his lectures on Leibniz:

> The concept of drops of water is applicable to all drops of water. Leibniz says, of course, if you have blocked off

analysis of the concept at a certain point, at a finite moment. But if you push the analysis forward, there will be a moment in which the concepts are no longer the same.[12]

In this example, you have to imagine yourself looking at a drop of water. From one point of view you can say, 'this is a drop of water' meaning that you *recognize* this drop as a drop insofar as it participates in the general concept 'drop of water', a concept which applies to all drops. But you could also say that this particular drop is different from all the others. It is, for example, here and not there, now and not later. And if you were God – and by no means am I implying that you aren't – you could extend the analysis all the way to infinity. You could understand not only the drop's relation to all other drops and to the rest of the universe at that moment, but you could see its future and you could follow the drop's descent in reverse, all the way back up into the clouds, through all of its various paths determined by the winds, to the point at which evaporated water molecules first condensed into that singular drop, and so forth. All of these moments in the individual drop's history and future taken together constitute its 'complete concept' – and, importantly, this concept excludes all other drops and their concepts.[13] The drop's individual difference is included in its concept.[14]

It is from this God's-eye point of view that the notion of the blocked concept takes on its sense. Only God knows the infinite concept clearly.[15] 'The beauty of the universe *could* be learnt in each soul, could one unravel all its folds', but us humans with our finite minds can only comprehend small and isolated patches of the universe.[16] God comprehends the infinite concept. We comprehend the blocked or 'limited' concept. This finite concept can be more or less limited. For example, we can extend analysis far enough to determine a concept for this singular drop, here and now, as we hypothetically did above. Or we can stop analysis relatively early so that the concept no longer designates a singular drop, but perhaps several – for example, those falling out of the sky right now. If analysis were even more limited, the concept would no longer be that of raindrops, but all drops. The more limited the concept, the more general it is.

How does 'repetition' block the concept? To understand the significance of this question it helps to turn from beings to that being with which we are most familiar. We are also substances. Like the raindrop we also express the entire universe, past, present and future. Like the raindrop we are finite, and therefore unlike God we only know the universe obscurely. We only know 'limited' concepts clearly.[17] In the *New Essays* Leibniz distinguishes between these two points of view – infinite and finite comprehension – in terms of unconscious 'minute perceptions' 'which involve the infinite' and a finite 'apperception' which involves our conscious, 'noticeable', or 'sensible' perceptions (NE 53–9).[18] Our unconscious is infinite, but consciousness is limited.

> To give a clearer idea of these minute impressions which we are unable to pick out from the crowd, I like to use the example of the roaring noise of the sea which impresses itself on us when we are standing on the shore. To hear this noise as we do, we must hear the parts which make up the whole, that is the noise of each wave, although each of these little noises makes itself known only when combined confusedly with all the others, and would not be noticed if the wave which made it were by itself. We must be affected slightly by the motion of this wave, and have some perception of each of these noises however faint they may be; otherwise there would be no perception of a hundred thousand waves since a hundred thousand nothings cannot make something. (NE 54)[19]

Apperception, our finite area of clear perception, hears the global roar of the waves. Minute perception, on the other hand participates in 'the immeasurable fineness of things, which always and everywhere involves an actual infinity'.[20] It hears each individual wave, and, at the limit, infinity itself. When we ask how repetition blocks the concept then, we are asking how an unconscious process, related to the infinite, can also be related to the clear area of expression presided over by apperception. What is the relation between minute perception and apperception?[21]

How would we pose this question in Deleuze's terminology? The Deleuzian equivalent to Leibniz's 'apperception' is the manifest consciousness in its apprehension of the represented thing (quality + quantity). The functional equivalent of minute perception would be the evanescent singularity at the beginning of the process of repetition. The question, then, is what is the relation between singularity and representation? We already know the answer in a general way. Repetition, the new dialectic, is the process in which a latent subject gives rise to a manifest subject by means of asymmetrical syntheses that begin in immediate singularity. It is this dialectic which relates the immediate object to a representational consciousness. Twice Deleuze is more specific: he says that it is the Idea that blocks the concept.[22] And indeed, if we follow the actualization of the Idea, we will see that it comes to an end precisely in a represented quality and an extensity. The Idea itself is only one moment in the new dialectic. Repetition produces the Idea. The Idea produces representation. These are the three main moments of the detective story: singularity or matter; the Idea; representation. This is also the path of the Deleuzian dialectic as it propels thought from singularity to representation.

CONCLUSION

This still only answers the question in a general way, and what we really want to know is *how* 'repetition' moves from evanescent singularity to the Idea, and from the Idea to representation. At this point the word 'repetition' is as vague as the word 'mediation'.[23] Repetition is a form of mediation, a 'new dialectic', which is no less more understandable than the Hegelian one. We could put this differently, however, and say that repetition is a form of synthesis. In opposing repetition to generality Deleuze brought to light three general characteristics of this synthesis which begin to give it a more determinate character.

1. From the point of view of conduct, synthesis bears on singularities. It gathers together the evanescent fragments of immediate intuition.
2. From the point of view of law, this synthesis takes place below or before laws. Repetition is 'essentially transgression', and it is woven 'in the depths of the earth and of the heart, where laws do not *yet* exist' (25/38/28–9; my emphasis).

3. From the point of view of concepts, repetition is unconscious, pre-conceptual and sub-representative. The blockage of concepts does indeed result in a superficial repetition within 'generality'. But it is only on the condition of a pre-conceptual 'repetition which has nothing to do with generality' that the concept is blocked in the first place.

As we will see below, these three characteristics are the three characteristics of passive synthesis in general.

SECTION 2. DIFFERENCE IN ITSELF

In a lot of ways the first chapter of *Difference and Repetition*, 'Difference in Itself', is still introductory. Like the introduction the reader again wanders through a rhapsodic survey of the central concepts of the book, with only one apparent difference: instead of centring around the concept of repetition, in this chapter Deleuze focuses on the concept of difference. In the introduction Deleuze distinguished between an everyday conception of repetition and a deeper, more 'secret' repetition which referred to a latent subject and its new dialectic. In this first chapter Deleuze will again distinguish between a technical use of the word 'difference' and our ordinary everyday understanding of difference as a difference between two things or as a difference in relation to something else. In both the introduction and this first chapter, however, these concepts are introduced outside of the systematic context which gives them their sense, and for that reason they remain largely indeterminate and meaningless in themselves.

This first chapter is substantially longer than the introduction. In what follows I will concentrate on three themes: the notion of a productive and potentially individuating difference, the critique of Hegel, and the question of Being.

INDIVIDUATING DIFFERENCE

The most important theme of this chapter and the one around which it is organized is the idea of difference as productive and individuating. Difference has always played an important role in individuation insofar as individuation is the process through which a being is both given its own characteristic unity and is *distinguished* from all other individuals. Deleuze will argue that individuating difference has also always been thought in relation to some larger and more fundamental identity. Even if it is productive, difference is still a difference 'within the concept'. Deleuze's procedure is thus quite simple. He first describes the various ways in which difference is productive (his particular cases are Aristotle, Leibniz, Hegel, Scholastic theories of being and Plato), but then shows how it remains constrained within the concept. He then suggests that difference can remain productive and individuating even outside of the concept.

The ultimate aim of this chapter is to develop a concept of what Hegel called 'difference in itself' – a difference which is 'in and for itself, not difference resulting from anything external, but *self-related*, and therefore *simple* difference'.[24] Hegel only discovers this difference through a process of dialectical opposition which renders it abstract and makes it only one moment in the movement of Being. Deleuze tries to develop a notion of difference which is not a difference between things, or in relation to other things, which is discovered not through dialectics, but through a 'crucial' lived experience of difference, and finally which is not just one moment in the movement of Being but is indistinguishable from Being as such.

Deleuze begins by describing the role of difference in Aristotle. In Aristotle, difference could be considered as productive in the sense that by predicating a difference of a genus, you end up with a species. This is probably best captured by Porphyry's famous tree. Porphyry writes,

> Substance is itself a genus. Under it is body, and under body is animate body, under which is animal; under animal is rational animal, under which is man; and under man are Socrates and Plato and particular men. (*Introduction* 6)[25]

Right down the tree it is always a difference which turns a genus into a species. The difference 'corporeal' (or 'extended'), when attributed to 'substance', produces the species 'body'. A body is an extended substance. 'Body' then becomes the genus which supports the next difference. The difference 'animate' turns the genus body into the species animal. When attributed to the genus animal, the difference 'rational' produces man.

As Porphyry puts it, 'A genus is like matter, a difference is like shape' (14). From this point of view difference appears to be individuating – or at least productive of the species (individuation is left to time, place and non-essential differences in general). 'Man' is defined by the genera and the differences which divide the genera.

There are several things about this notion of difference that Deleuze emphasizes and which will reappear later in his own concept of difference. Three are particularly relevant here. The first is that difference is productive. 'It is productive, since genera are not divided into differences but divided by differences which produce the corresponding species' (31/47/39; translation modified). The second characteristic is that with each division, the difference 'carries' both its own character and that of the genus with it: 'Difference carries with itself the genus and all the intermediary differences' (31/47/39). In other words, difference is invested with a power to not only articulate and divide, but also to bring together. It is at once synthesis and analysis. It divides the genus, but produces a species. This is related to the third characteristic. As we move down the tree from substance to individual, there is a connection of differences:

> A transport of difference, a diaphora of diaphora, the determination of species (*spécification*) links difference with difference across the successive levels of division until a final difference, that of the *infirma species*, condenses in the chosen direction the entirety of the essence and its continued quality, gathers them together under an intuitive concept and grounds them [. . .]. (31/47/40; translation modified)[26]

'Specification', which Paul Patton has translated throughout the work as the 'determination of species', relates difference to difference. Difference is related to difference and the last difference gathers together – you could almost say 'sublimates' – all of the previous differences. These are the three characteristics of difference that Deleuze finds in Aristotle: difference is productive, it is itself synthetic, but there is also a synthesis of difference in the act of specification. Specification relates one difference to the next.

Even if difference is given a productive and synthetic power, however, it still remains a difference which is caught within the concept. Difference is only productive when it divides the genus. In fact, as Jeff Bell points out, Aristotle will insist that difference will always be a difference between. Difference can only be thought in relation to something else, the concept it divides.[27] But there is also a second sense in which difference is caught within the concept. Notice that here difference itself takes the form of a general concept: it is a predicate, possessing a generality greater than that of the subject. In Aristotle, Deleuze says, 'Difference then can be no more than a predicate in the comprehension of a concept' (32/48/41). Difference is both a general concept and it is predicated of other concepts. There are of course other kinds of difference in Aristotle which are not predicates. For example, there are the differences between the categories, and there are individual differences which do not bear on the essence or definition of a thing. But, according to Deleuze, Aristotle never tried to develop a comprehensive concept of difference which would unite the other differences. He confused difference in the concept for a concept of difference.

Whereas Deleuze could say that Aristotle never created a full concept of difference because he left both the differences above the categories and below the *infirma species* undetermined, it is much more difficult to say this of Leibniz. In Leibniz difference, in the form of infinitesimal difference, is not only productive, but it really goes all the way to the infinite, and further it directly determines the individual. Even so, Deleuze will argue that for Leibniz too difference was no more than a predicate in the comprehension of the concept, even if the nature of this predicate was of a completely different nature.

We saw above that for Leibniz, everything that happens to a substance is contained within its concept.

There are in the soul [or concept] of Alexander, from all time, traces of all that has happened to him, and marks of everything that will happen to him – and even traces of everything that happens in the universe – though no one but God can know them all.[28]

If, like God, you could see this concept, you would also grasp the individuality of Alexander. God, 'seeing the individual notion or *haecceitas* of Alexander, sees in it at the same time the foundation of and reason for all the predicates which can truly be stated of him'.[29] Leibniz is alluding to Duns Scotus here. The individual notion, if it is extended to infinity, is also the haecceity or the *thisness* of Alexander. It constitutes his concrete individuality: God can see what makes Alexander different from all other beings. If there is only one concept for each individual, and if each individual has only one concept then, as Deleuze puts it, 'There is only conceptual difference. In other words, if you assign a difference between two things, there is necessarily a difference in the concept.'[30]

Perhaps the most important aspect of this theory of the individual is that the concept must extend all the way to infinity. '[I]ndividuality involves infinity, and only someone who is capable of grasping the infinite could know the principle of individuation of a given thing. This arises from the influence – properly understood – that all things in the universe have on one another'.[31] Individuation involves infinity and arises from the *influence* that all things in the universe have on one another. Put differently individuality is constituted by the way in which an individual is affected (and what distinguishes one monad from another if not its 'perceptions'[32]). If we turn from beings to our own being, we see that it is at the level of minute perceptions that both our own individuality and our connection with the universe is determined. Minute perceptions constitute 'those impressions which are made on us by the bodies around us and which involve the infinite; that connection that each being has with all the rest of the universe'.[33] These impressions do not simply affect us then pass. Rather, they are contained in our concept where they leave 'traces'. In the same way that the haecceity of Alexander was the support for all the predicates which could truly be stated of him, so too does our own notion contain traces of everything that has happened and will happen. 'These insensible perceptions also indicate and *constitute* the same individual, who is characterized by the vestiges or expressions which the perceptions preserver from the individual's former states, thereby connecting these with his present state.'[34]

Deleuze will constantly emphasize two points in this vulgarized Leibnizianism. First, our concept expresses the entire world, but this world precedes us and constitutes our individuality. At the level of minute perceptions 'the world' is an actual and continuous infinity which both *precedes* the individual and which *constitutes* the individual. The world is anterior to the individual, and the infinitely small differences which make up the continuum determine the finite differences which distinguish an individual from every other individual.[35] The problem for Deleuze is that this continuum of 'properties' and 'affections' is pre-selected by God. The world which we live is the best of all possible worlds, and God selected it, Deleuze explains, in order to ensure a maximum of continuity. This is the second point Deleuze emphasizes: there is a pre-established harmony which governs the continuum. If our individuality is determined by the entire set of affections which determine our concept, and if this continuum of affections is governed by a pre-established harmony, then our individual difference is already circumscribed by the identity of God and of the world. Leibniz thus went further than Aristotle (and Hegel) insofar as he developed a genuine concept of difference: the finite difference between individuals is directly determined and related to the infinitely small differences of the continuum. Put differently, difference is really individuating, but difference is also pre-selected by God so that this world exhibits a maximum of continuity or 'convergence'. 'Difference, both as infinitely small difference and as finite difference' is related to 'sufficient reason as the foundation which selects or chooses the best world' (48/69/59). Difference 'remains subject to the condition of the convergence of series' (49/70/60). It is not really difference which is individuating then, but God insofar as he orders the differences.

We can now begin to approach negatively what Deleuze might mean by 'difference'. In both Aristotle and Leibniz 'difference' was a predicate. Of course what each meant by predicate was radically different. For example, in Aristotle, the difference was still a general concept. Corporeality and rationality have nothing specific about them. Difference is a concept which determines another concept. In Leibniz, difference is still the property or affection of a concept, but it has become a worldly event which pre-exists the individual and

44

which completely lacks the character of generality. Deleuze will sometimes go even further and say that the predicate or the event is an infinitely small event which is better thought of as a relation than as a thing.[36] What Deleuze objected to in both cases however was that the affections were not free. They were limited either by the genera or by a principle of convergence. 'Leibniz's only error was to have linked difference to the negative of limitation [. . .] because he linked the series to a principle of convergence' (51/72–3/62).[37] For his own part, however, Deleuze wants to argue that every limitation of difference refers back to a 'swarm of differences, a pluralism of free, wild or untamed differences' (50/71/61). The very idea of a limit presupposes something that needs to be limited. What is this something, and might it be capable of producing and individuating by itself? Put differently, how is the concept itself which difference is said to determine and in relation to which it is always thought produced? Do we then approach Deleuze's concept of difference if we simply remove the constraint of convergence? Is Deleuze imagining a world of evanescent events which have no determinate relationship to one another, but which still constitute the individuality of the subject? We will see below that he is indeed thinking of such a world, but it is crucial to emphasize that this is not the world of quantum physics. The incompossiblity which Deleuze inscribes at the heart of the world does not refer to a principle of uncertainty at the heart of matter, for example. For Deleuze the evanescent matter upon which we are constructed as effects is the matter given to a transcendental sensibility. The disconnected series of events are still insensible perceptions, but now there is no pre-selection which determines the set of our affections.

Deleuze also emphasizes a second aspect of difference in both Aristotle and Leibniz: it is productive and constitutive. The insensible perceptions *constitute* individuality. Perhaps this is even more clear in Aristotle where the successive differentiae which are linked together in specification constitute the species 'man'. I have already said that for both Leibniz and Aristotle difference was a predicate, but not every predicate which is said of a subject counts as a 'difference'. 'Difference' describes a specific type of predicate, one that changes the nature of subject to which it is attributed. A difference is an event which causes the subject that it affects to evolve. It is in Hegel that Deleuze finds a truly genetic account of difference. Difference is not only what affects the subject, it is also the law of its development and self-transcendence. This very simple question cuts to the heart of Deleuze's criticisms of Hegel: does the difference which causes consciousness to evolve have to be a contradiction? Does a new predicate have to oppose or negate the proposition, or can it simply differ from it.

DELEUZE AND HEGEL

Deleuze's engagement with Hegel is far more complex than he would let us think. Unfortunately there is only enough space here to concentrate on the minor and polemic way in which Deleuze distances himself from Hegel.[38] This is always dangerous with Deleuze because his polemics are almost always indexes of a more profound and positive engagement. If I emphasize the polemic here, it is because it brings to light the nature of difference as it relates to genesis.

 In general Deleuze's engagement with Hegel is largely indebted to the work of Jean Hyppolite. There is no doubt that Deleuze differs from Hyppolite on significant points, but Hyppolite's reading sets the stage for Deleuze's encounter with Hegel on several fronts. There are two main points laid out by Hyppolite in the first chapter of his *Genesis and Structure* around which Deleuze's comments on Hegel tend to revolve in *Difference and Repetition*. First, Hyppolite describes the *Phenomenology of Spirit* as a *story* of the genetic development of consciousness. Hyppolite suggests that Hegel may have even drawn inspiration from the *Bildungsroman*:

> Hegel had read Rousseau's *Emile* in Tübingen and had found in it a preliminary history of natural consciousness rising to liberty through particularly educative experiences which were specific to it. [. . .] Hegel's *Phenomenology*, for its part, is the novel of philosophic formation; it follows the development of consciousness, which, renouncing its first beliefs, reaches through its experiences the properly philosophical point of view, that of absolute knowledge. (*Genesis and Structure* 11–12)

Deleuze will not abandon this general point of view. *Difference and Repetition*, as we have already seen, is the story of the progressive development of consciousness.[39] It is the story in which a latent subject raises itself from singularity to the world of representation by means of its power to repeat. Of course, all of the general coordinates change as you move between Rousseau, Hegel and Deleuze. Deleuze's story is neither the story of natural consciousness attaining freedom by virtue of its education, nor is it that of sense-certainty becoming absolute consciousness by virtue of the labour of the negative. The *Hegel* genetic structure, however, remains fundamentally important for Deleuze.

The second point Hyppolite makes is that the genetic development of consciousness proceeds by means of 'determinate negation'. Deleuze had already criticized this in the introduction: he claimed that the dialectic was only a false and abstract movement. Hyppolite would not agree. He points out that this dialectical movement of negation is hardly an abstract movement. In fact, the dialectic is 'the very experience of consciousness' (*Genesis* 19). In the following passage Hyppolite is still within the metaphor of the novel:

> What is most striking for the consciousness engaged in experience is indeed the negative character of its result: it initially posited a certain truth which had absolute value for it, but in the course of that journey that truth is lost. It trusted itself absolutely to 'immediate sensuous certainty', then to the 'thing' of perception, and to the 'strength' of understanding; but it discovers that what it thus took to be truth is not, and it loses its truth. (*Genesis* 13)

The process of education takes place by 'determinate negation', and consciousness is the lived experience of negation. Consciousness initially holds one thing to be true, finds that truth to be impossible, and then replaces it with a new truth. *Hegel*

At this point Hyppolite distinguishes the 'philosopher', Hegel and his readers, from the consciousness under examination. There is indeed a concrete consciousness which bathes in the negative and whose authentic experience is the movement of the dialectic, but this consciousness hardly grasps either the nature of this movement or its necessity. All it knows is that it transcends itself, but it doesn't understand why. Consciousness 'sees what it held to be the true and in-itself disappear, and at the same time sees a different object *appear* as though it were a new thing, something *discovered*' (24; original emphases). In its experience, consciousness does not grasp the law of its becoming as the dialectic. It sees an old truth disappear and a new truth appear, but it does not see the necessity of its education or the reason for negation. Both consciousness and the philosopher know that subjectivity is self-transcendence, but only the philosopher knows that transcendence unfolds through opposition.

Hegel

The definition of subjectivity as self-transcendence is one of the most important for Deleuze, and it motivates all of his works from *Empiricism and Subjectivity* to *What is Philosophy? Difference and Repetition* as a whole could be read as the story of the such a consciousness. The entire question is whether or not consciousness evolves by means of opposition.

As early as *Nietzsche and Philosophy* (1962) Deleuze had already criticized Hegel on this point. For Hegel, 'The speculative motor of the dialectic is contradiction and its resolution' (NP 160). For Deleuze, however, contradiction is only an 'abstract' form of difference. By saying contradiction is abstract Deleuze is not simply saying that consciousness doesn't live contradiction. He is saying that it is a produced form. It is a product of genesis and cannot therefore be the motor of genesis.

> Opposition can be the law of the relation between abstract products, but difference is the only principle of genesis or production; a principle which itself produces opposition as mere appearance. Dialectic thrives on oppositions because it is unaware of far more subtle and subterranean differential mechanisms [. . .]. (NP 157)

Opposition is a relation between abstract *products*. In fact it itself is a product: opposition is produced by 'subtle and subterranean differential mechanisms' which produce the dialectic as a 'mere appearance'. How then can it function, for either the philosopher or for the consciousness who undergoes the experience, as a principle of production? How can it explain the constitution of those products if it itself is constituted? For

Deleuze, it can't. The philosopher has simply taken a product and imposed it on the process of production as a model when s/he should have given priority to the 'crucial *experience* of difference' as it unfolds in concrete consciousness (50/71/61; my emphasis). Difference, not opposition, is the real movement of thought. It is the principle or origin of the dialectic. For this reason Deleuze writes, 'The negative expires at the gates of being. Opposition ceases its labor and difference begins its play' (NP 190). More informally: 'The labor of the negative is a load of crap'.[40]

Deleuze had already developed these ideas in a 1954 review of Hyppolite's *Logic and Existence*. The review concludes with a speculative remark regarding a chapter in which Hyppolite shows us that 'Hegel is going to do everything he can in order to reduce this indifferent diversity to opposition and to contradiction' (LE 114).[41]

> The richness of Hyppolite's book could then let us wonder this: can we not construct an ontology of difference which would not have to go up to contradiction, because contradiction would be less than difference and not more? Is not contradiction itself only the phenomenal and anthropological aspect of difference? (LE 195)

Here we see the same themes that were outlined in *Nietzsche and Philosophy* except the words have slightly changed: instead of 'abstract' Deleuze says 'phenomenal and anthropological'. For Deleuze, contradiction *is* only the phenomenal and anthropological aspect of difference. Consequently, in the place of contradiction Deleuze puts difference. Consciousness does not evolve by contradicting itself, but by differing from itself. Becoming is not governed by a rule.

These comments find their way straight into *Difference and Repetition*. Deleuze writes,

> It is not difference which presupposes opposition, but opposition which presupposes difference, and far from resolving difference by tracing it back to a foundation, opposition betrays and distorts it. Our claim is not only that difference in itself in not 'already' contradiction, but

that it cannot be reduced or traced back to contradiction, since the latter is not more but less profound than difference. (51/73/62–3)

It is true, as Hyppolite says, that the dialectic is the concrete lived experience of evolving consciousness. But for Deleuze Hegel began with an already constituted, phenomenal and anthropological, subject. 'The whole of Phenomenology is an epiphenomenology' (52/74/63).

We can get a better sense for what Deleuze means when he says that contradiction is an abstract product if we consider the distinction he made in the introduction between a latent and a manifest subject. A sub-representative subject repeats (or mediates) the singular and immediate object of intuition. In the introduction the fragmented objects of immediate intuition were simply referred to as 'singularities', but in this first chapter, Deleuze has expanded his account. What else could these singularities of intuition be but the evanescent and incompossible events which precede the subject and constitute its individuality? The latent subject comes after these events which affect it, and it contemplates or repeats them. It takes them up into its consciousness and by repeating them eventually produces its own determinate individuality after several important detours and failures. As it progresses, it moves from 'the sub-representative domain' of the latent subject to the represented object (quality + extensity) contemplated by the manifest subject. This development or becoming does not unfold by means of opposition or determinate negation because the entire development takes place in a 'sub-representative domain'.[42] Mediation cannot proceed by means of opposition because opposition itself presupposes something to which it can be opposed. In the latent subject there is neither a determinate subject nor object which could support negation.

It is not until the manifest subject appears that opposition even becomes possible. The identity of the represented object grounds what Deleuze calls the 'fourfold root' of representation, or the 'four dimensions which co-ordinate and measure' the world of representation. These four are identity, opposition, analogy and resemblance.[43] Opposition is the second of the four. In other words, opposition, the motor of the dialectic, presupposes the identity of the object – an identity, we will see, which is granted only by the actualization of an Idea:

> Hegelian contradiction appears to push difference to the limit, but this path is a dead end which brings it back to identity, making identity the sufficient condition for difference to exist and be thought. It is only in relation to the identical, as a function of the identical, that contradiction is the *greatest* difference. The intoxications and giddinesses are feigned, the obscure is already clarified at the outset. (263/338–9/331–2; original emphases)

It is in this sense that opposition is an abstract product and that 'opposition presupposes difference': it presupposes identity which is itself produced by difference. Difference is both the 'principle' or source of repetition and the law of genesis. It regulates the process through which repetition gives rise to representation – to phenomena and to the empirical-anthropological subject. These are the 'abstract products' of which opposition can then 'be the law' (NP 157).

Deleuze criticizes Aristotle, Leibniz and Hegel for the same reason. In each case difference is limited and constrained to function within some larger setting. Deleuze's project in this chapter is simply to think difference as a principle of individuation independently of some sort of overarching all-encompassing continuity. What then would this new notion of difference look like positively? What would a difference which wasn't a difference from or a difference between look like? Could it even be called a difference? Perhaps we would do better to simply invent a new word for it? In Aristotle, Hegel and Leibniz, it is easy to see how difference is individuating and to understand what the word 'difference' means. Difference articulates, separates and determines things in relation to an already given substance of some sort. When we use the word 'difference' in these three accounts we can still retain our everyday sense of difference as a difference *between* something. Difference comes between genus and species. If we take away that initial context, we are no longer dealing with difference between. Does it make sense to continue to use the word 'difference'?

ONTOLOGICAL DIFFERENCE

It the passages above I underplayed the ontological aspect of difference. In *Nietzsche and Philosophy*, Deleuze wrote that the 'negative expired at the gates of Being'. In the review of Hyppolite, Deleuze asked whether it was possible to construct an 'ontology of difference'. For Deleuze, productive difference has an ontological aspect to it, and Deleuze will spend a good part of the chapter arguing that difference is Being. Alain Badiou will even make this the cornerstone of his interpretation of Deleuze. 'Deleuze purely and simply identifies philosophy with ontology. One misses everything if one disregards such explicit declarations as "Philosophy merges with ontology"' (Badiou, *Deleuze* 20). Badiou is undoubtedly right, and his emphasis on this point is what makes his reading of Deleuze so strong, but there are two problems which immediately arise. The first problem is both unavoidable and must be avoided: nobody knows what that word 'ontology' means any more. This especially true when Deleuze uses it. Deleuze is a philosopher who rarely uses a word consistently or in its conventional sense, and further, his own concepts only take their sense from their position within his system. What does Deleuze mean by the word 'Being', and what kind of an ontology is he going to construct? How does he pose the question of Being? It is often difficult to tell how Deleuze approaches the question of Being. Is he returning to ontology pure and simple? Is he writing within the context of a modified Kantianism? Or Heideggerianism as the theme of transcendental empiricism might suggest? Has he made the celebrated phenomenological 'metaphysical decision'[44] to treat consciousness as primary (even if he interprets 'consciousness' in a way that is completely foreign to Husserl), or has he returned to a 'wild' or 'savage' ontology which no longer needs to make the decision? Or perhaps has he rejected it outright and simply taken up the jargon of classical philosophy in order to make another point as he does with so many other vocabularies from Proust to the cinema. Indeed, the fact that his narrative of the univocity of being ends in Nietzsche, the philosopher who proclaimed that God, or Being, is dead, would suggest that ontology is no longer an issue for Deleuze.

From this point of view it is important to emphasize as Foucault did that Deleuze's discussion of ontology follows directly on the heels of his accounts of limited difference in Aristotle, Hegel and Leibniz, and that it follows the same procedure. In one ontology difference is subordinated to identity. In another it is not. Deleuze's most general point in this section of the text is that an ontology which admits categories already situates difference in relation to these categories.[45] Only by saying the word being univocally, or with one sense, can one begin to think difference outside of the concept. However, even if you say being univocally there is still no guarantee that difference will be thought in itself. This is why, as we will see below, Duns Scotus will be surpassed by Spinoza who will be surpassed by Nietzsche.

Without deciding in what sense Deleuze uses the word being, as Badiou points out, we still cannot deny that Deleuze repeatedly says that philosophy merges with ontology. This is true, but one misses everything if the quotation is cut off there or if it is taken out of its context. Philosophy is ontology, but ontology is always an ontology of sense – and again, no body has grasped this more clearly than Badiou. What Badiou and countless others seem to have overlooked, however, is that for Deleuze *sense itself is produced*.[46] Being is not first. It is produced. This is why, after describing ontology as a tiring and 'interminable discourse', and after saying that Being can no longer be found in either God or man, Deleuze concludes in a Nietzschean register that 'It is thus pleasing that there resounds today the news that sense is never a principle or an origin, but that it is produced' (LS 72).[47] Being is not the originary moment from which we fall (as in *Being in Time*). Nor is it is the final prize won at the end of an epic genesis (as in *The Phenomenology of Spirit*). It comes in the middle between an unindividuated matter and an individuated matter (Badiou is therefore right to say that Being is the 'core' of Deleuze's thought). Being is wrested from unindividuated beings, and it returns to individuated beings. This is one of the most original aspects of Deleuze's thought. 'Univocity raises and extracts Being [. . .]. It wrests Being from beings in order to bring it to all of them at once' (LS 180). Philosophy is ontology. Ontology is an ontology of sense. Sense is produced. This will play an important role in Deleuze's distinction between the will to power and the eternal return.

UNIVOCITY

Deleuze's reading of Aristotle made two points. The first was that difference is productive: it defines individuals by specifying genera. Second, there are at least two other kinds of difference in Aristotle. Difference escapes the model of specification in two directions: above and below. Individuating difference within genera is not the same as the differences between the greatest genera, the categories, and further, specific difference seems unable to account for the non-essential and individual differences at the bottom of the scale. According to Deleuze, as we saw, Aristotle never tried to create a total concept of difference which would bring together all three kinds of difference. How does the difference between genera relate to generic difference, and how does generic difference relate to individual difference? Deleuze will therefore say that Aristotle mistook difference within the concept (within genera) for a concept of difference.

'Being' could be said in at least three different ways: it is said of Being which relates 'equivocally' to the genera; it is said of the genera which relate 'univocally' to the species; and it is said of the individual and the essential and accidental differences which define it. In other words, if you say 'Being is', 'Genus is' and the 'individual is', you have to use the word 'is' in three different, but related senses. You use the word 'analogically'.

There are several problems with this for Deleuze, but the most important is that it is particularly difficult to account for individuation within this model.

[A]nalogy falls into an irresolvable difficulty: it must essentially relate being it particular existents, but at the same time it cannot say what constitutes their individuality. For it retains in the particular only that which conforms to the general (matter and form), and seeks the principle of individuation in this or that element of fully constituted individuals. (38/56/47)

Deleuze is alluding to the persistent difficulty of explaining individuation in Aristotle which traditionally revolves around the question of whether or not the principle of individuation lies in the form – that is, in the condensed differentiae – or in the matter which this form actualizes.[48] Whether the principle of individuation is found in matter or in form or in both, however, is not the issue for Deleuze. What is at issue is that either way, the individual is 'constituted' only in relation to properties which pertain to already 'constituted individuals'. Socrates is defined as this or that rational animal, but neither Socrates nor the differentiae 'rationality' and 'animality' are generated themselves. They are pregiven outside of a genesis. However we decide that individuation is supposed to work in Aristotle, it will remain the case that matter and form 'conform to the general'. Every individual is already a particular. Now, Deleuze's claim seems to be that this will always be the case as long as being is said analogically because the ontological implication is that there is a being with various senses (the categories) that is transcendent to the individual and in relation to which the individual needs to be determined. There is then no room for an authentic genesis of the individual because the individual will always already be constituted by or in relation to pregiven forms.[49] Deleuze's preference for 'univocity' over analogy comes down to his insistence on the genetic point of view. The key word in the passage above is 'constitution', and Deleuze's distinction between a univocal and an analogical use of the word being ultimately turns on the implications such a decision has on the constitution of individuality.

In a discussion of Descartes' 'doctrine of being', Heidegger gives a characteristically clear account of the notions of univocity and analogy.[50]

A concept is univocal if its meaning content, that is, what it intends, what is addressed by it, is intended in the same sense. When I say, for example, 'God is' and 'the [created] world is', I certainly assert being in both cases but I intend something different thereby and cannot intend the term 'is' in the same sense, univocally; for if that were the case, then I would thereby either intend the creature itself as uncreated or reduce the uncreated being God to a creature [i.e. a created being]. Since according to Descartes there is an *infinite* difference between the kind of being of these two entities, the term 'being', which is still used for both, cannot be used in the same sense, not univocally, but [. . .] *analogously*. I can only speak of both God and the world as entities analogously. In other words, the concept of being, insofar as it is generally applied to the entire manifold of all possible entities, as such has the character of an analogous concept.[51]

There are two problems with saying that being is univocal. Heidegger points out the first: even though the word 'univocal' refers only to the *use* of the word 'is' and is perhaps better considered a logical problem than an ontological one, it still has substantial ontological implications – namely that God and created beings *are* in the same way. God is 'reduced' or 'degraded' to the status of a created being.[52] As Deleuze points out, people who said this in the middle ages got 'burned'.[53]

The second problem, however, is that it is still difficult to account for individuation even if you discard the categories and say being univocally. Even if the analogical conception of being cannot describe the generation of individuals without recourse to already constituted forms, it did have at least two advantages: not only do the categories and the differentiae introduce a distance between God and species that might save one from the flames (or today, from the ill-will of Aquinas scholars), but they also account for the production of species. Deleuze highlights this problem in a lecture:

> My question is, if I say being is univocal, it's said in the same sense of everything of which it's said, then what could the differences between [beings?] be? They can no longer be differences of category, they can no longer be differences of form, they can no longer be differences of genus and species. And why can they no longer be all that? Because, once again, if I say: the differences between beings are differences of form, are formal, generic, specific differences, at that moment I cannot escape from the analogy of being for this simple reason: the categories are the ultimate genera of being. If I say: there are several senses of the word 'being' which are precisely the categories, I must say that what is, that of which I say 'this is,' is distinguished by the form, the species, the genus. On the other hand, if I say that being is univocal and that it's said in one and the same sense of everything of which it's said, I fall into that which becomes the mad thought, the thought of infamy,

the thought of the formless, the thought of the non-specific, the thought of the non-generic. The only means of getting out of this is to say: of course there are differences between beings, and in any case being is said in one and the same sense of everything which is. Then what do the differences between beings consist in? The only difference conceivable at this very moment, from the point of view of a univocal being, is obviously difference solely as degrees of power [puissance]. Beings are not distinguished by their form, their genus, their species, that's secondary; everything which is refers to a degree of power. (*Anti-Oedipus* Seminar (14 Jan. 1974))

What is so fascinating about this passage is that it makes the distinction between analogical and univocal being from the point of view of the notion of difference implied in each. From an Aristotelian/Neoplatonic point of view, the categories or ultimate genera are the different senses of the word Being, and difference divides these. At the same time, difference is then contained within the concept, and you can define the individual in relation to its genera. But when you no longer have categories or genera, you no longer have anything in relation to which individuals can be determined. 'Then what do the differences between beings consist in?' What defines the individual? What is its essence and how is it different from all other individuals? This is the mad thought, and it is the same one we encountered above when we wondered what a difference might look like that was not between or within something larger.

What is the way out? Deleuze says it is to ascribe to each being a 'degree of power' or what Deleuze will call a 'capacity to be affected'.

Why is the idea of degrees of power fundamentally linked to that of the univocity of being? Because beings which are distinguished solely by the degree of their power are beings which realize a single univocal being, except for the difference in the degree of power or its withdrawal. So between a table, a little boy, a little girl, a locomotive, a cow, a god, the difference is solely one of degree of power in the realization of one and the same being. (*Anti-Oedipus* Seminar (14 Jan. 1974))

Things are no longer distinguished in relation to their genus, but according to their capacity to be affected or by their individual participation in Being. At risk of sounding Leibnizian, we could say that each individual is distinguished by its particular point of view on being. Each monad is distinguished from all others through its 'perceptions'.[54]

> Between a racehorse and a draft horse, which belong to the same species, the difference can perhaps be thought as greater than the difference between a draft horse and an ox. Which comes down to saying that the draft horse and the ox are taken in the same assemblage [agencement] and that their degrees of power are closer to one another's than is the draft horse's degree of power to the racehorse's. (*Anti-Oedipus* Seminar (14 Jan. 1974))

We can follow Deleuze to a degree: a being is defined not in relation to an eternal essence, but in relation to the concrete situation in which that being finds itself. The doctrine of univocity is fundamentally related to pragmatics. But something seems to be missing from this account. To say 'being' analogically implies a hierarchy of being, and thus a distinction of forms and a regulation of generation, but does it follow that when we say 'being' univocally that everything can be directly reduced to equal participation in being and a capacity to be affected?

This touches on what is without a doubt one of the most striking elements of Deleuze's characterization of univocal being in *Difference and Repetition*: being is said of a pre-individual, undeveloped world of individuating – and not individuated – factors. The move from analogy to univocity is more than a move from a hierarchical vision of the world to an equal vision of the world. It is the movement from a world of constituted individuals to an unconstituted world prior to the individual.

> Univocity of being, in so far as it is immediately related to difference, demands that we show how individuating difference *precedes* generic, specific, and even individual differences within being; how a prior field of individuation within being conditions at once the determination of species and forms [. . .]. If individuation does not take place either

by form or by matter, neither qualitatively nor extensionally, this is not only because it differs in kind but *because
it is already presupposed by the forms, matters, and extensive
parts.* (38/56–7/48; my emphases)

Deleuze repeatedly emphasizes this point. Individuation by form
and matter or by genera and differentiae presupposes a genetic
world of individuating differences which actually constitute the
individual. Individuating differences precede individual differences. Only univocity makes room for the genetic point of view,
but it is precisely this point of view which gives it its priority.
Deleuze often makes it sound as though analogy was opposed
to univocity in the sense that analogy went from the top down,
and univocity from the bottom up.

It is by no means obvious that this is either where the notion of
a univocal being leads you or that distinguishing between beings
according to their degree of power is the correct response. For
example, I said above that Deleuze preferred univocity to analogy because analogy predetermined generation in relation to
already given forms, but the same could be said of univocity.
Even on *Deleuze's* reading of Spinoza, individuation takes place
by means of a modal essence contained in the attribute, and further, given that a modal essence does not automatically lead to
modal existence (the attributes are real without being actual),
it would seem that individual essence is given in advance of the
individual.[55] From this point of view even in Spinoza, the 'Christ
of philosophers',[56] genesis already unfolds according to predetermined forms (the attributes).

This is the importance of Deleuze's short historical narrative
of the development of the notion of univocity (and the reason
why the Christ of philosophers is overtaken by the Antichrist).[57]
While a number of interesting themes arise across this narrative, it is perhaps more important to notice the general direction
it takes: the story progresses from the abstract to the concrete.
In general the notion of univocity is that the word 'being' is said
in one sense of everything that is. The notion of being, however,
and in particular its relation to individuals or modes, changes
dramatically between these three thinkers. In Duns Scotus,
being is 'neutral'.[58] He 'only *thought* univocal being' (39/57/49;
original emphasis). Being remains distant from the modes.

'With the second moment, Spinoza marks a considerable progress. Instead of understanding univocal being as neutral or indifferent, he makes it an object of pure affirmation. Univocal being becomes identical with unique, universal and infinite substance: *Deus sive Natura*' (40/58/49). In Spinoza, being is no longer neutral. It is concrete: 'God or nature'. However, even if ontology has taken a big step towards the concrete in Spinoza, the relation between substance (God) and the modes, between Being and the individual, is mediated by the attributes.[59] 'Spinoza's substance appears independent of the modes, while the modes are dependent on substance, but as though on something other than themselves' (40/58/50; original emphasis). Even though God is identified with the modes, the attributes introduce a distance between them, a distance which makes the modes dependent on substance, 'as though on something *other* than themselves'.

In Spinoza Being is univocal. It is said in one sense, but it is only said of the modes *by way of* the attributes. Consequently, 'All that Spinozism needed to do for the univocal to become an object of pure affirmation was to make substance turn around the modes' (304/388/377). 'Substance must be said *of* the modes and only *of* the modes' (40/59/50; original emphasis). Substance must be said of the modes without intermediary. Being must be said *directly* of the modes and it must belong directly to the modes. According to Deleuze it is Nietzsche who realizes this program in his thought of the eternal return.

'Being' is said directly of the modes. This does not mean that it is said of fully constituted modes. It is not said of individuals but of the incompossible events which precede the individual.[60] It is said of '*individuating* factors'. It is no longer a question of boys, girls, tables and oxen, as in Deleuze's examples, but of a world prior to them comprising their constitutive differences. This is why Deleuze turns to Nietzsche and to the eternal return to describe this world. Being is *form*less. There are no categories or genera which can support differences. There is no God to select differences according to a principle of convergence. There are no attributes that formally divide Being and which are themselves divided into modal essences. The real difficulty is not saying 'Being' with just one sense when it is said of individuating factors because these factors themselves are meaningless and fragmented. Indeed it would be much more difficult to say 'being' analogically of such a world. The real difficulty is to explain how form can arise from this world when there is no external reason, model or guide. When Deleuze says 'univocal being' he is referring to a world with two characteristics: (1) it is pre-individual; and (2) there is absolutely no hierarchy, but only individuating differences: Being is said directly of the modes, but the modes themselves are fragmented.

ETERNAL RETURN AND THE WILL TO POWER

Deleuze's interpretation of the eternal return is heavily indebted to three other thinkers: Klossowski, Blanchot and, derivatively, to Heidegger. In the introduction to *Difference and Repetition* Deleuze distinguished between a superficial repetition and a sub-representative 'secret' repetition which is responsible in some way for the genesis of the superficial repetition. Klossowski makes a similar move in his essay 'Nietzsche, Polytheism, Parody'. He starts with what he calls 'conscious life', the manifest subject. This is the set of acts which have been traditionally held to define thinking: 'the act of knowing, judging, or concluding'.[61] 'For the longest time, Klossowski writes, 'conscious thought was considered thought itself. Only now does the truth dawn on us that by far the greatest part of our spirit's activity remains unconscious and unfelt' (107). This unconscious and unfelt part of our spirit, the secret subject, is what he repeatedly calls the 'essential aspect of ourselves'. It is 'our pathos'. It is our body and its drives, 'the ensemble of our impulsive life' (111). Like Deleuze's secret subject, these drives *constitute consciousness*: 'The act of knowing, judging, or concluding is nothing but the result of a certain behavior of the impulses toward each other. [. . .] a precarious armistice between obscure forces' (108–9).

For Klossowski the unconscious subject which lives the impulses of the body is the 'will to power'. Klossowski translated Heidegger's lectures on Nietzsche, and he develops distinction that Heidegger mentioned but passed over: the will to power is a 'fact' but the eternal return is a 'thought'.[62]

The thought of the Eternal Return of the Same came to Nietzsche as an *abrupt awakening* in the midst of a *Stimmung*, a certain tonality of the soul. Initially confused with this *Stimmung, it gradually emerged as a thought* [. . .]. (*Nietzsche and the Vicious Circle* 44).

Klossowski develops his entire interpretation of the eternal return around this point. 'How can a tonality of the soul, a *Stimmung*, become a thought [. . .]' (47)? Klossowski will go on to give a detailed explanation of this process. He describes the way in which intensity folds back on itself, turning the pure designation of intensities into signification (thus suggesting that the eternal return cannot be thought outside of the context of the genesis of sense). The eternal return is neither intensity, our pathos, nor wakeful consciousness. Rather it is what mediates the relationship between body and consciousness. It is what brings about that precarious armistice between obscure forces which gives birth two consciousness. The thought of the eternal return is thus suspended somewhere between the will to power (the body, its impulses and intensities) and 'conscious thought' (knowing, judging, thinking). It is what regulates the relation between intensity and consciousness or 'communicable thought' and prevents the two from ever overlapping.

For his part, Deleuze puts the distinction between will to power and the eternal return this way:

> Difference in the will to power is the highest object of sensibility, the *hohe Stimmung*, sensed against the laws of nature (remember that the will to power was first presented as a feeling, a feeling of distance). Thought against the laws of nature, repetition in the eternal return is the highest thought, the *gross Gedanke*. (243/313/304; translation modified)

The influence of Klossowski is obvious. Difference in the will to power is *sensed*, it is the *hohe Stimmung*. Repetition in the eternal return is *thought*, it is the *gross Gedanke*. Indeed, it often seems as though Deleuze is less interested in the content of Nietzsche's thought than in the fact that it expresses the movement from the highest feeling to the highest thought. Deleuze will continually draw this distinction in different ways throughout the text. The will to power is becoming, but the eternal return is the Being said of becoming. The will to power is the in-itself of difference, but the eternal return is the for-itself.[63] The will to power is difference, but the eternal return is the affirmation, reproduction, repetition or return of difference (Deleuze uses all of these various expressions).[64] The will to power refers to a 'dissolved self' whereas the eternal return is the 'thought' of a 'fractured I'. This is a very subtle difference between the will to power and the eternal return which is sometimes undetectable, but it is absolutely essential.[65] It is the difference between intensity and virtuality.[66]

The important point for now is that the *thought* of Being is not first. It begins in 'sensibility' with a feeling of 'distance'. If Duns Scotus only thought Being, Nietzsche first felt it. The will to power is our pathos. It is the latent subject which apprehends singularities or is affected by the incompossible and insensible events. Being itself is 'wrested' from unindividuated beings. Being emerges from our pathos as the thought of our own affection. This is not a well-determined conscious thought. It remains enveloped in a mist. Eternal return is suspended between our pathos and our conscious thought, and it regulates the relationship between the two. The eternal return, the infamous 'virtual', is neither the first nor the last thought. Wrested from unindividuated beings, Being will produce Ideas which will 'bring Being back to all beings at once'. In returning to beings, it individuates them. Being arises at the midpoint of the Deleuzian dialectic.

How does this thought relate to anything that might have traditionally been called Being? In a review of Klossowski's essay, Blanchot describes the *thought* of the eternal return as a 'movement of intensity that always returns to itself, like the circle' (Blanchot *Friendship* 173). The word 'intensity' here expresses the way in which the body is experienced in the will. At the heart of this movement and ensuring the return of intensity to itself – ensuring that it fold back on itself – there is a 'unique sign in which *thought designates itself*' (173; my emphasis).

This sign, the strangest one, signifies only itself. A sign that one could call arbitrary, mysterious, secret (without secret), like a living point that would express and affirm the energetic life of thought reduced to the unity of this point.

63

A sort of intense coherence, in relation to which everyday life, the one that is content with the everyday system of signs, becomes, both within and without, the place of an intolerable coherence. (173; cf. 182)[67]

Thought is a self-designating sign, a sign which designates nothing but itself and which possesses an 'intolerable coherence'. There are at least two important historical allusions caught up in Blanchot's definition. The first refers to Kantian apperception. Thought is a unique sign which designates itself and which marks out a zone in which my representations are my representations. The second allusion is to Spinoza's definition of substance. 'By substance I mean that which is in itself and is conceived through itself' (Spinoza EID4). Spinoza points out that only one thing actually meets this definition: God (since everything else ultimately refer back to God). Only God or being is in itself and conceives only itself. When Blanchot (and Deleuze who will follow Blanchot on this) speaks of a sign, the strangest one, that signifies only itself, he is referring to the self-knowledge of Being.

Being is no longer the one above beings, but the unity of thought which emerges from the impulses of the body and from the unindividuated fragments which affect the body. This is the importance of the narrative of the history of univocity. From Duns Scotus to Spinoza to Nietzsche we go from the neutral infinite to the body and its being. Everything is reversed between Duns Scotus and Nietzsche. If Deleuze's doctrine of the eternal return means anything, it means that sensibility is raised to the power of thought and that Being is felt before it is thought. If Deleuze is a thinker of the infinite – and this is still very much an open question – then the infinite must emerge from within the finite.[68] It would therefore be a mistake to think that with the thought of the eternal return we have reached Deleuze's most fundamental thought. Difference in the will to power and repetition in the eternal return do not found Deleuze's thought, and ontology is no longer first philosophy. As we will see, the will to power presupposes the latent subject, the entire unconscious and its three passive syntheses. The third synthesis *as third* produces difference in intensity.

All of this belongs only to the first part of the detective story or to the first movement of the Deleuzian dialectic. In the second part of the story, the eternal return sublimates the will to power and by repeating it produces Ideas. But the eternal return is not Deleuze's last thought either, and it therefore points on to the third part of the story and to the second movement of the dialectic. Once produced in the eternal return, Ideas are actualized, thus producing conscious, representative thought – that part of thought which for the longest time was taken to be thought itself.

SECTION 3. CRITICAL AND DOGMATIC IMAGES OF THOUGHT

The theory of thought is like painting: it needs that revolution which took art from representation to abstraction. This is the aim of a theory of thought without image. (276/354/346)

'The Image of Thought' is the third chapter of *Difference and Repetition*. I am describing it before the second chapter for two reasons. First, it is primarily in chapters two, four and five that Deleuze describes in detail the main structure of his system, and I want to be able to present that process linearly in what follows. The second reason is that the third chapter is still preparatory and introductory. It has two functions. First, it is a negative presentation of the entire system. It covers each moment of the genesis of representation as it moves from the latent subject's singularity to the manifest subject's quality and extensity, but it only describes this genesis by contrasting it to a set of presuppositions. The second, and I would argue, primary function of the chapter is to outline a methodology. This goes hand in hand with the negative presentation of the system: by what means will Deleuze avoid all the presuppositions which define the tradition?

This chapter presents Deleuze's system in its entirety. This system has two main parts. I briefly described the path of the Deleuzian dialectic above: it is first the movement from singularity to the Idea; second, it is the movement from the Idea to representation. Repetition repeats singularities and in so doing produces the Idea.[69] When an Idea is actualized, a representation is produced. Following Deleuze in *The Logic of Sense* we can separate these two movements into two geneses. He called the genesis which moves from singularity to the Idea the 'dynamic genesis'. He called the genesis which followed the actualization of Ideas to representation the 'static genesis'.[70] This distinction is crucial to understanding the formal structure of the third chapter of *Difference and Repetition*.

In this chapter Deleuze describes eight 'postulates', or 'subjective presuppositions'. The first four postulates bear on the dynamic genesis. The last four bear on the static genesis. The chapter itself therefore has a relatively straightforward structure. First Deleuze presents a postulate (or sometimes two or three in a row) which characterizes a 'dogmatic' image of thought. He then pretends to remove that presupposition and to describe a new 'critical' image of thought which is supposedly free of presuppositions. Because my ultimate aim in this book is to describe the structure of *Difference and Repetition*, in what follows I will focus less on the dogmatic image and Deleuze's descriptions and criticisms of individual postulates and instead emphasize some characteristics of this new, critical image of thought.[71]

POSTULATES

What is a postulate? 'Postulates in philosophy are not propositions the philosopher asks us to accept. On the contrary, they are propositional themes which remain implicit and are understood in a pre-philosophical manner' (131/172/167). Postulates are not explicit propositions which one can contemplate and then affirm or deny in an active judgement. We are not asked to accept them. They are implied and remain 'pre-philosophical' – even though they might have important philosophical consequences. Deleuze uses an example from Descartes' *Meditations*. Descartes writes in the second meditation,

> What then did I formerly think I was? A man. But what is a man? Shall I say 'a rational animal'? No; for then I should have to inquire what an animal is, what rationality is, and in this way one question would lead me down the slope to harder ones, and I do not now have the time to waste on subtleties of this kind. (*Meditations* 25/81)

Descartes avoids the Aristotelian definition of 'man' as a rational animal because, as Deleuze puts it, 'such a definition explicitly presupposes the concepts of rationality and animality' (129/169/164). These constitute what Deleuze calls 'objective presuppositions'. The presupposition is explicit and the presupposed are 'concepts', or 'propositions'.

According to Deleuze it is in order to avoid these objective presuppositions that Descartes decides to define man not as a rational animal, but as a thinking being. While this avoids objective presuppositions, it still contains 'subjective or implicit' presuppositions. 'It is clear', Deleuze writes, 'that [Descartes] does not escape presuppositions of another kind – subjective or implicit presuppositions contained in opinions rather than concepts: it is presumed that everybody knows, independently of concepts, what is meant by self, thinking and being' (129/169/164). Deleuze's claim is that the expression, 'I think, therefore I am' presupposes three notions: that of 'self', that of 'thinking' and that of 'being'. These presuppositions are no longer explicit and propositional (or conceptual). They are not 'objective' presuppositions which are capable of further definition and refinement. Here the presupposition is implicit. The presupposed are opinions. They rest on what everybody already knows.

This becomes clearer if we remember Descartes' reply to an often repeated objection to the *cogito*:

> When someone says 'I am thinking, therefore I am, or I exist', he does not deduce existence from thought by means of a syllogism, but recognizes it as *something self-evident by a simple intuition of the mind*. (*Objections and Replies* 127; my emphasis)

This is what Deleuze means by an implicit or subjective presupposition: the idea that in the end being and thinking are treated not as a philosophical concepts but rest on a principle of 'self-evidence', on a 'simple intuition of the mind', when it is not at all self-evident what Descartes means by thinking, being, or the self.

This is precisely the problem with subjective presuppositions. Even though they are pre-philosophical and remain hidden as a consequence of their 'self-evidence' or obviousness, they still

67

determine the transcendental structures of thought. Deleuze will therefore describe, for each of the eight postulates, the way in which a certain presupposition does not remain at the level of opinion but finds its way into the transcendental. Each of the eight postulates 'presupposes a certain distribution of the empirical and the transcendental, and it is this distribution or transcendental model implied by the image that must be judged' (133/174/168). Even if these presuppositions are pre-philosophical they still determine philosophy, and it is at the level of the characterization of the transcendental that Deleuze ultimately places the importance of developing a critical image of thought.

An initial reading of the chapter would frame it as a critique of certain themes across the history of philosophy, and from certain point of view it is. Deleuze constructs across eight postulates what he calls the 'dogmatic image of thought'. This image doesn't belong to any particular philosophy in the tradition, and it would be a mistake to read his comments on certain philosophers as though they were well developed critiques of a philosophy. Perhaps a good comparison to his technique would be the way Merleau-Ponty, in the *Phenomenology of Perception*, describes two tendencies in thinking about thought – 'empiricism' and 'intellectualism' – between which he puts forward his own way of thinking about thought. In the same way that Merleau-Ponty's 'intellectualism' doesn't correspond in its specifics to any historical instance of idealism, Deleuze's dogmatic image of thought doesn't correspond in all of its particulars to any specific thinker. At times we recognize elements of Plato, Aristotle, Descartes, Kant, Hegel and above all Husserl. Deleuze's description of a dogmatic image of thought doesn't characterize any of these thinkers in particular. *It characterizes a set of tendencies in philosophical descriptions of thinking which causes philosophers to describe thought in relation to certain presuppositions.*[72]

REDUCTION

It is from this point of view that the third chapter of *Difference and Repetition* could be read as Deleuze's methodology. The specific problem which Deleuze has staged in this chapter is this: historically, in the attempt to determine and describe thought and its transcendental structures, various presuppos-itions have crept in and determined everything in advance, pre-philosophically, and before any real work had even begun. Of course throughout the history of philosophy, we can find other philosophers saying the very same thing. Descartes him-self, for example, found that the ideas his school teachers had implanted in his head as a boy continually recurred in his mature philosophy. Bergson found that our familiarity with space determined what we said about time. For Nietzsche, it was a moral image of thought which determined philosophy in advance, and so forth. It was ultimately Husserl and the phenomenological tradition, however, which both posed the problem of presuppositions and provided a method for avoid-ing these presuppositions in a way that Deleuze takes up in this chapter. It is true that the language Deleuze uses throughout the chapter is self-consciously Kantian – Kant claimed to ground 'dogmatic' metaphysics with a 'critical' one – and that the claim to have elaborated a presuppositionless science can be found in every major thinker of the critical tradition from Kant to Fichte to Hegel. And indeed, with this chapter, Deleuze places his philosophy firmly within the 'critical' tradition initiated by Kant. This distinction, however, is not at all foreign to phenom-enology, and if there is an essential tie to Husserl, it is because both Deleuze and Husserl use the same method in order to avoid the onslaught of presuppositions.

From its inception one of phenomenology's central projects was the description of thought. It could be described as an attempt to paint an image of thought. Husserl wanted to stick to thought itself and to describe its contours and textures, but for Husserl thought was not a homogenous field. There were many different levels or 'strata' of experience, some more prominent than others.[73] In the lowest depths of the ego, for example, there is an internal flow of time. On top of this flow is a second flow of unorganized data. The data from these flows is progressively organized through a combination of 'passive syntheses'. This progressive organization results in yet another flow: that of affections and intensities which populate the 'life world'. A further set of 'active' syntheses, which character-ize determinate, judgemental thought, is constructed upon the foundation of the life world.[74] These active syntheses can go very far into the determination of universals and abstract truths.

The project of describing thought is not, therefore, as simple as describing the contents of consciousness as they appear – a white piece of paper, a piece of wax or the red of a lampshade. Rather, the problem is how to describe the lower, *constituting* levels of thought *without thinking them in relation to the constituted products that populate our 'natural attitude'*. One cannot 'remain with the piece of wax itself, describe only what is given without presuppositions' as Lyotard has suggested, because as the lower depths are penetrated the object dissolves.[75] From this point of view Husserl's problem wasn't childhood or space but that we take for granted the fact that consciousness constructs our world for us. We have before us in our natural attitude an already constituted, meaningful world populated by determinate and unified objects fading off into their halos potentiality. But this world of unity and meaning is produced, and underneath the constituted world are many different strata of thought characterized by intensive becomings, potentialities and temporal horizons. All of these lower depths need to be described in themselves without importing the characteristics of the constituted world given in the natural attitude.

Husserl found that it was all too easy to talk about this constitutive life of consciousness in terms of the constituted life of consciousness. For example, in perception we are confronted with unified objects, but this unity is a produced unity which arises out of various levels of becoming. We can only discover becoming if we bracket unity and try to avert the direction of natural perception. He therefore needed a method in order to prevent himself from prejudging his analyses. The method which allows us to describe these lower levels without tracing elements of the natural attitude is the phenomenological reduction. At its most general, it 'brackets' the natural attitude and asks us to turn reflectively and without presupposition to the life of consciousness. We turn, as Merleau-Ponty puts it, from 'a thought obsessed with the world and the object' (PP 299) to the 'problem of the constitution of the world' (69).[76] The last thing we want to do as we make this turn away from the object is determine our new point of view, the constitution of the world, in the image of the object.

We could describe the reduction in another way. Because consciousness actually creates the world according to Husserl, he described constituting conscious as 'transcendental'. The ultimate goal of phenomenology then is to provide a 'scientific' description of the transcendental. The specific function of the reduction is to allow us to describe the transcendental without *epoche* importing characteristics of the empirical. As Deleuze would put it, the reduction prevents us from 'tracing' the transcendental from the empirical. This is the only characteristic that all eight postulates of the dogmatic image of thought have in common: *they all trace the transcendental from the empirical.* They all determine the constitutive life of thought in the image of the natural attitude. 'We discover in all the postulates of the dogmatic image the same confusion: elevating a simple empirical figure to the status of the transcendental, at the risk of allowing the real structures of the transcendental to fall into the empirical' (154/200–1/193). Regardless of the specific characteristic of each individual postulate, then, we can say that each postulate mistakes an empirical figure of thought for a transcendental figure, and it projects this empirical figure onto the transcendental structure of thought.

If we invert this situation we can formulate one of Deleuze's central projects: instead of elevating the empirical to the transcendental, he will describe the 'real structures of the transcendental' without reference to the empirical. He will paint a critical image rather than a dogmatic image of thought. We already saw him begin to do this in the introduction and first chapter of the book. The introduction freed up the notion of repetition so that it would be able to function as a new theory of mediation. Repetition is not the repetition of identical elements, but what functions below these elements and actually constitutes them. The first chapter began a liberation of the concept of difference from everything that was in fact constituted by difference (the concept, identity and opposition) so that difference might take on a new role in individuation. In this chapter, for the first time in the book, Deleuze provides a systematic account of his method. He brackets the empirical and describes the transcendental. In place of an 'Image which already prejudges everything' (131/172/167), he clears the field for a presuppositionless account of thought (130/171/166). But

71

it is this specific method, the phenomenological reduction, which allows Deleuze to articulate a 'critical image of thought' in opposition to each postulate of the dogmatic image. The reduction is, for Deleuze as it was for Husserl, the lever which allows us to displace the entire weight of the tradition – and, of course, Deleuze would have been well aware that Husserl himself characterized the natural attitude as 'dogmatic' and the phenomenological attitude as 'critical'.[77]

DYNAMIC GENESIS: THE DOCTRINE OF THE FACULTIES

The first four postulates all bear on Deleuze's characterization of the dynamic genesis, or the movement from the immediate object of intuition to the Idea. They characterize the latent subject of repetition. The first postulate, 'the principle of the *Cogitatio natura universalis*', bears on thinking in general. It states that we are all born with a capacity to think and that once this capacity is actualized it naturally wants the truth or has a natural orientation towards the true. The second postulate, 'the ideal of common sense', says that thought in general functions harmoniously. All of the various faculties – sensibility, imagination, memory and thought – work together in their attempt to explicate the object. The third postulate, 'the model of recognition', is the objective correlate to 'common sense'. Instead of finding unity in the harmonious exercise of the faculties, the unity now lies in the object: the object is supposed the same for each faculty: sensibility, imagination, memory and thought all confront one and the same object. The fourth postulate, 'the element of representation' states that all of the previous postulates – the search for the true, the relations among the faculties, and the relation of the faculties to the object – take place within the 'element of representation'. If we simply invert these four postulates we end up with four of the dominant characteristics of the dynamic genesis, many of which we have already encountered as the characteristics of the subterranean world of repetition laid out in the introduction: the dynamic genesis is sub-representative; the contemplated object is fragmented, not unified; the faculties do not work harmoniously; and thought is neither given nor synonymous with the good-natured pursuit of truth.

All four of these characteristics are brought together in Deleuze's doctrine of the faculties. But is this doctrine really even necessary to a comprehensive account of *Difference and Repetition*? It is both strange and marginal. Not only does it resuscitate an old-fashioned faculty psychology that would seem to no longer have any relevance today, but it also seems to be an isolated incident in the work. Deleuze elaborates his theory of the faculties never to return to it again in any great detail. These two points become even stranger in light of the fact that he attaches a *systematic importance* to the doctrine of faculties and claims to resurrect it even though it is currently unfashionable: 'Despite the fact that it has become discredited today, the doctrine of faculties is an entirely necessary component of the system of philosophy' (143/186/180). What are we to make of this return to faculty psychology?[78]

Much of what Deleuze says regarding the faculties comes straight out of his earlier work *Proust and Signs*. In a chapter of that book titled 'The Image of Thought', Deleuze describes 'Proust's' criticism of 'classical philosophy of the rationalist type' (PS 94). He begins by countering the notion of thought as a pure faculty with the notion of thought as genesis:

> The act of thinking does not proceed from a simple natural possibility; on the contrary, it is the only true creation. Creation is the genesis of the act of thinking within thought itself. This genesis implicates something that does violence to thought, which wrests it from its natural stupor and its merely abstract possibilities. (PS 97)[79]

We find the same idea in *Difference and Repetition*, only here it is Artaud speaking, not Proust.

> [Artaud] knows that thinking is not innate, but must be engendered in thought. He knows that the problem is not to direct or methodically apply a thought which pre-exists in principle and in nature, but to bring into being that which does not yet exist [. . .]. To think is to create – there is no other creation – but to create is first of all to engender 'thinking' in thought. (147/192/185)

'Creation' in both books is genesis. More specifically, it is the 'genesis of the act of thinking within thought itself'. If genesis is called '*true* creation', it is because it has nothing to do with pre-existent forms or faculties. It brings into being that which has never before existed: thinking. In *Difference and Repetition*, Deleuze calls this creation the 'principle of a transcendental empiricism' (147/192/185).[80] genesis

Thinking is not a simple possibility, but is born of a 'violence'. What is the nature of this violence which is at the origin of the entire genesis? In the words of Proust, this violence is the 'violence of an impression' (PS 97). In the words of Deleuze interpreting Proust, it is an 'encounter' with a '*material* impression' (PS 98, my emphasis). In *Proust and Signs* then, the object of this encounter which does us violence is clearly a material impression. It takes the form of a 'sign'.

This sign forces us to think, but 'thought' is only one faculty, the last, in a line of faculties which is created in attempt to interpret this violence. The material impression transmits a violence to sensibility which in turn transmits a violence to memory which in turn transmits a violence to thought.

> The sensuous sign does us violence: it mobilizes the memory, it sets the soul in motion; but the soul in its turn excites thought, transmits to it the constraint of the sensibility, forces it to conceive essence, as the only thing that must be conceived. Thus the faculties enter into a transcendent exercise, in which each confronts and joins its own limit: the sensibility that apprehends the sign; the soul, the memory, that interprets it; the mind that is forced to conceive essence. (PS 101)

Here Deleuze arranges the faculties along a genetic line which moves from sensation to thought. They are not arranged according to the model of 'common sense' or of the 'harmonious exercise' in which 'what we perceive we could just as well remember, imagine or conceive' (PS 99). Rather the violence of the sensible sign 'leads us in spite of ourselves to Essences' (PS 100), and it *has* to follow this line: from sensibility to memory to thought. Nor is the object unified. The violence is a material impression, but it is by no means a unified object which could support the convergence of the faculties.

Deleuze resurrects this model of the faculties in his description of the critical image of thought in *Difference and Repetition*, and he uses it to outline a critical image of thought.[81] Thought here is not a general faculty, as in the first postulate, or a collection of harmoniously functioning faculties, as in the second postulate, but is a series of faculties arranged along a 'discordant' genetic line. As in *Proust and Signs*, this genetic line begins with sensibility: 'on the path which leads to that which is to be thought, all begins with sensibility' (144/188/182).[82] And again, Deleuze is careful to point out that while thought begins with an experience of the world, this world is not populated by those unified objects of recognition which he had disqualified in the third postulate: 'Something in the world forces us to think. This something is not an object of recognition but of a fundamental *encounter*' (139/182/176; original emphasis). This unrecognizable object, this 'something in the world', doesn't depend on our goodwill as thinkers. It 'forces us to think', and under the shock of the fragmented object, sensibility sets off a discordant genetic line of the faculties. Finally, in opposition to the fourth postulate, the one which says that the general element of thought is representation, Deleuze introduces a distinction between an empirical sensibility and a transcendental sensibility. The fragmented object isn't experienced by the 'empirical sensibility' (140/182/176). Empirical sensibility is what apprehends the represented thing (quality + extensity). It never feels the violence of the encounter which remains, like Leibniz's 'insensible perceptions', 'imperceptible (*insensible*)' (144/187/181). Only a 'transcendental sensibility' grasps the fragmented object in its violence. It apprehends the object 'in the world' (139/182/176).

We can immediately recognize the way in which this image of thought corresponds to Deleuze's distinction between repetition and representation in the introduction and the way it recuperates a vulgarized Leibnizianism. What Deleuze called the 'secret' or 'latent' subject there is now called 'transcendental sensibility'. What I temporarily called the 'manifest subject' is now called 'empirical sensibility'. We learned in the introduction that the secret subject encountered singularities – not mathematical points, but the immediate object of intuition. We see here, that this is indeed the case: transcendental sensibility is born in a violent encounter with the world. It apprehends 'material impressions'. These material impressions are precisely the incompossible, insensible events which precede the subject and which account for its individuality. What transcendental sensibility encounters, we will see, is an *intensity* – a difference which is not contradiction, and this asymmetrical difference is transmitted along the genetic line of the faculties awakening each in its turn (144/186/181).

This allows us to further expand on some of the ideas hinted at in the first chapter. I suggested above that the Deleuzian dialectic jumped from singularity to the Idea and then from Idea to representation. In the introduction, the latent subject repeats or mediates singularity, and this repetition supposedly gives rise to the Idea (which in turn gives rise to representation). Here Deleuze tells us a second time that this subject indeed repeats the object of its encounter, but he fleshes out the path that leads from sensible singularity to the Idea. As the latent subject repeats the fragmented object, it passes this object on to other faculties. Between singularity and the Idea we pass through the faculties. The doctrine of the faculties therefore elaborates the entire first half of the Deleuzian dialectic. This process clearly deserves much more attention.

Deleuze gives two versions of the genetic line of the faculties in *Difference and Repetition*. The first, which echoes the distribution of faculties in *Proust and Signs*, is here attributed to Plato:

> sensibility, forced by the encounter to sense the *sentiendum*, forces memory in its turn to remember the *memorandum*, that which can only be recalled. Finally, the third characteristic of transcendental memory is that, in turn, it forces thought to grasp that which can only be thought, the *cogitandum* or *noēteon*, the Essence. (141/183/177)

Just as in *Proust and Signs* we proceed from sensibility to memory to thought or to the contemplation of Essence. And again, as in *Proust and Signs*, Deleuze opposes this to the harmonious exercise of the faculties:

> Rather than all the faculties converging and contributing to a common project of recognizing an object, we see divergent projects in which, with regard to what concerns it essentially, each faculty is in the presence of that which is its 'own'

Discord of the faculties, chain of force and fuse along which each confronts its limit, receiving from (or communicating to) the other only a violence which brings it face to face with its own element, as though with its disappearance or it perfection. (141/184/178)

Each faculty confronts its own limit. From the point of view of Deleuze's rewriting of the *Critique of Pure Reason* we could say that there is an experience of the sublime proper to each faculty, and that that experience is what ignites a particular faculty. Each faculty is overwhelmed by the violence which is passed on to it, and it is this feeling of vertigo which awakens it.

We should keep in mind, however, that in *Difference and Repetition* these statements on the faculties comprise a commentary *on Plato*, and they cannot be directly carried over into Deleuze's own system. They are Deleuze's slightly odd synthesis of Book VII of the *Republic* and the *Theaetetus* according to which knowledge begins with a contrary perception which then causes the knower to recollect and eventually, by means of this transcendental memory, to come to know Ideas. Immediately after these quotations Deleuze raises several objections both to Plato's characterizations of the object of the encounter and to his understanding of the respective faculties.[83] It would be a mistake then to treat Deleuze's version of the faculties in Plato as his own version.

There are two corrections which we must make to this model before we can get to the properly Deleuzian 'doctrine of the faculties' as it is presented in *Difference and Repetition* – and thus to his version of the 'system of philosophy'. The first change Deleuze makes regards the object of the encounter. In Deleuze's Plato, it is a 'contrary perception' which perplexes us, and which moves the soul to recollect (141/184/178). In place of the contrary perception, Deleuze will put 'intensity', a free difference rather than a difference which is pushed all the way to contrariety. Transcendental sensibility only encounters the fragmented object. The differences between fragments are not ordered or organized differences, and sensibility is not confused because it is caught between two judgements.

Deleuze also makes one more almost imperceptible change that makes all the difference for our understanding of how the doctrine of faculties relates to the rest of the book and to 'the system of philosophy' in general. For 'Proust' and Plato, the genetic line of the faculties goes from sensibility to memory to thought. But almost in passing, for the last formulation of the series of faculties in the book, Deleuze adds the imagination. In the final formulation the doctrine of the faculties reads as follows: 'transcendental sensibility' 'apprehends [an intensity] immediately in the encounter'. Then 'sensibility transmits its constraint to the *imagination*' (144/188/181; my emphasis). Imagination transmits its constraint to memory, and memory to thought.

Why is this so important? Because it allows us to answer two crucial questions. The first is, what does the doctrine of faculties have to do with the rest of the book? Clearly, if the order of the faculties is sensibility-imagination-memory-thought, we can see that the doctrine of faculties is simply a reformulation of the three passive syntheses. As we will see below, the first passive synthesis is brought about by the imagination, the second by the memory, and the third by thought. The entire chain of syntheses begins in the sensibility. This brings us to the second question, one which has plagued readings of *Difference and Repetition*: in what order do the three syntheses take place. James Williams and many others, for example, read the third synthesis as operating prior to the first. In both *Proust and Signs* and *Difference and Repetition*, however, Deleuze insists on the importance of a particular order. Thus he writes 'There is indeed a serial connection between the faculties and an *order in that series*' (145/189–90/183; my emphasis). We have to insist that the syntheses follow this particular order: beginning with the intensity given to a transcendental sensibility a 'forced and broken connection' 'traverses the fragments of a dissolved self' from imagination to memory to thought, and not the reverse (145/190/183).

STATIC GENESIS: THE ACTUALIZATION OF SENSE

The first four postulates bear on the dynamic genesis, and the new image of thought which Deleuze constructs in relation to these four postulates depicts the first movement of thought or the first part of Deleuze's detective story – the movement from sensible singularity to the Idea. The last four postulates bear on the second movement of thought. They bear on the static genesis or the movement from the Idea to representation. This static genesis begins more or less where the dynamic genesis left off. The dynamic genesis is the 'volcanic line' which leads from one faculty to the next. The last faculty in this chain is 'thought', the faculty of 'essences'. However, 'essence' is just another word for the Idea.[84] Of course 'thought' and 'Idea', 'cogito' and 'essence', words burdened by long histories, will take on entirely new meanings within the context of Deleuze's system. For now I simply want to make the point that the dynamic genesis ends in the faculty of thought, and that this new cogito is precisely the origin of Ideas, and therefore of the static genesis which actualizes Ideas.

In this last part of the chapter Deleuze does two things that will be essential for the rest of the book. First he outlines the contours of an epistemology.[85] He tells us – even if only in a general way – how a representation truthfully relates to its object. Second, he establishes an important set of synonyms which all express in different ways the movement between Ideas and representation. Table 1 outlines those synonyms.

The entire static genesis unfolds between these two dimensions. It goes from Ideas to representation, from sense to the proposition, from the problem to its solution, or from learning to knowledge.

The fifth postulate is difficult to understand at this point in the book. It describes thought's 'misadventures', where it goes wrong. Its empirical figure is 'error', and as it is prone to do, the dogmatic image of thought inscribes error at the heart of the subject.[86] If the 'negative' of the dogmatic image is error, the negative or misadventure of the critical image is 'stupidity'.[87] What does Deleuze mean by a *transcendental* stupidity? 'How is stupidity (not error) possible? It is possible by virtue of the link between thought and individuation (151/197/189). Stupidity is possible by virtue of the link between thought, the faculty of Ideas, and individuation. We will only be able to register

Table 1 Synonyms for 'Idea' and 'Representation'

3].	*Representation:*	Proposition	Solution	Knowledge
2].	*Ideas:*	Sense	Problem	Learning
1].	Singularity		Question	

(handwritten marginalia): tatic gen. { 3], 2] ; ynamic gen. { 1]

the full significance of this statement after a close reading of the last two chapters of *Difference and Repetition*. For now we can simply notice that stupidity is the lack of communication between two fundamentally different elements of subjectivity. 'Thought' is the faculty of Ideas. 'Individuation' refers to the incarnation of Ideas within a field of intensity, or within transcendental sensibility. In other words, 'individuation' is the act in which thought returns to what was sensed. It is a synthesis of Idea and intensity, of thought and sensibility.[88] An Idea is a form, but the field of intensity is formless. If everything works correctly, when Ideas return to sensibility they will also give their form to it. Ideas will be plugged into intensities and will be able to give rise to determinate representations, or 'individuals'. Hence the name 'individuation'. In stupidity the synthesis of thought and intensity fails to take place. Rather than contemplating an 'individual' (quality + extensity) that is 'differenciated' or formed by the Idea, we are given a formless individual. Thus stupidity is the 'relation in which individuation brings the ground to the surface without being able to give it form' (152/197/190).

The last three aspects of the critical image of thought become relevant only insofar as actualization or individuation actually takes place. Assuming that stupidity is not an issue, and assuming that thought suffers no misadventures, to what degree can thought then be said to possess truth?

In the sixth postulate Deleuze draws a distinction between sense and the proposition, and Deleuze's remarks on this postulate will go a long way towards clarifying what he means by 'sense'. He begins with by distinguishing two dimensions of the proposition: 'two dimensions may be distinguished in a proposition: *expression*, in which a proposition says or expresses some idea; and *designation*, in which it indicates or designates the objects to which what is said or expressed applies' (153/199/191; original emphases). In order to make a similar distinction Frege, for example, pointed out that the expressions 'morning star' and 'evening star' both denote the same object – the planet Venus – but each expression has a completely different sense. Imagine that you knew someone who was aware that the morning star was the planet Venus, but still thought that the evening star was in fact a star. If, to borrow Frege's riveting example, you were to propose to that person the proposition, 'the Morning Star is a planet with a shorter period of revolution than the Earth', they will no doubt agree with you and consider that proposition to be true. As long as they consider the substitution of 'Venus' for 'Morning Star' to be valid.[89] If you said the same thing of the evening star, given that they still think the star is a star, though they would consider the proposition to be false.

When Deleuze complains that 'sense conditions the true' but does not ground truth itself, he is alluding to this phenomenon. The only way you can talk about the morning star with your imaginary friend is on the condition that they *grasp* what you mean by the expression 'morning star', and one has to grasp the sense of an expression before it is judged to be true. There is no question that from this point of view it is ultimately denotation, and not sense, that determines the truth of the proposition, but sense still conditions the relation. In other words, the imaginary friend can think what they like about the evening star, but it will ultimately be the characteristics of the object itself, and not the sense your friend has, that determines what can be said about the star.

Deleuze will develop an alternative concept of sense in which sense, and not designation, determines the truth of the proposition. It is not so much that he 'attacks' this vision of language. Rather, like Husserl, he tries to ground it, and in doing so he utilizes a completely different notion of sense than the one employed in the analytic tradition immediately following Frege.[90] Deleuze characterizes the Fregean notion of sense as being too loose: 'Sense is defined as the condition of the true' but the condition retains 'an extension larger than that which is conditioned' (153/199/191). In contrast to this, in his notion of sense, Deleuze is trying to conceive of a condition which is strictly coextensive with the conditioned – sense as a condition of 'real experience' (154/200/192).[91]

This has broad implications for what Deleuze means by 'sense'. The Fregean version bordered on the concept. Sense had a certain generality which allowed it to be present during multiple instances of encountering the morning star, but Deleuze explicitly denies that sense has any relation to the concept or to generality (155/201/193). In saying that sense is a condition tied to real experience, that *it is no wider than that experience,* and that it is a plastic principle which changes with experience, he is suggesting that sense is generated here and now in the immediate presence of the object. The 'sense' of an object was never seen prior to the object, but was created upon the appearance of the object and will fade upon its disappearance. Deleuze goes even further however: for him the object is not yet constituted. 'The nature of ideal sense is to point beyond itself (*se dépasser*) towards the object designated' (154/200/192). Sense transcends itself towards the object, and in its transcendence it actually constitutes the object. Sense does not refer to an object or a concept, but is what produces the very object itself in the first place.

From this point of view we can see how much Deleuze's notion of sense differs from the Fregean: sense is not the presupposed concept, but what generates the object itself. We can also see how Husserlian Deleuze is. It is worth quoting Husserl on this point because it touches on several of the themes which follow. For Husserl, the act of judgement *constitutes* propositions. Once constituted and deemed as true, these propositions take the form of repeatable, communicable pieces of 'knowledge'.

> Knowledge of what? Speaking quite generally, knowledge of what-is, of the existent [*das Seiende*]. But if the striving for knowledge is directed toward the existent, if it is the effort to formulate in a judgment what and how the existent is, then the existent must have been given beforehand. And since the act of judgment requires something 'underlying' about which it judges, an *object-about-which*, it is necessary that the existent be so pregiven that it can become the object of a judgment. (E&J 19; original emphases)

This passage is organized according to the regression which I outlined in the first chapter above. Knowledge is an affirmative statement. As affirmative it presupposes a judgement, but judgement is always a judgement about something. Judgement itself therefore presupposes an object-about-which judgement is passed. This object is given by the passive syntheses. Reversing the order, we can say from the point of view of constitution, that in order for there to be knowledge, there must first be a set a passive syntheses which constitute the concrete object. Judgement itself is an active synthesis which operates on these objects produced in passivity. If the judgement is affirmative, the proposition is stored as knowledge. This is perhaps too schematic, but we can see two things here that Deleuze will draw on. The first is Husserl's characterization of knowledge as propositional. Genesis ends with the truthful proposition. We can already see that Deleuze alludes to this characterization in Table 1, and we will return to this below. The second thing that Deleuze will draw on is related to Husserl's claim that judgement bears on an object which is assumed as pregiven. The object-about-which a judgement is made is an already given object, provided in advance of the judgement. This is clearly the case in Frege's example. The morning star and Venus are already there, and what is at issue is not how they came to be there, but how a proposition truthfully relates to what is already given. Husserl's expressed project, however, is a 'genealogy of logic' which is undertaken with the sole purpose of grounding this relation of the proposition to its object. It is not therefore enough to treat the object as pregiven by passive syntheses. The object itself must be 'so pregiven', or given in such a way 'that it can become the object of a judgment'. In other words it has to be given truthfully. In order for judgement to actively attribute truth to an object, we must first be certain of the object about which judgement is made. The truth of the judgement is derived from our certainty about the object. Husserl thus says that the object must be given 'in simple certainty' or in the 'certainty of being'. Since 'every thinkable judgment *ultimately* refers to individual objects' (E&J 26), the genealogist of logic must trace and describe the emergence of the individual object as it is formed in the horizon of the life world with the 'certainty of being'.

It is this latter project which Deleuze seems to be concerned with in the final sections of the third chapter. For Deleuze, truth is not found in the adequacy of the proposition to the denoted. 'In every respect, truth is a matter of production, not of adequation' (154/200/192). Adequacy is grounded in sense, as is denotation:

Designation, in so far as it is achieved in the case of a true proposition, would never be grounded unless it were

understood as the limit of the genetic series or the ideal connections which constitute sense. (154/200/192)

How does this grounding take place? We will see below that it
depends in part upon the actualization of Ideas. The 'ideal connections which constitute sense' in the virtual Idea produce the
determinate object whenever an Idea is actualized.
The seventh postulate is closely related to this set of concerns.
Here 'sense' is called a 'problem' and the proposition is called a
'solution'. Deleuze writes that '[t]he problem or sense is at once
both the site of an originary truth and the genesis of a derived
truth' (159/207/198). At one level, this repeats the claim Deleuze
made above: a true proposition must be understood as the limit
of a genetic series. However Deleuze adds something here. Such
a proposition, which is tied to its conditions of production, has
only a derived truth. There is in fact an 'originary' truth, close
to what Husserl called the 'certainty of being'. This is the truth
specific to sense itself or to the problem, and it is independent of the truth of the proposition. Deleuze will often say, for
example, that 'We always have as much truth as we deserve in
accordance with the sense of what we say' (154/200/193); or 'A
solution always has the truth it deserves according to the problem to which it is a response, and the problem always has the
solution it deserves in proportion to *its own* truth or falsity'
(159/206/198; original emphasis). The solution of a problem is
an effect which is true only in proportion to the truth of the
problem.
The consequences of this are important. If sense is the
originary truth which gives rise to the proposition as an effect
and as a derived truth, the truth or falsity of sense has to be
determined within sense itself. It has to be determined without
relation to the proposition or the solution since the solution is
only produced afterwards.
Here we can clearly recognize the importance of the phenomenological reduction. Deleuze consistently remarks that
we cannot in any way let the product prejudice our understanding of the production. Problems cannot be determined
in 'the shadow of pre-existing solutions but, on the contrary,
because the solution necessarily follows from the complete
conditions under which the problem is determined as problem'

(159/206/198). What, then, does this process of production look like? How is the problem determined as problem or without any reference to solutions? Deleuze's answer is that it is determined by an 'ideal synthesis' (164/213/204). The description of this ideal synthesis will be the major project of chapter four of *Difference and Repetition*, but Deleuze already points towards it in the eighth postulate.

So far Deleuze has made two closely related claims. In the sixth postulate he claimed that the proposition has to be grounded in a 'genetic series or *ideal relations* which constitute sense'. In the seventh postulate he claimed that that set of ideal relations needed to be determined by an 'ideal synthesis' which determined sense without any relation to representation. Truth needs to be determined in the problem, not the solution. At first sight, in the eighth postulate where Deleuze opposes knowledge to learning and says that knowledge can in no way determine our understanding of learning, he seems to simply repeat what was said in the previous two.

What does Deleuze mean by 'learning' and 'knowledge'? In the fourth chapter Deleuze will describe the 'ideal synthesis' in much greater detail. The ideal synthesis is a synthesis which progressively establishes 'ideal connections' between virtual elements. It is these relations that 'constitute sense'. Insofar as these relations progressively constitute sense, the process of establishing them can be called 'learning'. Learning is the process in which we make sense of something. Learning gives rise to knowledge. The end of learning is knowledge. As we saw above, for Husserl, knowledge is the set of affirmative propositions that we have made about objects.[92] In other words, knowledge is the proposition. Learning is the progressive determination of the Idea which will give rise to knowledge. The eight postulate therefore seems a simple repetition of all the others: don't let the product determine the process of production in its image. Just as the sixth postulate warned against creating sense in the image of the proposition, the eighth warns us against modelling learning after knowledge.

However, this postulate goes beyond the relation between sense and representation. This postulate is the one 'which incorporates and recapitulates all the others in a supposedly simple result' (167/216/207). Learning does not bear only on the static genesis, or on the birth and actualization of Ideas. It begins back at the very beginning of everything. It begins with an 'apprentice' (the latent subject of repetition) which follows the volcanic line of the faculties up until the production of Ideas in 'thought', and it ends when Ideas are actualized into determinate representations (164/213–14/204).[93] In fact the apprentice is nothing other than the set of faculties. Learning 'is the true transcendental structure which unites difference to difference, dissimilarity to dissimilarity, without mediating between them; and introduces time into thought' (166–7/216/206–7). The unification of difference to difference describes the faculty of imagination. The unification of dissimilarity refers to the faculty of memory. The introduction of time into thought refers to the faculty of thought. In thought the Idea is born. And once the Idea is born, it is actualized in propositions. If these propositions are affirmed they constitute knowledge. Knowledge, 'the supposedly simple result' is the final telos of the entire genesis – of the entire book.

From this point of view it is tempting to say that *Difference and Repetition* is Deleuze's *Bildungsroman*, it is Deleuze's *Emile*, or maybe even his *Phenomenology of Spirit*. But we could just as well say that it is his *Critique of Pure Reason* rewritten from the vantage point attained in the *Critique of Judgment*.

SECTION 4. THE THREE PASSIVE SYNTHESES

Chapter two of *Difference and Repetition* is the first chapter in which Deleuze begins to lay out the structure of his system step by step. In chapter three we caught a glimpse of the total structure of *Difference and Repetition* for the first time. A dynamic genesis begins in sensibility and sets off the 'explosive' line of the faculties as it travels from the imagination to memory to thought. Thought is the faculty of Ideas or of essences. In it, Ideas are born. These Ideas lead to a second genesis. The static genesis follows the actualization of Ideas as they move from thought to the world of representation. Chapter two of *Difference and Repetition* is related only to the first of these geneses. It is Deleuze's account of the dynamic genesis. We saw above how this genesis was filled out by the faculties. The latent subject does not jump from singularity to Ideas. Rather the fragmented object is passed from one faculty to the next. In this chapter each of the faculties are reformulated as passive syntheses, and these syntheses move from the discontinuous matter of sensibility up to thought, the faculty of Ideas.

The title of chapter two is 'Repetition for Itself'. This refers us back to the introduction. In the introduction, Deleuze developed a concept of repetition which, following Kierkegaard and Gabriel Tarde, was supposed to function as an alternative to Hegelian mediation. Despite the fact that 'repetition' remained just as vague as 'mediation' we were still able to settle on three characteristics of this new dialectic: (1) it repeated 'singularities', or the immediate objects of intuition; (2) it was prior to the law, 'essentially transgression'; and (3) it was pre-conceptual, giving rise to the Idea which would block the concept. Deleuze described yet another characteristic of repetition as it differs from mediation in the first chapter, 'Difference in itself'. Mediation in Hegel proceeds by means of a symmetrical synthesis, or a thesis which is confronted by its opposite. For Deleuze, however, each synthesis is asymmetrical.[94] In this chapter Deleuze draws all of these elements together and finally shows us how this process unfolds. He describes in detail the way in which three passive syntheses take up the object of immediate intuition and transform that object into an Idea.

It is not hard to see how things are beginning to come together. The three characteristics of repetition (from singularity to the Idea) are clearly related to the dynamic genesis outlined in chapter three (from sensibility to thought), and I am about to describe the way in which the three passive syntheses are the detailed and systematic exposition of these two processes. But as things become more clear they also become more complicated. This complication takes off in two directions in this chapter. First, there is a further proliferation of technical vocabularies. We have already encountered the syntheses in the languages of repetition and of the faculties. In this chapter Deleuze adds *three* more ways to talk about the dynamic genesis. Second, despite the early emphasis on Hegel, he is by no means the most important historical figure behind these syntheses. Like Leibniz – and Hegel himself – Deleuze is the great synthesizer of philosophy. This chapter in particular manages to bring together thinkers as diverse as Hume, Leibniz, Kant,

Hegel, Bergson, James, Freud, Husserl, Heidegger, Levinas, Merleau-Ponty, Lacan and Ricoeur – and there are probably more. This makes the text extraordinarily rich, but also unspeakably dense. Of course it would be impossible to untangle all of these lines, not to mention counter-productive. There are however three inescapable figures in the background of the chapter: Husserl, Kant and Heidegger. In order to understand what goes on in this tremendously important chapter, we have to understand the way that each of these three figures contributes to the theory of 'repetition'.

HUSSERL, KANT AND HEIDEGGER
Husserl
Throughout this chapter (and indeed, throughout the book) Deleuze constantly appropriates Husserlian concepts. At the same time that he appropriates these concepts, however, he often changes them in ways that tend to obscure their lineage. The one concept that he does take from Husserl without significantly altering it is the notion of a passive synthesis. Husserl himself derived this notion from Kant.

In *Ideas I* Husserl makes the clearly uncontestable claim that 'phenomenology is, so to speak, the secret nostalgia of all modern philosophy' (*Ideas* 142). The first philosopher to 'correctly see' this was Kant even if he was unable to recognize phenomenology as a legitimate field of work. Consequently, only a small portion of the *Critique* is relevant to phenomenology.

> Thus, for example, the transcendental deduction in the first edition of the *Kritik der reinen Vernunft* was actually operating inside the realm of phenomenology, but Kant misinterpreted that realm as psychological and therefore he himself abandoned it. (*Ideas* 142)

This almost throwaway sentence contains the germ of what would become one of Husserl's most influential and important ideas. Here Husserl reclaims the transcendental deduction of the first edition of the *Critique* for phenomenology. In particular he has in mind the second section of that deduction in which Kant develops his account of the three syntheses.[95]

In addition to singling out only an extremely small portion of the *Critique*, Husserl also emphasizes that it is only 'the first edition' of the deduction that carries any relevance for phenomenology. The transcendental deduction underwent significant changes between the 1781 edition of the *Critique* and the 1787 edition. By specifying that it is only in the so-called A edition that Kant gives in to his secret nostalgia and becomes a phenomenologist, Husserl first hits on the idea of a passive synthesis.

It is worth describing this in some detail since it will also shed some light on what Kant himself contributes to this chapter of *Difference and Repetition*. In the 1781 edition of the *Critique of Pure Reason*, there were three syntheses that belonged to three separate faculties. Kant suggests this distribution of the syntheses in the titles of each section dealing with a particular synthesis: '(1) On the synthesis of apprehension in the intuition;' '(2) On the synthesis of reproduction in the imagination;' and '(3) On the synthesis of recognition in the concept'.[96] He states it explicitly in this preliminary formulation of the syntheses:

> There are, however, three original sources (capacities or faculties of the soul), which contain the conditions of the possibility of all experience, and cannot themselves be derived from any other faculty of the mind, namely **sense, imagination,** and **apperception**. On these are grounded 1) the **synopsis** of the manifold *a priori* through sense; 2) the **synthesis** of the manifold through the imagination; finally 3) the **unity** of this synthesis through original apperception. (CPR A94; original emphasis)[97]

Synopsis, synthesis and unity are the three aspects of synthesis, and each belongs to a specific and original faculty – sense, imagination and apperception. Synopsis, synthesis and unity will become the three different syntheses of apprehension, reproduction and recognition, and we will return to the specific character of each of these syntheses below, but notice here that of these three moments, 'original apperception' enters the picture only in the third moment. 'Original apperception' is the transcendental ground of all subjectivity, the 'absolutely first and synthetic principle of our thinking in general' (A117). It is what gives the I its numerical unity outside of and prior to any experience (A107). Further, it is characterized by freedom and spontaneity. The transcendental I isn't mechanistically determined, but is free and acts spontaneously. The other two faculties – sense and imagination – only receive this freedom in a mediated form insofar as they are subject to the volition of the active subject. Otherwise they do not participate in the activity of apperception, but function *passively* (A124). They take what is given to them. They are 'blind' syntheses 'of which we are seldom ever conscious' (A78/B103).

By the 1787 edition however all three syntheses fell under the jurisdiction of apperception.[98] Thus at the opening of the B deduction Kant writes,

> the **combination** (*conjunctio*) of a manifold in general can never come to us through the senses, and therefore cannot already be contained in the pure form of sensible intuition; for it is an act of the spontaneity of the power of representation, and, since one must call the latter understanding, in distinction from sensibility, *all combination, whether we are conscious of it or not, whether it is a combination of the manifold of intuition or of several concepts [. . .] is an action of the understanding* [. . .]. (CPR B129–30; original emphasis)

In the A deduction there was always an implied possibility of an unconscious synthesis, of a synthesis brought about by a passive faculty under the radar of the spontaneity and self-conscious 'self-activity' (B130) of the cogito. In this passage however Kant completely and unequivocally revokes that possibility. Sense, a passive faculty, does not combine. There is no combination outside of original apperception.

For Husserl this move obscured Kant's 'brilliant insight' of the A deduction into a type of synthesis that was operated by a passive faculty which functioned independently of our activity (APS 410). Husserl thus goes on to recuperate this notion of synthesis and to put it to profound use in his later writings. Deleuze directly adopts this notion from Husserl in *Difference and Repetition* in his terse definition of passive synthesis as one which 'is not carried out by the mind, but occurs *in* the mind' (DR 71; original emphasis). A passive synthesis is a synthesis that is not carried out by an active faculty but by a passive faculty. It is a synthesis of which we are seldom ever conscious.[99]

The fact that these syntheses are unconscious is not at all what is most interesting about them for either Deleuze or Husserl. What is far more interesting is that they are not rule-governed syntheses. They are essentially transgressive. *passive syntheses*

Kant

This aspect comes out nicely in Deleuze's reading of Kant. In his lectures on Kant, Deleuze paints a general picture of Kant's thought which I will summarize here both because it touches on several aspects which will recur over the next few chapters of *Difference and Repetition*, and because it is often easiest to start with the bigger picture.

According to Deleuze, Kant distinguishes between 'two types of determination'. Every object has conceptual determinations and every object has spatio-temporal determinations. For example, we can have a pure concept of a straight line, but we can also say that a straight line is the shortest distance between two points. This latter proposition goes beyond the concept ('straight line') insofar as it embodies spatial determinations ('shortest distance'). This distinction between kinds of determination takes on a systematic importance when Kant argues that the two types of determination, spatio-temporal and conceptual, cannot at all be reduced to one another, as the example of enantiomorphic bodies is supposed to show.[100] In fact, the two types of determination belong to two separate faculties. Spatio-temporal determinations are given by the forms of sensibility (space and time). The conceptual determinations are given by the understanding (the categories).

In order to *know* something, these two types of determination need to be brought together. For Deleuze, this is the importance of Kant's definition of knowledge as a synthetic proposition. An analytic proposition is one in which the determination or the predicate is contained within the concept. By analyzing the concept, you discover the predicate. By contrast, in a synthetic proposition a determination which is beyond the concept is added to it. In the Kantian synthetic proposition, it is the spatio-temporal determinations which are beyond the concept and which are added to conceptual determinations, or vice versa.

The question of whether a synthetic proposition is possible is therefore the question of the relation between two different faculties and their respective determinations. What is the relation between intuition and the understanding? Between spatio-temporal determinations and conceptual determinations? This relation takes place in two directions, both of which will play a significant role in *Difference and Repetition*. Either conceptual determinations are added to spatio-temporal determinations, or spatio-temporal determinations are added to conceptual determinations. In the first case, the relation is called the schematism. In the schematism a concept is given spatio-temporal determinations: the concepts of the understanding are applied to the forms of sensibility. In the second case it is called synthesis. In synthesis spatio-temporal diversity is taken up into the unity of a concept.

In my first chapter I said that *Difference and Repetition* was structured along the lines of a conceptual experiment: what would Kant's first *Critique* look like from the point of view of the third? This experiment led Deleuze on a double adventure. The first was a reconfiguration of the Kantian syntheses as faculties arranged along a genetic line. The second was a reconfiguration of the Kantian schematism. This second chapter of *Difference and Repetition* is Deleuze's account of the first adventure. It takes up the Kantian syntheses and describes them from the point of view of a transcendental genesis. Each synthesis, and in particular the third, will undergo significant revisions in Deleuze's hands. Even so, the conceptual structure of the second chapter as a whole, as well as the various relations between Deleuze's three syntheses, is largely indebted to the structure of Kant's three syntheses. It is therefore necessary to briefly describe the way in which the syntheses function in Kant, and especially in Deleuze's reading of Kant.

In Kant, each synthesis has two forms: transcendental and empirical. As transcendental syntheses, the syntheses move from the pure forms of intuition, space and time, to the form of the understanding, concepts or the categories. Synthesis moves from the spatio-temporal diversity of intuition to the concepts of the understanding. In their empirical aspect, the syntheses move from the unorganized appearances which fill out the forms of intuition to the unity of an object. Empirical synthesis moves from the 'indeterminate object' of intuition to the determinate object of the understanding, and this is why Deleuze will often refer to it as a 'perceptual' synthesis. (It is also for this reason that Husserl likens the Kantian syntheses to his passive syntheses: they both constitute the object of perception or the object-about-which judgement is passed (APS 410).)[101]

Synthesis therefore begins in a manifold, or diversity.[102] And like synthesis, diversity has an empirical aspect and a transcendental aspect. As Deleuze puts it, there is 'diversity as it *appears* in space and time' (empirical diversity), and there is 'the diversity of space and time themselves' (transcendental diversity) (KP 15). Synthesis bears both on empirical appearances and on the forms of sensibility themselves.

With regard to the first empirical synthesis, Kant writes that 'it is necessary to run through and then to take together this manifoldness, which action I call the **synthesis of apprehension,** since it is aimed directly at the intuition' (CPR A99; original emphasis). This is only the empirical synthesis. It gathers together the diversity that appears in space and time in an apprehension. It is a synopsis or survey of the manifold. Kant describes the transcendental synthesis, on the other hand, as a 'synthesis of the manifold that sensibility in its original receptivity provides' (A100). In contrast to the empirical synthesis, this synthesis gathers together not the appearances, but the diversity of 'original' time and space as such. In so doing, Kant says, it 'generates' or produces representations of space and time. From here we can understand Deleuze's definition of the first synthesis, a definition which exercises more economy of expression than most poets: the first 'aspect' of synthesis is 'apprehension, by means of which we pose the manifold as occupying a certain space and a certain time [i.e. in the empirical synthesis], by means of which we "produce" different parts in space and time [i.e. in the transcendental synthesis]' (KP 15).

At an empirical level, the second synthesis of 'reproduction' conditions association. In experience a present perception causes me to *reproduce* a previous representation with which it is associated. The transcendental synthesis, on the other hand, conditions reproducibility in general. It is what makes empirical association possible in the first place. It is necessary because, as Kant tells us at the beginning of his exposition of the syntheses, time is the form of inner sense, and everything that happens in thought is subject to the passage of time. This is especially true of the syntheses. What we apprehend in the first synthesis passes in time. A second synthesis is therefore necessary.

> [I]f I were always to lose the preceding representations [. . .] from my thoughts and not reproduce them when I proceed to the following ones, then no whole representation and none of the previously mentioned thoughts [. . .] could ever arise. (CPR A102)

The second synthesis of reproduction addresses this problem. It reproduces in the present apprehension what was previously apprehended. 'The synthesis of apprehension is therefore inseparably combined with the synthesis of reproduction' (A102). Deleuze tersely summarizes this second synthesis as well: the second aspect of synthesis is 'reproduction, by means of which we reproduce the preceding parts as we arrive at the ones following' (KP 15).

Kant describes the need for a third synthesis as follows: 'Without consciousness that that which we think is the very same as what we thought a moment before, all reproduction in the series of representations would be in vain. For it would be a new representation in our current state' (A103). In other words, one has to *recognize*, in the 'unity of the synthesis', that what was reproduced is the same as what was apprehended. The third synthesis appears here as a synthesis of the representations produced in the first two. Because time is the form of inner sense, if we apprehend something, we will have to reproduce it, or else we will lose it forever. But if we don't recognize what was reproduced as what was apprehended, we will simply treat the reproduction as a new appearance.[103] All three syntheses seem inseparably bound. It is at this point that Deleuze's reading of Kant becomes interesting. Recognition is not at all like the other two syntheses.

On Deleuze's reading only the first two syntheses make up the process of synthesis. 'Synthesis has two aspects': apprehension and reproduction (KP 15). He says this for a number of reasons, but primarily because the third synthesis, that of recognition, belongs to an entirely different faculty than the first two (passive) syntheses.[104]

> [S]ynthesis, as both apprehension *and* reproduction, is always defined by Kant as an act of the imagination. But the question is: can we say with complete accuracy, as we did above, that synthesis is sufficient to constitute knowledge? In fact knowledge implies two things which go beyond synthesis itself: it implies consciousness, or more precisely the belonging of representations to a single consciousness within which they must be linked. Now, the synthesis of the imagination, taken in itself, is not at all self-conscious (CPR A78/B103). On the other hand, knowledge implies a necessary relation to an object. That which constitutes knowledge is not simply the act by which the manifold is synthesized, but the act by which the represented manifold is related to an object (recognition: this is a table, this is an apple, this is such and such an object). (KP 15; original emphasis)

Recognition goes beyond synthesis in two directions: it points towards the unity of the subject, or towards original apperception, and it points towards the unity of the object, the object = X, or what Deleuze sometimes calls the 'object-form'.[105] How are these three things related: recognition, apperception and the object = X?

Deleuze first asks what the relation between the object = X and the unity of consciousness is. His answer is somewhat surprising. The unity of apperception is what lets me say that my representations are mine. It grants me a numerical unity, and this unity provides what Heidegger describes as a 'zone'.[106] In this zone, all my representations are 'linked', and only insofar as they are linked in the unity of this zone can they be called *my* representations. Deleuze suggests that my representations could not be linked in consciousness unless they were themselves unified in the first place. The zone itself is populated by determinate objects. 'Now, representations are not *united* in a consciousness in this way unless the manifold that they *synthe-size* is thereby related to the object in general' (KP 15; original emphasis). Representations are not linked in the unity of apperception *unless* they are related to the object. Deleuze seems to be in the process of subordinating the unity of consciousness to the unity of the object = X. The object = X is what unifies the manifold, and apperception is simply consciousness of this unity. The way Deleuze achieves this is quite simple. It turns on understanding the categories as 'predicates of the object in general' (KP 16).

How do these predicates determine the object in general? This is the crucial point: they determine the object in general by determining the third synthesis. After the first synthesis apprehends diversity, and after the second synthesis reproduces what was apprehended, recognition *unifies* the synthesis insofar as it synthesizes according to the category. Recognition is not a passive or unconscious synthesis like the first two. Recognition is a rule-governed synthesis, and the categories are precisely the rules for the unity of synthesis. 'Thus the category provides unity for the synthesis of imagination' (KP 16). It is the 'unity of the rule' which grants the third synthesis its unity. This is how the categories determine the object: they determine the synthesis, enabling it to bring unity to appearances. Finally, apperception is *consciousness of* the unity of synthesis (A108).[107] Apperception is made possible by the unity of the synthesis.

There are a number of themes in this narrative that will become important below. The two worth noting right away are the structure of the syntheses, and the relation to Husserl's notion of a passive synthesis. The syntheses move from an indeterminate object dispersed in diversity to the determinate object of cognition. The first synthesis apprehends diversity itself. The second synthesis reproduced what was apprehended, and only by virtue of the categories understood as rules, does the third synthesis unify the synthesis. The fact that this synthesis is rule-governed returns us to the theme of passive synthesis. The first characteristic of a passive synthesis was that it was unconscious. It took place in the mind but was not carried out by the mind. This type of synthesis characterizes the first two Kantian syntheses which Deleuze described above as being 'not at all self-conscious'. The third synthesis however, insofar as it is governed by the categories, is carried out both in the mind and by the mind.

Here we can see two of the three characteristics of 'repetition' that Deleuze outlined in the introduction taking shape: repetition is unconscious; it unfolds in a latent subject; and repetition is before the law, essentially transgressive: it is not a rule-governed synthesis. As Heidegger puts it, synthesis 'underlies' the categories.[108]

Heidegger

The final figure underlying this second chapter of *Difference and Repetition* is Heidegger. Deleuze will adopt a fundamental aspect of Heidegger's interpretation of Kant in *Kant and the Problem of Metaphysics*.[109] On Heidegger's reading, the Kantian syntheses have to be read as constitutive of time. While Kant occasionally suggests this (e.g. CPR A143/B182), he doesn't develop it. According to Heidegger, there are two reasons for this. The first is that Kant never thought through and clearly grasped the truly productive nature of synthesis.[110] The Kantian notion of synthesis possesses what Heidegger calls an 'ominous ambiguity' which prevented it from ever being fully thought out.[111] Second, Heidegger famously claims that Kant couldn't handle what he saw: 'Kant shrank back from this unknown root' (KPM 112). Lacking courage and clarity, Kant himself was unable to fully describe the transcendental syntheses. Consequently, Heidegger re-presents and clarifies the authentic transcendental character of the syntheses in a way Kant was unable to. He also clarifies them in a way that ends up sounding a lot like *Being and Time*.

Heidegger's reading differs from Deleuze's in that Heidegger tends to underplay Kant's descriptions of transcendental synthesis and proceeds as though Kant described the empirical nature of the syntheses in great detail, but only gestured towards the transcendental. This causes Heidegger to put forward a crucial distinction. In contrast to the empirical syntheses which take place in time and are subject to its passing, the transcendental syntheses do not 'take place within the horizon of time' (KPM 126). Instead, they come before time. They are an 'original forming' of time which lets time itself 'spring forth'. The arguments Heidegger makes to defend his reading, while fascinating, are not essential for what follows. I simply want to note the temporal character Heidegger ascribes to each of the three syntheses and the relations he establishes between them.

In contrast to the empirical synthesis of apprehension which is concerned with an immediate object given here and now in intuition, Heidegger says that the '*pure* apprehending synthesis' has nothing whatsoever to do with objects or their 'nows'. Instead it comes before all appearance and constitutes the general dimension in which appearances can be said to appear as present. It constitutes the present not as a particular instant, but as the general 'horizon' in which instants 'have the look of the now'. As Heidegger describes it, the 'pure synthesis, as apprehension, as that which offers the "present in general," is time-forming' (KPM 126). It does not produce a present moment. It produces the 'look' of the 'present in general'.

The same thing can be said of the second, reproductive synthesis. In its empirical form the synthesis of reproduction deals with present and past *moments*. It reproduces what was apprehended. The transcendental synthesis, on the other hand, does not reproduce specific moments, but 'forms the possibility of reproduction in general' (127). Such a possibility depends on the mind's ability to retain what was once present, but it cannot retain these present moments in the modality of the present. This space of retention cannot have the 'look of the now'. It is still a general horizon of time, but Heidegger describes this new horizon of reproduction in general as *a pure past which was never present* (128). It is the general element of the past. 'Pure synthesis in the mode of reproduction forms having-been-ness as such' (127). Each former present, when it appears in this horizon, has the look of the past. This pure past, 'having-been-ness as such', conditions empirical association. It retains what was apprehended in such a way that we can return to what was apprehended when we need to. It 'opens up in general the horizon of the possible attending-to' (128).

Perhaps Heidegger's greatest innovation comes in his characterization of the third synthesis. In the empirical synthesis, recognition recognized what was already given. It brings unity to the two other aspects of synthesis, apprehension and reproduction. In Heidegger's version of the transcendental synthesis, the third synthesis does not come after the other two, 'it pops us in advance of them, so to speak' (130). The third synthesis comes in advance and instead bringing about a synthesis of recognition between a past present and a present present, it brings about a synthesis among the two syntheses themselves: 'For at the ground of both syntheses, and *directing them*, a unifying (synthesis) [. . .] is already found' (130; my emphasis). The third synthesis *comes before* the other two and coordinates them. '[W]hat emerged as the third synthesis in the characterization of the empirical genesis of conceptual development is in fact the first, i.e., the synthesis which in the first place directs the other two characterized above' (130). Whereas empirical recognition had very little to do with the future, insofar as this third synthesis is a coordination of what is to come it is always directed towards the future. In two unforgettable expressions, Heidegger writes that this synthesis 'reconnoiters' and that it explores the 'horizon of being-able-to-hold-something-before-us' (130).

These three figures will all play a dominant role in what follows. In fact, by simply having run through these three figures, we have already encountered the general themes and structure of Deleuze dynamic genesis. Deleuze takes the notion of a passive synthesis of Husserl. He takes the overall structure of synthesis from Kant. He takes the time-forming character of synthesis from Heidegger. However he also makes some important changes which turn everything upside down.

THE FORMAL STRUCTURE OF CHAPTER TWO

The second chapter of *Difference and Repetition* is one of the most difficult in the book, and it is especially difficult if one is not aware of its formal structure. Deleuze's presentation of the three syntheses is divided into three parts.[112] Each of these three parts is a different account in a different technical vocabulary of the dynamic genesis, or what Deleuze calls here the 'unconscious' (the unconscious is the set of three passive syntheses). Deleuze gives three accounts of these syntheses. The first account (70–96/96–128/90–119) makes use of terms and concepts from the history of philosophy. I will therefore refer to it as the philosophical account. The second account (96–116/128–53/119–42) makes use of the language of psychoanalysis. I will therefore refer to it as the psychoanalytic account. The third account (116–28/153–68/142–56) makes use of the language of physics. I'll refer to this as the physical account. This division adds three new sets of words with which we can talk about the syntheses. We have already talked about the syntheses in the language of repetition, and in the language of the faculties, and Deleuze's set of syntheses is modelled on the Kantian account and is a direct engagement with Heidegger's reading of Kant. In other words, when we talk about the syntheses, we have to traverse *at least* seven different vocabularies: (1) that of the doctrine of the faculties; (2) the language of difference and repetition discussed in the introduction and first chapters; (3) the language of Kant and (4) Heidegger; and finally the three new vocabularies belonging to this chapter: (5) philosophy, (6) psychoanalysis and (7) physics. Table 2 is intended to provide a basic framework for moving between these languages. It outlines the dominant expressions and their relations across various vocabularies.

Despite the verbal complexity of the chapter, what actually happens is relatively simple, and almost straightforwardly Kantian. A first synthesis apprehends what was given in sensibility. A second synthesis reproduces what was apprehended. A third synthesis *tries* to recognize what was apprehended and reproduced, but it fails. In the failure of recognition a new synthesis, the 'ideal synthesis of difference', emerges. The advent of this new synthesis marks the end of chapter two and the beginning of chapter four.

Of course, given the complexity of the chapter this structure is not immediately apparent in Deleuze's text. In what follows, I explain how this structure is played out across chapter two of *Difference and Repetition*.

SENSIBILITY: MATERIAL DISCONTINUITY

Our first question when faced with a set of syntheses is what do the syntheses synthesize, or, to put it another way, where does the entire genetic process which I have continually referred to begin? Many of the difficulties associated with Deleuze's account of the syntheses can be avoided simply by determining this starting point. In the introduction Deleuze already hinted at this origin. Repetition began with singularities. A latent subject repeated singularities which we understood as

Table 2 Vocabularies of the Dynamic Genesis

	Kant	Doctrine of Faculties	Philosophical Account	Psychoanalytic Account	Physical Account	Temporal Dimensions (of Deleuze's syntheses)	Heidegger
Sensibility	Spatio-temporal Diversity	Sensibility	Evanescent Matter	Intensity as Excitation	Excitation	Death	N/A
First Synthesis	Apprehension	Imagination	Imagination	Binding	Coupling	Present	Present
Second Synthesis	Reproduction	Memory	Memory	Mnemosyne	Resonance	Past	Past
Third Synthesis	Recognition	Thought	Thought	Thanatos	Forced Movement	Future	Future

the immediate objects of intuition. From the point of view of a vulgarized Leibnizianism, these singularities were the minute perceptions which expressed incompossible worlds which precede us. Deleuze also said that this latent subject was entirely sub-representative. This means that it cannot repeat an already constituted object. The immediate object is therefore a fragmented object (we also saw this in the third postulate of the image of thought). None of these characteristics seem to be present in this chapter, however. Can we still say that repetition begins in the fragmented object of immediate intuition?

In the philosophical account of the syntheses, Deleuze gives this starting point several ambiguously related names: 'repetition-in-itself', 'repetition in the object', 'repetition of instants', 'material repetition' and 'matter'.[113] 'Object', 'matter', 'repetition' and 'instant' are the four words which characterize this origin. Perhaps all of these expressions come together under Deleuze's claim that this originary matter is subject to the 'rule of discontinuity'. This rule says that one material instant does not appear without the other disappearing. It divides matter into a series of 'unthinkable' 'homogeneous instants' (70/96–7/90–1). In the philosophical account then, everything begins with a discontinuous matter which is, strictly speaking, unthinkable. This instantly brings to mind Leibniz, for example. The idea of a discontinuous matter plays an important role in his writings on the continuum, and in the *New Essays* Leibniz clearly related his minute perceptions to this discontinuous matter. We have also seen that Hegel's *Phenomenology* began in 'death' or in consciousness's contemplation of the immediate object. Following Hegel to a degree, Merleau-Ponty wrote that 'Each *sensation*, being strictly speaking, the first, last and only one of its kind, is a birth and a death' (PP 250; my emphasis).[114] Above all we think of Kant and the temporal discontinuity which sensibility imposes on all representations which causes the synthesis of apprehension to lead to reproduction and recognition. These historical associations – minute perceptions, singularity, sensation, sensibility – already go a long way to confirming that Deleuze's description of discontinuous matter is also his description of what is given to a transcendental sensibility. But as associations they don't go far enough. Can we find Deleuze himself saying that everything begins in sensation?

We already saw in the doctrine of the faculties that thought had its origins in a transcendental sensibility which endured the imperceptible violence of intensive encounters: 'on the path which leads to that which is to be thought, all begins with sensibility' (144/188/182). As I suggested above, and as I will continue to develop below, the doctrine of the faculties maps directly onto the philosophical account of the three passive syntheses. The genetic line of the faculties ran from sensibility to imagination to memory to thought. Likewise, the first passive synthesis takes place in a 'spontaneous imagination' (70–9/96–108/90–100); the second passive synthesis is a 'passive synthesis of memory' (79/108/100–1); and the third synthesis raises memory to the level of the 'pure thought'. By mapping the syntheses onto the faculties, we can account for all of the faculties with the exception of the first, sensibility. Can we say then, by analogy, that Deleuze's brief descriptions of a discontinuous and instantaneous matter in chapter two are characterizations of the transcendental sensibility at the origin of thought in chapter three?

If we leave the philosophical account of the syntheses behind and consider the psychoanalytic and physical accounts, we can see that these suspicions are clearly justified. In the psychoanalytic account, the entire genetic line of the syntheses begins in a 'field of individuation in which differences in intensity are distributed here and there in the form of *excitations*' (96/128/119; my emphasis). Here Deleuze names the correlate of discontinuous matter 'excitation' and says that these excitations, just like the object of the encounter, take the form of intensities. He does the same thing in the physical account: 'psychic connection (Habitus) effects a coupling of series of excitations' (118/155/144). From this point of view the doctrine of the faculties is easily reconciled with the account of passive synthesis. The discontinuous matter at the base of the three syntheses is nothing other than the transcendental sensibility of the doctrine of faculties.

The three syntheses, and with them, the entire genesis of thought, begin in a transcendental sensibility. In *Proust and Signs* the object of encounter took the form of a 'material impression'. Here that impression is called an 'excitation' or 'material repetition'. Sensibility apprehends matter, but

Deleuze is quite clear that the object of the encounter is not a quality as in Plato (139–40/182/176). One doesn't encounter the colour red. Red is what is given to an empirical sensibility only after the genetic process has run its course. In a transcendental sensibility one encounters matter without qualities. This is what Husserl called hyletic data. It is the content of sensation prior to that content taking on any determinate form or quality. By calling this matter 'intensity' however Deleuze prevents us from imagining hyletic data as a static set of distinct dot-like impacts which consciousness gathers together. Instead matter constantly unravels itself according to the rule of discontinuity. There are no material terms. There is simply a pure evanescence in the instantaneous birth and death of matter. It is worth noting here that this state of matter is not at all 'difference-in-itself', or 'univocal being', or 'virtuality' though it has definite resonances with these concepts. We will see that all of these concepts make their appearances much later in the course of genesis. Here, we are simply in the presence of a unique description of matter as the content of sensation.

IMAGINATION: THE FIRST SYNTHESIS

From this point of view we have to ask what would seem to be a very un-Deleuzian question, but it is one which Deleuze himself asks: if sensibility is defined as the evanescence of matter, what would be required in this situation in order for representation to become possible?

> [I]n order to represent [material] repetition, contemplative souls must be installed here and there; passive selves, sub-representative syntheses and habituses capable of *contracting* the cases or elements into one another [. . .]. (286/366/357; original emphasis)

There is a proliferation of expressions here: 'contemplative souls', 'habituses', 'passive selves' and 'sub-representative syntheses'. *What they all describe is simply the first passive synthesis*, which, like all of Deleuze's concepts, goes by many names.[115] If sensibility gives us discontinuous matter, the first synthesis is a synthesis of those very discontinuous instants – a first step on the road to representation. In the doctrine of faculties, it was the imagination that took up the difference given by sensibility. In the philosophical account of the syntheses, a 'spontaneous imagination' (the contemplative soul) 'contracts' discontinuous matter. 'The imagination is defined here as a contractile power: like a sensitive plate it retains one case when the other appears' (70/96/90–1).

contracts

The first passive synthesis, undertaken by a spontaneous imagination, does nothing more than gather together sensibility's passing instants. In doing so, it produces the temporal dimension of 'the present': 'The synthesis of time constitutes the present in time' (76/105/97). As in Heidegger's reading of Kant, the present produced here is not a present object or instant. Rather according to Deleuze, it 'constitutes the general possibility of any present' (81/110/102). It constitutes the 'present in general'.

In what sense can we say that a synthesis, by gathering together instants, constitutes time? Remember that sensibility only gives us discontinuous instants. It is impossible for any one of these by themselves to constitute a present 'now' because the spontaneous imagination attached to just one instant would pass with that instant. As Heidegger puts it, 'at most it would be able to "intuit" just the current now, and never the sequence of nows as such and the horizon formed in it' (KPM 122). This 'horizon' which lets a now appear only as situated within a series of nows is what Heidegger calls the 'present in general'. It is in the sense of constituting a temporal extension over a series of nows that a synthesis of instants can produce a dimension of time, a present of indeterminate extension:

A succession of instants does not constitute time any more than it causes it to disappear; it indicates only its constantly aborted moment of birth. Time is constituted only in the originary synthesis *which operates on the repetition of instants*. This synthesis contracts the successive independent instants into one another, thereby constituting the lived, or living, present. It is in this present that time is deployed [*se déploie*]. (70/97/91; my emphases)[116]

This quotation summarizes all of the major points regarding the first synthesis discussed so far. The first sentence describes sensibility: the succession of instants which represent the constantly aborted birth of time. The second sentence describes imagination: the originary synthesis which synthesizes the discontinuous instants given by sensibility. Finally, we read in the third sentence that, through the contraction of instants, the present in general is produced not as a present instant or object but as a living present, a present with a temporal horizon or extension.[117]

Before moving on to the second synthesis we should note one crucial difference between the Kantian and Heideggerian accounts of synthesis and Deleuze's. In Kant/Heidegger the first synthesis operates on the purely formal and empty form of intuition. It apprehends the diversity of space and time as such. In Deleuze, there is no such form, but only a vanishing content. The first synthesis begins with the imagination's experience of a discontinuous matter. On the basis of this contemplation the first synthesis produces the first dimension of time, the present.

MEMORY: THE SECOND SYNTHESIS
In the doctrine of the faculties, sensibility transmitted its constraint to the imagination, and the imagination transmitted its constraint to memory. We see the same relation in the passive syntheses. After the imagination synthesizes the discontinuous instants given by sensibility, it is 'extended [*s'approfondit*]' (108/144/134) in a second passive synthesis which 'constitutes' a transcendental memory (79–80/108/101). We will return to this characterization of the second synthesis as a memory below, but first we should ask, what does the second synthesis synthesize?

The philosophical account of this synthesis tells us surprisingly little about the second synthesis. It confirms that this synthesis constitutes a transcendental memory, and further, it describes the temporal dimension of this synthesis as 'the pure element of the past, understood as the past in general, as an *a priori* past' (81/110/103). But it then goes on to develop the relationship between the pure past and the *represented* present (the 'present which passes' and not the sub-representative present of the first passive synthesis) in the form of three paradoxes. These paradoxes do not pertain to our question because we are not yet interested in the relationship between passive, 'sub-representative' syntheses and representation. What exactly is the second synthesis a synthesis of and how does this synthesis relate to the first passive synthesis?

If we look at the psychoanalytic and physical accounts of the syntheses, it turns out that these two questions are in fact one and the same: the second passive synthesis is a synthesis of the product of the first passive synthesis. What was apprehended by the imagination is reproduced by memory. In order to see this we have to consider Deleuze's characterizations of first synthesis as well as the second in both of these accounts.

Perhaps the relation between first and second synthesis is most clear in the physical account. At one point in each of the three accounts, Deleuze describes the first synthesis as one which 'draws off' a difference. The difference which the imagination draws off in the philosophical account is the difference between discontinuous instants. You could say that it draws off discontinuity itself and thus gathers together successive instants into a continuous present. In the physical account, this act is called 'coupling' (117–18/154–5/143–4). Coupling brings together the discontinuous instants by drawing off the difference between them. In doing so, it produces a '*series*' of 'excitations'. Instead of vanishing, excitations are now linked in a series. The second synthesis in the physical account is called 'resonance'. Resonance is a synthesis of precisely those differences which were previously drawn off. Deleuze says that resonance 'relates differences to other differences' or 'first-degree differences to one another' (117/154/143). The first-degree differences are the differences drawn off in the first synthesis. In the second synthesis, these differences 'resonate' under the influence of a 'dark precursor'. From this point of view it becomes clear that the second synthesis is a synthesis of the first synthesis.

We reach the same conclusion if we look to the psychoanalytic account, although things are slightly more complicated. We saw above that in this account sensibility was characterized as a 'field of individuation in which differences in intensity are distributed here and there in the form of excitations' (96/128/119). The first synthesis takes the form of a 'binding'. A local ego, the spontaneous imagination, 'binds' the differences in intensity. Deleuze describes this synthesis as a 'reproductive synthesis' (96/128/120). It is reproductive because the ego literally becomes what it synthesizes, and thus reproduces the excitation in the contemplation of the excitation: 'the eye that binds light is itself a bound light' (96/128/120; cf. 74–5/102/96–6). For this reason Deleuze describes the ego of this first synthesis as 'narcissistic': it sees itself in what it contemplates.

> The fact that these egos should be immediately narcissistic is readily explained if we consider narcissism to be not a contemplation of oneself but the fulfillment of a self-image through the contemplation of something else: the eye or the seeing ego is filled with an image of itself in contemplating the excitation that it binds. It produces or 'draws itself' from what it contemplates [. . .]. (97/129/120)

What is the relationship of the second synthesis to these narcissistic egos? Deleuze only says it once: '[T]he first synthesis extends itself (*s'approfondit*) in a second passive synthesis which gathers up the particular narcissistic satisfaction and relates it to the contemplation of virtual objects' (108–9/144/134; translation modified). 'Particular narcissistic satisfaction' refers to the ego of the first synthesis which becomes what it synthesizes. The 'virtual object' is the 'principle of the second passive synthesis' (109/145/135). It is what constitutes the pure past in general, a horizon of having-been-ness, in which what was apprehended finds the conditions of its reproducibility.[118] In the second synthesis, narcissistic egos are 'gathered together' in the virtual object. Here too, then, the second passive synthesis is a synthesis of the product of the first passive synthesis.

There are several difficulties which present themselves here. First, why is this second synthesis necessary? Why does the product of the first synthesis need to be gathered together in a second synthesis? Deleuze's reasons for introducing the second synthesis very closely resemble Kant's arguments for a second synthesis. Kant had two motivations for introducing another synthesis, one relating to the empirical, one to the transcendental. First, he argued that the second synthesis could ground empirical association. If a present perception causes me to reproduce a prior perception according to the laws of association, there must be something which conditions reproducibility in general. This role is filled by the second synthesis (CPR A101–2). As Heidegger put it, the having-been-ness of the past makes possible my attending-to.

Deleuze follows Kant/Heidegger almost to the word on this point. For Deleuze too, the second synthesis grounds empirical association. It does so insofar as it produces the 'past as the general element in which each former present preserves itself'. In preserving past representations, the pure past is the condition of reproducibility in general. It provides the element in which a former present is preserved and can be reproduced alongside a future perception (80/109/101–2). He even goes so far as to say that 'The limits of this representation or reproduction are in fact determined by the variable relations of resemblance and contiguity known as forms of association' (80/109/102). In the psychoanalytic account of the syntheses, Deleuze names these two aspects of the synthesis 'Mnemosyne' and 'Eros'. Mnemosyne is the 'treasure' of the pure past; it is Heidegger's 'having-been-ness'. Eros, 'who allows us to penetrate this pure past', is 'the seeker after memories'; it is Heidegger's 'attending-to'.[119] The second synthesis therefore conditions empirical association in Kant and Deleuze alike.

These arguments turn only on the relation of a transcendental ground to the empirical state which that ground conditions. They still don't answer the question of why a second synthesis would be necessary in the first place. Kant's second motivation however doesn't bear on the empirical. As we saw above, for Kant the first synthesis apprehended the immediate present, but because time was the form of inner sense or of all that happens in thought (including synthesis) this synthesis itself passed in time. A second synthesis was therefore needed to prevent us from always loosing our prior apprehensions. What was apprehended in the first synthesis must be able to be retained and reproduced.

Again, Deleuze follows Kant almost to the word. Deleuze's first synthesis faces the same problem as Kant's: it passes. In fact Deleuze reminds us, just as Kant did, that the syntheses pass in time. 'Habit' is the foundation of time insofar as it produces the look of the present in general, but it is a foundation which is built on a 'moving soil' (79/108/101). A great difference between Kant and Deleuze appears here, however: there is no form of inner sense in Deleuze, but only evanescent matter. Habit passes for a different reason than apprehension did. Deleuze's first synthesis passes because it has a 'contractile range'. It can only comprehend so many material instants before 'fatigue' forces it to let go of the apprehended discontinuity (77/106–7/98–9). There is thus a '*finitude of contraction*' which determines the extent of the living present's duration, and when that duration is up, when fatigue sets in, the living present itself passes (79/108/101).[120] Our contractile range is the index of our finitude.[121]

This is why Deleuze invokes the second synthesis of memory. 'Although it is originary, the first synthesis of time is no less intratemporal. [. . .] We cannot avoid the necessary conclusion – that there must be another time in which the first synthesis of time occurs (*s'opère*)' (79/109/100–1; original emphasis, translation modified). Just as in Kant, the first synthesis passes in time. A second synthesis is therefore required, without which none of our thoughts could arise. This passage is often misinterpreted as suggesting that the second synthesis brings about the first, and that the first is not, as Deleuze said, 'originary', but Deleuze is quite clear: the second synthesis doesn't bring about the first. Rather it 'appropriates the present and habit (*approprie le présent et l'habitude*)' (79/108/101; translation modified).[122] As the psychoanalytic and physical accounts of the syntheses make clear, by 'appropriates' Deleuze means 'runs through and gathers together'.

If this second synthesis constitutes the temporal dimension of the past in general, it is because it sets itself up as the synthesis of what was previously present. It gathers together finite imaginations. For the same reason it *constitutes* a memory. But notice that in neither of these first two syntheses was the data given in sensibility organized according to content or in order to determine a content. These are 'blind' syntheses which, even if they synthesize sensible matter itself, take no regard of that matter. They synthesize without regard to content. The past they produce is not a particular past moment, but a past in general. The memory which is constituted does not contain past moments, but the form of the past as such. Heidegger had described the second synthesis in Kant as a pure past which was never present – the horizon of the past in general – because Kant's second synthesis grounded both empirical and transcendental reproducibility. Deleuze too describes this transcendental memory as the 'past in general' or the 'pure past' or 'the past that was never present': 'The past is not the former present but the element in which we focus upon the latter' (80/109/101). Again, in contrast to the Kantian/Heideggerian syntheses, Deleuze's second synthesis is a synthesis of a determinate content, not an empty form, and further, that content is the one handed down to it from the first synthesis. Even if the content has not yet become important, it has been passed on from one faculty to the next.

VIRTUALITY AND THE PROBLEM

There is a further difficulty associated with the second synthesis. This concerns the extent to which this synthesis can be described as constituting the 'virtual'. There are several reasons why readers of *Difference and Repetition* have equated the pure past of the second synthesis with the virtual. First of all, in both *Bergsonism* and *Proust and Signs* Deleuze had described the Bergsonian notion of the virtual in just these terms: it is a past that has never been present, it enters into various paradoxical relationships with the represented present, it preserves and maintains itself, it forms a Bergsonian cone, and so on.[123] In fact Deleuze's discussion of the second synthesis in the philosophical account draws directly and in great detail from the third chapter of *Bergsonism*. However, we should be wary of immediately concluding that with the second synthesis we have arrived at the Deleuzian notion of the virtual. In both of these earlier works Deleuze is writing about another writer, and his use of free indirect discourse makes it nearly impossible to tell where Bergson or Proust ends and Deleuze begins. Where the virtual is clearly the pure past for Bergson, it may not be for Deleuze. The fact that Deleuze emphasizes this point in *Bergsonism* does not mean that the pure past will also constitute the Deleuzian virtual, but only that he was writing on Bergson. He may well adopt aspects of Bergson's thought for his description of the second synthesis in *Difference and Repetition*, including the word itself, but it in no way follows from this that we have reached the properly Deleuzian notion of the virtual. As we will see below, it is only after the third synthesis has done its work that the Deleuzian notion of the virtual has been *produced*.

There is a second and more sophisticated reason that this second synthesis has been equated with the Deleuzian virtual. In the philosophical account, Deleuze describes the pure past as a 'field of problems' (85/115/107). In the psychoanalytic account he develops this description in great detail (106–8/140–4/130–2). If we then notice that Deleuze begins chapter four of *Difference and Repetition* by describing the virtual as the field in which problems – or Ideas – are progressively determined, it would seem undeniable that the pure past of the second synthesis, insofar as it is a field of problems, is virtuality itself.

We should notice, however, that it is not the second synthesis alone that constitutes a 'question-problem complex'. In fact, *all three syntheses have their own question-problem complex*. 'To the first synthesis there corresponds a first question-problem complex' (78/107/99); the outcome of the third synthesis 'is the last form of the problematic' (112/148/137–8). It is not just the second synthesis that is 'problematising', but all three syntheses or the 'unconscious' as a whole: 'the structure of the unconscious is [. . .] questioning and problematising' (112/148/137). At the opening of chapter four, when Deleuze speaks of Ideas as problems, the problems he is referring to correspond only to 'the last form of the question-problem complex' in the third passive synthesis – not the problems of the second or first syntheses. From this point of view it is clear that the second synthesis is not the fully developed Deleuzian notion of the virtual since it points towards the third synthesis and even beyond it. This raises a more pressing question: what are we to make of the fact that 'the problematic' has three distinct forms?

Deleuze is alluding to Merleau-Ponty and Bergson here. In *The Structure of Behavior* Merleau-Ponty pointed out that one particular stimulus called for many different reflex responses, and further, that those responses depended upon the overall context in which the stimulus appeared and were by no means specific to the stimulus itself. A causal link between stimulus and response could not therefore be established, and instead of describing the reflex arc in terms of cause and effect, Merleau-Ponty described it according to a '*dialectical*' or problematizing model.[124] Here the stimulus appeared as a '*problem*' which called for a 'response'.[125] In the *Phenomenology of Perception*

112

he extends this dialectical model of the reflex arc to perception as a whole:

> The sensible datum which is on the point of being felt sets a
> kind of muddled problem for my body to solve. I must find
> the attitude which will provide it with the means of becoming
> determinate, of showing up as blue; I must find the reply to a
> question which is obscurely expressed. (PP 248–9; cf. 90)[126]

A sensible datum does not first appear as the determinate quality blue. Rather, it appears as a muddled problem, and only
after my body has found the appropriate 'attitude' to solve this
problem does blue as a determinate quality appear. *The act of
turning a vague sensation into a determinate perception is here
likened to the act of solving a problem*. Merleau-Ponty, however,
likely had Bergson in mind when he formulated sensibility as
a faculty for apprehending problems (to borrow Descombes'
expression). In *Matter and Memory*, Bergson describes each
'perception' or excitation as a '*question*' which 'makes an appeal'
or 'invites a response'. This question is asked in two directions:
first, each perception puts 'so to speak, an elementary question
to my motor activity' (MM 45), but since a 'choice of reaction'
'is likely to be inspired by past experience' this question or
appeal is also addressed to memory (MM 65).[127]
    When Deleuze then refers to a series of 'question-problem
complexes' which begins in sensibility, it is hard to deny that
he has this discourse in mind. The 'problem' is an excitation.
'Every such question is a perception' (MM 55). It is true that
at the beginning of chapter four Deleuze explicitly describes
his notion of the problem as a development of the Kantian
theory of Ideas, but this relation to Kant pertains only to a
particularly developed moment of the problem, and perhaps
the Idea in the Kantian cannot even be found there. The
first appearance of the problem is in the first synthesis, or
in the ego's apprehension of that which was given by sensibility. Sensibility poses the problem to the imagination. The
imagination passes it on to memory. The crucial point is that,
as Merleau-Ponty put it, the goal is to 'find the reply to a question which is obscurely expressed'. The problem is a 'muddled
problem', and neither imagination nor memory is able to

determine exactly what the problem is. We will see below that this is precisely the role given to *thought*. If sensibility is the faculty of apprehending problems, thought is the faculty of determining problems. It is only in thought that the properly virtual Idea first appears.

Before moving on to the third synthesis we should bring together the various points regarding what has unfolded so far in the linear advance of synthesis.

1. In all three accounts of the syntheses, everything begins in sensibility. In the philosophical account the given is called 'discontinuous matter'; in the psychoanalytic and physical accounts, it is called 'excitation'.
2. In all three accounts, the first synthesis is a synthesis of this given. In the philosophical account, imagination contracts successive instants; in the psychoanalytic account, local egos bind excitations; in the physical account, a coupling of instants occurs which orders excitations into series.
3. In all three accounts, the second synthesis synthesizes what was produced in the first synthesis. In the philosophical account, memory 'appropriates' the imagination; in the psychoanalytic account the local egos of the first synthesis are related to the virtual object; in the physical account the first-degree differences resonate with one another.

Despite the immense mobility of Deleuze's language, the Kantian model of the syntheses is very clear. Everything begins with discontinuity. The first synthesis apprehends discontinuity and draws off its difference. Since this synthesis itself passes, a second synthesis is required to gather together the passing apprehensions. This leads us to the third synthesis.

THOUGHT: THE THIRD SYNTHESIS

Deleuze's comments on the third synthesis are among the most opaque of the entire book. His descriptions are extremely difficult to follow, and at times they seem incoherent and contradictory. Deleuze himself gives us a clue as to how to proceed in the face of difficult texts: make distinctions.[128] Indeed, one reason this particular moment is so difficult to follow is that Deleuze himself does not make enough distinctions and pushes too much information and too many elaborate allusions into too few lines. In order to come to terms with the third synthesis we have to follow Deleuze's own advice: the interpreter must multiply distinctions. In addition to making distinctions, it also helps to say what we would expect at this point in the genesis of thought.

Given the Kantian structure of the first two syntheses, we might expect a third synthesis of recognition to follow. The first synthesis apprehended a discontinuous matter. The second synthesis recorded that apprehension in a pure past or a space of reproducibility. The third synthesis should unify these other two syntheses in a synthesis of recognition. Following Heidegger's reinterpretation of the Kantian syntheses, we might also expect to discover that the third synthesis is in fact the first. What is recognized would be precisely the compatibility of the first synthesis and the second synthesis. The third synthesis would come before and coordinate the other two and from this point of view it constitutes a transcendental future. In fact, none of these things will happen, and this leads to one of the most novel and interesting aspects of Deleuze's philosophy: the third synthesis is a failed synthesis.

In contrast to the Heideggerian interpretation, Deleuze's third synthesis cannot come first for two reasons. First, from the point of view of genesis, there simply would not be anything to synthesize at the beginning except matter – in which case synthesis would be a synthesis of apprehension. The obvious reply to this is that in Heidegger, transcendental recognition is actually regulation. It anticipates and directs the other two syntheses: it is in this sense that it has a relation to the future. This points to Deleuze's second departure from our expectations. In contrast to Kantian recognition, we encounter the impossibility of recognition in the third moment of synthesis. This is because in *Kant recognition and the unity of the synthesis depended entirely on the categories of the understanding*. The categories regulated recognition, and the unity of the synthesis was in fact the unity of a rule. In Deleuze, however, there are no such categories and there is no transcendental ground of the I. Consequently there is no guarantee of the unity of synthesis and therefore no hope for a coordinating synthesis even if it had the best of intention.

In place of a numerically identical I, there is only a passive and changing 'self' at this point in the Deleuzian system. There is only an 'ego', and this ego is capable of only one action: it contemplates. Being a passive ego, it can only contemplate what is given to it. At first this is simply matter itself. Contemplation is then an apprehension, and the ego is called an imagination. Having apprehended matter, the ego now has before it something other than matter. It now contemplates its previous apprehensions. The ego is then called a memory. In the third synthesis the ego has two things before it: apprehension and reproduction, imagination and memory. The third synthesis will therefore bring these other two faculties into one contemplation, and insofar as it is the unity of the faculties, the ego has become the faculty of Thought. Of course this synthesis does not go as planned.

In order to see how this plays out we need to follow Deleuze's advice and draw a series of distinctions. The third synthesis as a whole is called the 'empty form of time'.[129] It would be difficult to overemphasize that 'the empty form of time', despite the name, is not another synthesis which produces another dimension of time (the future) or even time as a whole. Further, the 'empty form of time' in *Difference and Repetition* has nothing in common with its Kantian counterpart. In Deleuze, the form of time is a synthesis, not a determinable diversity which relays appearances. As a synthesis, the form of time comprises three moments:

1. a formal and static order,
2. a totality (*ensemble*) and
3. a series.

The *order* of time is the static distribution of a before, a during and an after.[130] The *totality* of time is something Deleuze mysteriously calls the 'action = x', the 'formidable action' or the 'image of the act'. The *series* of time is the succession of past, present and future. Organized schematically the main components of the third synthesis are represented in Table 3.

By clarifying what each of these terms mean, we will eventually be able to get a sense for the way in which this third synthesis operates. In order to do this, however, we have to follow out some complex allusions to Kant.

116

Table 3 The Main Components of the Third Synthesis

Formal Order of Time	Totality of Time	Series
Before	Formidable Action	Past
During (Caesura)		Present
After		Future

The first allusion is already present in Deleuze's general distribution of time into an order, a totality and a series. Kant makes this distinction himself within the context of the schematism:

> The schemata are therefore nothing but *a priori* **time-determinations** in accordance with rules, and these concern, according to the order of the categories, the **time-series**, the **content of time**, the **order of time**, and finally the **sum total of time** (*Zeitinbegriff*) in regard to all possible objects. (CPR A145/B184–5; original emphasis).[131]

Deleuze's allusion to this passage is strange for two reasons. First, for Deleuze it is *empty* time which has an order, a totality and a series, but for Kant, these are time-determinations. This means that when time takes on an order, totality and a series it is no longer an empty time. It is a schematized time, or a time which is gathered together in determined representations. The second reason this allusion is strange is that the schematism is the process in which concepts are applied to intuitions, not the process through which spatio-temporal determinations are raised to conceptual determinations.[132] It is true that the very division of the subject into sensibility and receptivity which gives the procedures of synthesis and schematism their sense cannot be found in Deleuze, and that the systematic context in which the schematism appears would therefore be irrelevant. However, Deleuze does maintain an analogous distinction between a passive subject and an active I, and we will see below that he does indeed revive the schematism in order to explain the way in which this I determines the passive subject. Given the fact that we are in the middle of Deleuze's account of synthesis, or the movement from a passive self to an active I it seems that his allusion is particularly misplaced. Why, then does Deleuze allude to it here?

It is because the schematism represents the way in which the I affects the self. Deleuze alludes to this notion not for the specifics of the schematism, but because of its formal structure. What matters is that in it, a concept, or a category, is applied to time, or sensibility. The understanding is turned back on sensibility. The activity of the I is brought to bear on the passivity of the self. This refers us to a second allusion to Kant.

When Deleuze first introduces the third synthesis, he does so in the context of an interpretation of Kant's 'paradox of inner sense' as it bears on the Cartesian cogito. This paradox rests on a distinction between intuiting and thinking. I *intuit* appearances, but these appearances are not yet determinately related to one another. As Kant puts it, in sensibility there is 'no combination of the manifold' (CPR B154). The manifold remains a simple diversity. In contrast to intuiting, *thinking* is the thought of a determinate and unified object. We have seen how this object is produced above: all appearances are given through the forms of intuition; transcendental synthesis bears directly on these forms; and in so far as the third synthesis is determined by the categories, the given diversity is related to the object = X in which the appearances are unified and therefore *thought* (rather than intuited) by the subject of apperception.[133] The important point in relation to the paradox of inner sense is that in synthesizing these forms of intuition, we can be said to be *affecting* or determining ourselves: 'the understanding therefore does not **find** some sort of combination of the manifold already in inner sense, but **produces** it, by **affecting** inner sense' (B155; original emphasis). The understanding fashions an object out of appearance by ordering the forms of intuition. The active part of the subject affects the passive part.

The paradox of inner sense arises when we turn our attention away from objects and try to *think* rather than intuit *ourselves*. The same scenario is played out here. Kant says that I am 'given to myself in intuition', but, just as other phenomena, I am given 'not as I am for the understanding but rather as I appear to myself' (CPR B155). I am not given to myself in the form of a unified and substantial thought, but as an appearance dispersed in time. If I then want to *think* myself, as Descartes did when he said, 'I think', I have to unify the appearances of myself. '[W]e must order the determinations of inner sense' (CPR B156). The paradox, then, in that 'the I that I think' is different from the 'I that intuits itself', but yet the two are one and the same I. Put differently, the paradox is that receptivity, a passive faculty and the understanding, an active faculty, belong to one and the same subject which thinks itself only by affecting or synthesizing its self.[134]

Deleuze often describes the distinction between these two faculties in terms of the 'self' and the 'I'. The understanding, in its unity of apperception, constitutes an 'active I'. The sensibility, in its receptivity and passivity constitutes a 'self'.

The Self (*moi*) is in time and is constantly changing: it is a passive, or rather receptive, 'self' that experiences changes in time. The *I* is an act (I think) that actively determines my existence (I am), but can only determine it in time, as the existence of a passive, receptive, and changing *self*, which only represents to itself the activity of its *own* thought. (EC 29–30; original emphasis; cf. KP viii–ix)

Deleuze distinguishes between two aspects of the Kantian subject: a passive self, and an active I. The I is an active faculty which determines a passive faculty. Time is simply the form under which the two are related to one another. Time is nothing more than 'the formal relation through which the mind affects itself' (EC 31). At this point, these distinctions between a passive faculty, an active faculty and the condition of their relation characterize only the Kantian subject. The active I is the apperceptive understanding. The passive self is sensibility. Time is the determinable form of intuition.

How does this relate to the Deleuzian subject? In *Difference and Repetition*, Deleuze writes that '[t]he Kantian initiative can be taken up [. . .] *but in the course of a quite different understanding of the passive self*' (87/118/109; my emphasis). In other words, the same structure is at play in the Deleuzian subject, but the three terms have changed their characters. The 'passive, receptive and changing self' is no longer sensibility and its empty forms. In Deleuze it is the spontaneous imagination, or the contemplative soul of apprehension.[135] It is the subject which synthesizes in its passivity. What does Deleuze substitute for the other two elements: time and the I? Receptivity is replaced by passive synthesis. What replaces the numerical unity of the I, and by what form are the self and I related?

Before answering these questions – or rather, in order to answer them we should first note that what Deleuze means by 'the empty form of time' is becoming a little clearer. This form is not a temporal dimension like the other two syntheses. In fact, it has very little to do with time as such. Rather, it is a synthesis whose failure will open up not time as a whole, but only the future. There are two reasons why Deleuze will call this *synthesis* the empty form of time. The first is that as a synthesis, empty time tries to gather together the other two times: the present and the past. It therefore contains and orders time as a whole. The second, and more important reason is that Deleuze is working with an extremely broad definition of empty time in Kant:

> If the I determines our existence as a passive self changing in time, time is the formal relation through which the mind affects itself, or the way we are internally affected by ourselves. Time can thus be defined as the Affect of the self by itself, or at least as the formal possibility of being affected by oneself. (EC 31)

Time is simply the formal possibility of self-affection (or as Derrida so prudishly put it, of onanism). It is the form by which the mind affects itself. (There is indeed another aspect of time in Kant which Deleuze emphasizes – time as a form of determinability – but in his own system, as we will see, Deleuze clearly separates the form of self-affection from the form of determinability.[136]) Right now Deleuze is concerned solely with time as the form of self-affection. This is where the third synthesis begins: with the affection of the self by the self.

The third synthesis begins when the ego which contemplated other objects now turns back on itself and contemplates its self (these other objects were the singularities which it apprehended in the first synthesis and the apprehensions that it recorded in the second).[137] When the ego turns its attention to itself, Deleuze says that 'the passive ego becomes entirely narcissistic' (110/145/135). It is no longer narcissistic in the sense that it sees itself in some other object that it contemplates.

Now the ego literally contemplates its self. In its self-contemplation and its attempt to unify the self, this new ego becomes the Deleuzian I, or the faculty of thought. This faculty has a very short lifespan. Deleuze will say that this new ego 'walks with a limp on one green leg and one red leg' (110/145/135). These two legs are the two previous faculties, imagination and memory. If the ego walks with a limp, it is because these faculties are not at all equals. In the language of the philosophical account, Deleuze calls the new ego the 'caesura'. And again, the other two faculties 'are distributed unequally on both sides of the "caesura"' (89/120/111). We can already see that thought is going to attempt to bring about an asymmetrical synthesis of two unequal faculties. From the start, the possibility of recognition looks slim.

The 'caesura' constitutes the faculty of thought, and as such it has two functions. The first is that it divides or determines the self. 'The formal static order of before, during and after marks in time *the division of the narcissistic ego* [. . .]' (110/146/136 translation modified). In this capacity it is called the 'order of time'. The during is the caesura itself, but the before and after are the other two faculties which are unequally distributed in the caesura. These three faculties taken together, imagination, memory and thought, constitute what Deleuze calls the 'order of time', or the first aspect of the synthesis.

In its second aspect, the caesura is the unity of the self, and this unity sets it apart from the self. It now stands for '*the identity of the concept in general, or that of the I*' (296/378/368; my emphasis). In this capacity, as the unity of the self (or of the before, during and after) the caesura stands for the second moment of the third synthesis, the *totality* of time. Deleuze often describes the caesura in this capacity as a 'formidable image'. For example, at one point he writes,

In the first place, the idea of a totality of time corresponds to this: that any caesura must be determined in the image of an action, of a unique and formidable event, adequate to time as a whole. This image itself is divided, torn into two unequal parts; nevertheless it draws together the totality of time' (88/120/111–12; translation modified).

This language, as well as the expression 'caesura', has a complex history: it is drawn from Deleuze's variation on Jean Beaufret's interpretation of Hölderlin's 'Remarks on Oedipus'.[138] We do not need to follow this history here for the simple reason that Deleuze maps Hölderlin's comments directly onto the paradox of auto-affection. Oedipus and Hamlet are passive characters who await determination from the outside. Hamlet is the passive self. He is the receptive subject which changes in time. Not only does he lack the ability to act, but from his point of view the action is indeed 'formidable': to kill the king. The I or the caesura, however, is the active faculty. It designates the moment at which the subject becomes active. Thus Deleuze writes 'Hamlet displays his eminently Kantian character whenever he appears as a passive existence, who, like an actor or sleeper, receives the activity of his own thought as an Other [. . .]' (EC 30).[139] The story of auto-affection is the properly Deleuzian Oedipus complex.[140] It is important to emphasize from this point of view that when Deleuze speaks of the 'totality of time', the 'caesura', or the 'formidable' action, event or image, he is speaking of the I, of an active faculty which attempts to determine a passive self. To 'determine' in this context is also to 'unify' because the entire subject is swept away in the action of the I.

The first two aspects of the third synthesis are the 'order of time' and the 'totality of time'. In the first, a passive self is divided into three parts: imagination, thought and memory. In the second thought, the I, or the caesura which divides the self, maintains its unity in the image of a formidable action – in other words it takes its unity from the act of determining the passive self.

The third moment of the synthesis, the temporal series, expresses the relationship between these first two moments. 'The temporal series designates the confrontation of the divided narcissistic ego with the whole of time or the image of the action' (110/146/136). Put differently, the temporal series designates the confrontation of the passive self with the active I. It is the story of what happens when the active I affects the passive self. This temporal series has three aspects: a past, a present and a future. In the first moment, Deleuze says, the action appears 'too big for me'. The I is beyond the self, and determination has not yet taken place. Deleuze describes the second moment as a becoming-equal to the action. It is a 'present of metamorphosis. In other words, the self takes on the determination granted by the I. It becomes equal to the I. It is the moment of synthesis itself, when the self and I are brought into unity. But in the third moment, both the self and the I dissolve. We will return to this below, but for now it is worth taking a closer look at the first two moments of the synthesis.

Both of these moments express the relationship of a passive faculty to the active I. It is important to realize that the 'past' in the series of time does not refer to one faculty alone, but to the unity of a passive faculty and an active faculty. The same is true of the 'present' or the moment of determination. It too is the synthesis of a passive faculty and an active faculty. Which faculties? Interestingly, Deleuze changes it with each presentation of the third synthesis. In one case it is the synthesis of memory and the I which constitutes the past, while the synthesis of the imagination and the I makes up the present (94/125–6/117–18). Sometimes the opposite is the case. The past is determined by the synthesis of the I and imagination while it is memory which becomes equal to the I (296/378/368). And still other times the unity of sensibility (or the Id) and the I defines the past while the ego as a whole becomes equal to the I in the present (110/146/136). Whatever the case, the same scenario unfolds: when a faculty is related to the I it changes its function. For example, in one case, synthesis changes 'the ground of memory into a simple condition by default, but also the foundation of habit into a failure of "habitus", a metamorphosis of the agent' (94/125–6/117–18). Here the past is the relation of memory to the I. The present is the relation of habit to the I. In both syntheses, the faculty in question looses its character. Memory no longer functions as the ultimate ground of empirical association as we saw above. Rather, when it is determined by thought, it becomes subordinated to the interests of thought. It becomes a condition by default. Similarly, habit can no longer repeat its blind synthesis. The synthesis is asked to change, or become equal to the determination. Change, however, is antithetical to habit.

In the series of time, imagination and memory are brought together in the unity of a thought, but this synthesis fails. In Kant the third synthesis was guaranteed by apperception and the categories. The synthesis of recognition was a rule-governed synthesis, but there is nothing here to guide or regulate the syntheses. Interestingly, Deleuze doesn't emphasize this point here. Recognition doesn't fail because it is an attempt at the recognition of *two* unequal faculties. It fails because there are *three* unequal faculties. Thought is not in a harmonious relationship with the other two faculties it wishes to synthesize. Here we confront again the importance of second postulate of the dogmatic image of thought: the presupposed common sense of the faculties. Deleuze claimed to have avoided this postulate when he described a harmonious discord among the faculties. Instead of communicating under the pretence of a mutual goodwill or compatibility, in the Deleuzian version, the faculties transmitted constraints to one another. When the third synthesis turns around and contemplates the other two and tries to bring them under its unity, their mutual incompatibility becomes insurmountable and synthesis disintegrates. The synthesis of recognition is not accomplished and the cogito legislating over the third synthesis becomes an 'aborted cogito'.

ETERNAL RETURN AND THE IDEAL SYNTHESIS OF DIFFERENCE

If the will to power for Klossowski was the corporeal world of intensities and impulses, for Deleuze it is the world of the three passive syntheses which open up onto an evanescent materiality. What is this materiality if not a 'field of individuation in which *intensities* are distributed here and there'? What are the three syntheses (in the psychoanalytic account at least) if not the impulses or drives? Deleuze will also call this ensemble the 'system of the dissolved self'. As a whole, this system, the will to power, or the unconscious of passive synthesis, represents the movement from sensibility to thought, or the movement through which Being is wrested from beings. This thought is not achieved in the unity of the faculties. Instead it involves their dissolution.

The eternal return appears in the third time of the series and only in the third time, after the synthesis of self and I fails. 'Eternal return, in its esoteric truth, concerns – and can concern – only the third time of the series' (90/122/113). Deleuze is rigorous on this point. The eternal return has nothing to do with the present of the imagination, with the past of memory, or with the empty order and totality of time. It belongs only to the third time of the series. We 'simplify matters in expounding the doctrine of eternal return as though it affected the totality of time' (91/122/114). In fact it actively forgets the passive subject.

The first function of the eternal return is to 'expel' the entire system of the dissolved self. Deleuze will often say that the self is 'smashed to pieces', or, alluding to Klossowski, that 'the event and the act possess a secret coherence which excludes that of the self' (89/121/112). The nature of this coherence is less important than the fact that it is secret. In becoming equal to the I *the subject cannot discover any coherence in itself*. There may be a secret coherence, but it goes *unrecognized* by the self and the I alike. Eternal return 'expels' both memory and habit 'in the name of the work or product' (94/126/118). Eternal return 'causes neither the *condition* nor the *agent* to return: on the contrary, it repudiates these and expels them with all its centrifugal force. It constitutes the autonomy of the product, the independence of the work' (90/122/113; original emphases).[141] The work is autonomous. It requires neither agent nor condition, and is constituted only in their absence.

The second function of the eternal return is to inaugurate a new synthesis: the 'ideal synthesis of difference'. In the third time of the series, self and I dissolve, and the subject transcends itself towards a new synthesis. The third synthesis 'makes use of' habit and memory, but 'leaves them in its wake' (94/125/117). In this 'death' two things happen. First, the differences which the imagination had drawn off from matter and the differences which memory had included are 'liberated'. The 'death' of the self 'refers to the state of free differences when they are no longer subject to the form imposed upon them by an I or an ego' (113/149/138). Difference enters into a state of *determinability*. It is freed from the constraints of the passive imagination and memory. The same thing happens to synthesis. The 'libido' becomes 'desexualized' and forms a 'neutral *displaceable* energy' (111/147/136–7). If the principle of the second synthesis was the 'phallus', the principle of the third synthesis is the castrated phallus. If the 'still intact phallus' gathered together passing narcissistic egos into one great memory, now 'the scattered members' of the dissolved self 'gravitate around the sublime image' of the aleatory point (90/121/112). Difference enters into a state of *determinability* and synthesis or the libido is no longer governed by a principle.

This state of determinability defines the third dimension of time: the future. What does the eternal return have to do with the future? It was relatively easy to see how the other syntheses constituted time. The first synthesis gathered together the evanescent and incompossible events of sensibility into a living present of finite duration. The second synthesis gathered together passing presents and thus constituted a kind of past. The third synthesis rejects these other two. Or rather, it gathers together their 'scattered members' in a new synthesis. If the third synthesis has a link to the future then, it is not because it comes before and directs the other two syntheses as in Heidegger. It is because the future is the form of determinability, 'of the multiple, of the different, and of the fortuitous' (115/152/141). It is the dimension of time in which anything can happen. Deleuze will underscore this by closing the psychoanalytic account of the syntheses with a brief description of the 'divine game':

> The system of the future [. . .] must be called a divine game, since there is no pre-existing rule, since the game bears already upon its own rules and since the child-player can only win, all of chance being affirmed each time and for all times. (116/152/142).

There is no rule. All of the scattered members of the dissolved self or the liberated differences are dispersed in a '*formless*' field of pure chance, and the agent of synthesis, the aleatory point is a child-player, precisely because it has forgotten it past.

This 'system of the future' or field of determinability which unfolds in the third time of the series is nothing other than the virtual – a concept which makes no sense at all unless it comes after the three passive syntheses.

SECTION 5. THE IDEAL SYNTHESIS OF DIFFERENCE

But there's a consolation; at the moment that the imagination finds that it is impotent, no longer able to serve the understanding, it makes us discover in ourselves a still more beautiful faculty which is like the faculty of the infinite. So much so that at the moment we feel for our imagination and suffer with it, since it has become impotent, a new faculty is awakened in us, the faculty of the supersensible.[142]

The fourth chapter of *Difference and Repetition*, 'The Ideal Synthesis of Difference' takes up the genesis where chapter two left off. Despite its complexity, chapter two can be easily summarized. The three passive syntheses were modelled on Kant's syntheses. The first apprehended a discontinuous materiality. The second recorded that apprehension. The third attempted to recognize a common object between apprehension and memory. In Kant recognition was grounded in apperception and its categories, but in Deleuze there is neither a harmonious self-reflective subject nor rules for the unity of synthesis. Consequently, the third synthesis failed. There was, however, a consolation. The failure of imagination, memory and thought 'makes us discover in ourselves a still more beautiful faculty which is like the faculty of the infinite'. In the aftermath of recognition, a new cogito, the 'aleatory point' or castrated phallus, and its new synthesis, the eternal return, appear. The fourth chapter of *Difference and Repetition* is a detailed account of this new synthesis. The 'ideal synthesis of difference' is the 'eternal return' or the 'divine game of the future'.

This new synthesis and the Ideas that it will give rise to marks the end of the dynamic or passive genesis and the beginning of the static genesis. We move from the first four postulates of the image of thought to the last four. The latent subject has just passed away and we are on the trail of the manifest subject. From the point of view of the detective novel we are at the beginning of the second part of the story and looking towards the third. In the second part of the story we will see that Ideas are produced in a genesis. In the third part we will see that once produced, Ideas themselves will produce representation. The 'virtual', in which the ideal synthesis takes place, is clearly not the primary moment of the system. It comes halfway through. Everything began with a latent subject repeating singularities in a sub-representative domain. There were three repetitions. First an apprehension, second a recording, third a liberating expulsion. The virtual appears only after the third synthesis has failed.

Throughout chapter four, Deleuze is going to oscillate back and forth between the 'virtual' and the 'actual'. It would be a mistake to confuse the 'actual' with the unindividuated evanescent materiality with which everything began. The incompossible events which affected the latent subject were sub-representative, fragmented and dissolved objects. They were objects as they appear to the body or the will to power. The actual which follows from the virtual, however, is no longer fragmented. It is individuated. It is circumscribed within the limits of a quality and an extensity. In other words, rather than moving from an unindividuated materiality to an ideal synthesis, when we go from virtual to actual, we go from the virtual to representation. The movement of 'actualization' or 'differenciation' is the movement from the virtual object or 'the object in the Idea' to the actual, represented object. It does not go back to the sub-representative object.[143]

In this chapter too, we face the same problem that affected the previous chapters: the multiplication of technical vocabularies. Notice the way these three sentences all describe the same thing: the relationship between virtual and actual.

1. 'Vice-diction has two procedures which intervene both in the determination of the conditions of the problem and in the correlative genesis of cases of solutions [. . .]' (190/244–5/239).
2. These two aspects are also called 'differentiation' and 'differenciation': 'We call the determination of the virtual content of an Idea differentiation; we call the actualisation of that virtuality into species and distinguished parts differenciation' (207/267/258).
3. 'real events on the level of engendered solutions, and ideal events embedded in the conditions of the problem' (189/244/237).

Virtual is to actual as problems are to solutions, as differentiation is to differenciation, as ideal events to real events. Instead of saying that the chapter oscillates between virtual and actual, we could just as well say that it moves between Idea and knowledge, event and representation, sense and proposition, problem

Table 4 Synonyms for the 'Virtual' and 'Actual'

Virtual	Actual
1. Idea	1. 'Proposition of consciousness' or 'representation in/of knowledge'[a]
a. Structure-event-sense	a. Representation[b]
2. Problem	2. Solution[c]
3. Differentiation	3. Differenciation[d]
4. Ideal/Divine Game	4. Human Game

Note:

[a] Cf. (197/256/247).

[b] Cf. (191/247/240).

[c] '[T]he propositions of consciousness are engendered affirmations which constitutes cases of solution' (206/266/257). 'We can therefore treat representations like propositions of consciousness, designating cases of solution in relation to the concept in general' (178/231/225).

[d] Technically, differenciation is the process by which the actual is constituted. Propositions of consciousness or representations or solutions are what populate the actual. Differenciation explains how you get there from the virtual. The human game explains the rules and coordinates of the represented world.

and solution, and so on. These examples are by no means exhaustive, but they make one thing clear: if we are going to get anywhere in this chapter we have to be attentive to the play in language. Table 4 shows the distribution of some of the more dominant expressions as they divide up along the virtual/actual distinction.

The chapter itself is divided unequally into two parts. The first (168–208/218–69/214–60) deals entirely with Ideas in their virtuality – the second moment of the detective novel. The second part (208–21/269–85/260–74) begins to describe the actualization of Ideas and the movement towards representation – the third and final part of the novel.

DIFFERENTIAL CALCULUS?

At the beginning of the chapter, Deleuze introduces Ideas within the context of a history of differential calculus. We should be careful of attributing too much importance to Deleuze's discussion of calculus however. The fate of Ideas is in no way tied to Deleuze's mathematics. We know this for two reasons. First, throughout his works Deleuze repeatedly made use of the notion of a differential relation to describe *other* moments of the system. In *The Fold*, for example, the differential relation is invoked in order to explain the evanescent matter contemplated by the latent subject. In *Anti-Oedipus*, however it returns to explain the 'capitalist axiomatic' or the relations between representations in the manifest subject. In *Difference and Repetition*, we find it at the mid-point between those stages. Deleuze does this with nearly every major concept, and, as a result, we need to learn to not take his vocabulary too seriously and to focus on the structure of the works instead. This chapter is still very much written in the mode of free indirect discourse.

The second and closely related reason is simply that Deleuze repeatedly emphasizes that mathematics only appears here as a 'technical model' (220/285/273). Alain Badiou is absolutely right to say that mathematics is only a metaphor which Deleuze puts at the service of something else (Badiou, *Deleuze* 1). This something else is a 'dialectic superior to mathematics': 'an important point must be specified. Differential calculus obviously belongs to mathematics, it is an entirely mathematical instrument. It would therefore seem difficult to see in it the Platonic evidence of a dialectic superior to mathematics' (179/232/226).[144] We therefore have to be careful to not give undue privilege to these technical models which in themselves remain actual and never attain virtuality.[145]

IDEAS AND THE PASSIVE SYNTHESES

Ideas are problems, but we saw in the above that there was more than one question-problem complex. There were three: one for each passive synthesis. To which of these complexes does the properly virtual idea belong? For several reasons we can say that it belongs to the third synthesis, or to 'the last form of the problematic' (112/148/137). We can say this in the first instance in relation to the faculty involved. In a certain sense Ideas belong to each and every faculty. As Deleuze puts it, they constitute the link between each, and take each faculty to its limit (194/251/243–4). If Ideas belong to each and every faculty, however, it is only in the sense of the progressive development of the problem. Sensibility presented, in the words of Merleau-Ponty, a 'muddled problem' to the imagination. Imagination passed the problem on to memory. Memory passes the problem on to thought. Ideas understood as problems do, from this point of view, participate in every faculty. 'It is nevertheless true that Ideas have a very special relationship to pure thought' (194/251/244). 'Ideas are exactly the thoughts of the cogito' (169/220/216). Why? Because it is in the faculty of thought that what was sensed ceases to be muddled and becomes *determined*. This is why, even if problems were there from the start, Deleuze can still say that they have their 'origin' in thought (194/251/244). Thought is not the origin of muddled problems, sensibility is. Thought is the origin of determined problems. Deleuze often says that we get the answer we deserve according to the question we have asked or the problem we have posed.[146] If we pose only a muddled problem, the answer itself will be muddled. In the ideal synthesis we finally encounter the conditions which enable the mind to progressively determine a problem and to therefore 'find the reply to a question which is obscurely expressed' (PP 249).[147]

These conditions are figuratively outlined in Deleuze's characterization of the ideal game. The third synthesis left the thinker playing a 'game of the future'. The third time of the series in which the eternal return appeared had several characteristics, one of which was the dissolution of the subject and with it any possibility of a unifying synthesis of recognition. This is why Deleuze called it 'death'. The virtual, or the conditions under which the problem can be progressively determined, appears only in the aftermath of this failed synthesis, in a kind of game which transcends the human game. The following quotation is taken from Deleuze's discussion of the third passive synthesis.

The system of the future, by contrast, must be called a divine game, since there is no pre-existing rule, since the game bears already upon its own rules, and since the child-player can only win, all of chance being affirmed each time and for all times. Not restricted or limiting affirmations, but affirmations coextensive with the questions posed and with the decisions from which these emanate: such a game entails the repetition of the necessarily winning move, since it wins by embracing all possible combinations and rules in the system of its own return. (116/152/142)

These are the general conditions in which the problem can be determined. There can be no pre-existing rule. Only the child-player can win. 'All of chance' (*tout le hasard*) must be affirmed. The game constitutes a 'system of its own return'. We will touch on all of these points below, but for now I want to emphasize two: the absence of rules and the child-player.

For Deleuze thought is not defined by a conformity to rules but by a 'throw of the dice' which affirms all of chance. Kant is the obvious target here. In Kant, the act of thinking was conditioned by the understanding and its categories which were, precisely, *rules*.

We have above explained the **understanding** in various ways – through a spontaneity of cognition (in contrast to the receptivity of sensibility), through a faculty for thinking, or a faculty of concepts, or also of judgments – which explanations, if one looks at them properly, come down to the same thing. Now we can characterize it as the **faculty of rules.** (CPR A126; original emphasis)

The faculty for thinking is a faculty of rules. These rules, the categories, governed the third synthesis of recognition. Insofar as this third synthesis on Deleuze's reading related appearances to the object-form, we can characterize the categories in slightly phenomenological way as the *rules for the constitution of any possible object of experience.* But in Deleuze, as we saw, the third synthesis falls apart because there is neither this categorical model which would unify the third synthesis nor a subject of apperception to ground synthesis. Consequently, Deleuze cannot, like Kant, define thought as a faculty of rules. Thought, in the failure of synthesis, is characterized by the absence of rules: chance. The act of thinking is a 'throw of the dice'.

Deleuze doesn't leave rules entirely out of the picture, however, and in a certain sense thought is still a faculty of rules. Thought may not operate according to an already given rule. It does however 'invent its own rules' (283/263/354; my emphasis). From this point of view we will see that the Idea still has a fundamental relationship to the constitution of objects. Its systematic function is nothing other than *to produce rules for the constitution of objects in the absence of any pre-existing rule.*

Deleuze says that only the 'child-player' can win the divine game. Who is this child-player? The expression itself is an allusion to Zarathustra's parable on the three metamorphoses of spirit. 'I name you three metamorphoses of the spirit: how the spirit shall become a camel, and the camel a lion, and the lion at last a child' (Nietzsche *Thus Spoke Zarathustra* 54). It is easy to see why this parable was attractive to Deleuze. For Deleuze, spirit also undergoes three metamorphoses. The imagination is like the camel. It becomes what it synthesizes and is thus directly bound to the weight of the world. In its synthesis of fatigued contemplative souls, however, memory, like the lion, becomes the master of the world. Even so, it still lacks the power to *create*. It is only in the third metamorphosis, when spirit becomes the faculty of thought, that it acquires the ability to create – precisely because, like the child, spirit no longer knows rules or pre-established values. The eternal return has expelled both the condition and the agent. The 'work' is approached only in death and remains autonomous in relation to its past. In its innocence and forgetfulness the child is synonymous with the new:

> The child is innocence and forgetfulness, a new beginning, a sport [*un jeu*], a self-propelling wheel, a first motion, a sacred Yes [*une sainte affirmation*].
>
> Yes, a sacred Yes is needed, my brothers, for the sport of creation [*le jeu divin de la création*]: the spirit now wills *its own* will, the spirit sundered from the world now wins *its own* world. (Nietzsche 55; original emphasis)[148]

The parable of the metamorphoses of spirit repeats the story of the progressive development of the problem across the faculties, and in the final metamorphosis we encounter many of the themes already discussed: the notion of a the divine game of creation; the notion of eternal return, or the self-propelled wheel which turns around itself; affirmation, or the sacred Yes. Most importantly, we find here the idea of an innocence which conditions the 'divine game of creation', an innocence which is granted by forgetting and which is given only to a spirit sundered from the world. Distanced from the world in the failure of the third synthesis, the child-player is the thinker who can progressively determine problems outside of rules. Which of Deleuze's many concepts would correspond to all of these characteristics? What is Deleuze's philosophical formulation of this 'lyrical' concept? And what does the child-player create? The child-player is Deleuze's *cogito.* Its thoughts are Ideas.

VIRTUAL MULTIPLICITIES

There is a tendency to turn the Deleuzian notion of the Idea (or the multiplicity, or the event, or the structure) into something stable: we say that it is an assemblage of differential elements, differential relations and singularities. Deleuze himself sometimes takes the lead in this: 'An Idea [. . .] is neither one nor multiple, but a multiplicity constituted of differential elements, differential relations between those elements, and singularities *corresponding to* those relations' (278/356/348; my emphasis). The assemblage itself, however, is a process. The Idea is indistinguishable from its genesis, and at the origin of that process lies a strange cogito.

At an abstract and formal level nothing could be easier to describe than the genesis of the Idea. Everything begins with a set of undetermined 'ideal elements'. These elements are then subject to a synthesis which reciprocally determines them or puts them in relation to one another. Finally the various relations between elements are cemented by 'singularities'. Singularities give the Idea its concrete form and consequently represent a stage of 'complete determination'. There are thus three degrees of determination – undetermined, reciprocally determined and completely determined – which correspond to the three constitutive moments of the Idea – elements, relations and singularities. The problem with this abstract presentation is that it leaves some of our most basic questions unasked. Who or what brings about the ideal synthesis? What are these 'ideal elements' and where do they come from? What is the 'Idea' an idea of?

The first question is the easiest to answer but one of the more difficult to grasp. Who brings about the ideal synthesis if not the Deleuzian cogito? When we try to follow Deleuze's peregrinations around the origin of Ideas, we inevitably end up reading about a throw of the dice which is grounded in an 'aleatory point' (283/363/354; 198/256/248). In the language of the ideal game, the aleatory point is what throws the dice. It is the aleatory point which actually produces Ideas. For example, Deleuze says that the throws '*animate* ideal problems determining their relations and singularities' (283/363/354; my emphasis), or that the 'throw of the dice *carries out* the calculation of problems, the determination of differential elements or the distribution of singular points which constitute a structure' (198/256/248; my emphasis). In both quotes Deleuze clearly establishes an active role for the throw: it 'animates' and actually 'carries out' the genesis of multiplicities. It determines elements. It distributes points. It calculates problems.

Deleuze often refers to Blanchot here. The aleatory point is 'that point of which Maurice Blanchot speaks endlessly: that blind acephalic, aphasic and aleatory point which designates "impossibility of thinking *that is thought*"' (199/257/249–50; my emphasis). Georges Poulet grasps the essential in relation to this point. The aleatory point is Blanchot's *cogito:*

> *consciousness* for Blanchot, since it is always irreparably sep-
> arated from everything including itself, could never be other
> than the awareness of infinite isolation, if the very fact of
> existence did not offer unmistakable evidence of presence, a
> constant affirmation looming behind all separate negations,
> a unique spot, a point without space or duration, where
> there were no more contradictory terms, where the objective
> and subjective meet, therefore a singularly felicitous site, the
> only one where truth and our consent to truth can be situ-
> ated. (Poulet 80; my emphasis)[149]

This point is Blanchot's 'I think'. The I think doesn't think itself as a determinate subject nor does it think particular objects. It is infinitely isolated from the world. It is an impersonal consciousness which thinks at a felicitous site prior to objectivity and subjectivity. It is an empty thought which is nothing but a 'constant affirmation' of Being.[150] Poulet situates this new conception of consciousness in relation to Descartes, but given the systematic place in which it appears in Deleuze – after the three syntheses and, and as I will suggest below, just before the schematism – we should perhaps situate it in relation to Kant. In several important ways the aleatory point functions in Deleuze as an alternative to Kantian apperception. The third synthesis disintegrated, we said, because there was no unity of apperception. There was nonetheless a synthesis in the third time of the series, and with that synthesis a new form of consciousness. This new cogito, the aleatory point or the child-player, cannot be characterized in any of the traditional ways. It is neither pure, original nor unchanging; it does not participate in the apodicity of inner sense according to which I know my self better than I know any other thing; and finally, it cannot function as the necessary ground of all subjectivity. As Deleuze puts it, this new *cogito* is acephalic (headless), aphasic (speechless) and aleatory (contingent rather than necessary). In the *Logic of Sense* it is 'non-sense' incarnate. It does however possess two of the most fundamental characteristics of Kantian apperception (beyond the fact that is the agent of synthesis which is constantly poring over appearances looking for rules (CPR A126)).

First, as Blanchot puts it in his characterization of the eternal return, it is a self-designating sign. The aleatory point is a 'unique sign in which *thought designates itself*' (Blanchot *Friendship* 173; my emphasis). It is a movement that always returns to itself like the circle. Second, it still functions as an odd form of unity. The throw of the dice only animates particular Ideas, and Deleuze says that the question remains of an Idea of Ideas – in other words, of an Idea which contains and is the essence of all of the other Ideas.[151] This Idea of Ideas is the aleatory point. In *The Logic of Sense* Deleuze describes this point as the '*Eventum tantum* [i.e. the Event as such] for all events, the ultimate form for all the forms which remain disjointed in it' (LS 179). Each throw of the dice determines a particular Idea, but the 'circulation' of the aleatory point is both the genetic principle itself behind these particular throws and what unites all throws into one throw.[152] This means two things. First each Idea is produced only in relation to all other Ideas and as a function of a changing totality.[153] Second, the unity of this field is governed by the aleatory point. It is the form of forms, the Idea of Ideas. It is not only the genetic principle of each particular multiplicity in relation to which differential relations take on their absolute value, but it is also that which gathers

together and holds all of the particular Ideas in one consciousness, the thought of the eternal return.
The aleatory point is what determines Ideas to be produced.
It brings about the ideal synthesis. What is this synthesis a
synthesis of? Where do the ideal elements come from? In its
undetermined state, an Idea is a set of *determinable* elements.
These elements are the very elements that were originally
sensed at the very beginning of the passive syntheses, only now
they are freed from the limits of the contemplating ego. After
the synthesis of recognition failed, we saw two things happen.
First, the subject and the possibility of a unified object dissolved. The self was 'smashed to pieces', 'as though the bearer
of the new world were carried away and dispersed by the shock
of the multiplicity to which it gives birth' (89–90/121/112).
Second, even if the self was smashed to pieces, this moment
did not represent the *annihilation* of the self. It represented a
metamorphosis in which the self took on a new form. Not only
were the differences which were originally drawn off liberated, but synthesis too became free. In a particularly morbid
image Deleuze describes the new situation this way: 'scattered
members gravitate around the sublime image' (90/121/112). The
scattered members of the body are determinable elements at the
origin of the Idea's genesis. They are the 'liberated differences'
or the 'ungrounded' fragments the self which is 'dispersed' in
the '*formlessness*' of the 'eternal return' (91/122–3 /114). The sublime image is the new cogito which contemplates its dissolved
but liberated body. This is the first moment in the genesis of
Ideas: a new 'I' contemplates its dispersed self.
  This gives rise to a new synthesis for which Deleuze has many
names. It is the 'ideal synthesis', the 'fluent synthesis' or the
process of reciprocal determination. Whatever it is called, it is
the second moment in the genesis of Ideas. If the ideal elements
were the 'scattered members' of the dissolved self, this synthesis is the 'search for fragments' (190/245/239). It reintegrates the
fragmented body within a space of determinability. Deleuze
describes the synthesis in several ways.
  Perhaps the most precise description of this synthesis is his
description of it as the constitution of a differential relation
between elements. Why is this precise? Deleuze far more frequently speaks of the synthesis as the establishment of 'ideal

connections' (*liaisons idéals*) – and this is the easiest to think. In the first moment of the Idea there are determinable elements. In the second there are ideal connections which bring these elements together. In the first there are the dispersed fragments of the self, in the second there is a search for fragments. If this is the easiest to think, it is because it lets us maintain the priority of perception. It lets us think of the relation as a relation between two elements which are external to one another. As Deleuze puts it, it 'has too much of the aspect of a spatio-temporal relation' (184/239/232–3). This is why Deleuze begins the chapter with an account of differential relations. These are much harder to think of as relations between external elements.[154]

Deleuze describes the differential relation this way: '*dx* is strictly nothing in relation to *x*, as *dy* is in relation to *y*' (171/222/218). *dx* represents an infinitely small difference from *x*. It is nothing in relation to *x*. Even if *dy* and *dx* by themselves are vanishing quantities and thus 'zeros', when the two are put in relation to one another, for example, in the equation *dy/dx*, they are subsumed in the relation itself – in this case they now, by virtue of the relation which unites them, express the tangent of a given curve, even if this relation is between two 'nothings' or vanishing quantities.[155]

This differential relation has less of the aspect of spatio-temporal relations about it. As Deleuze says, it is not a relationship between *actual* 'intuited' or *possible* 'algebraic magnitudes of quantities'. These have 'particular values; and even when they are united in a fractional relation each maintains a value independently of the relation' (171/222/218). Rather, in a differential relation, '[e]ach term exists absolutely in its relation to the other: it is no longer necessary, or even possible to indicate an independent variable (172/223/219).

like
#

This is the ideal synthesis: a set of reciprocal relations are established between the scattered members of the dissolved self which leaves none of the fragments untouched. Each term exists solely in relation to the other and, lacking value in itself (Deleuze repeatedly emphasizes that ideal elements are thoroughly *meaningless*); each element takes its value from the relation which subsumes it.

by
dx
dy

If the language of 'differential relations' is the most precise, and the language of 'ideal connections' the easiest to think, there is still one more description of the ideal synthesis that may be the most illuminating. Deleuze sometimes leaves the language of ideal connections behind and turns to the language of group theory. In the example of group theory, progressive determination takes the form of successive variations on a 'problem':

> starting from a basic 'field' (R), successive adjunctions to this field (R', R'', R''') allow a progressively more precise distinction of the roots of the equation, by the progressive limitation of possible substitutions. (180/233/227–8)

In this example, the 'basic field' is the set of ideal elements. The successive adjunctions represent the progressive establishment of ideal connections. The example brings to light an essential function of ideal synthesis: to progressively limit the number of 'possible substitutions'. It allows one to extract a 'structure', an 'invariant' or an essence from the group.[156] Deleuze is clearly making use of group theory to reformulate Husserl's famous notion of 'imaginative variation'. Husserl claimed that it was possible to discover the essence of an object by taking that object up in a 'structure of arbitrariness' (determinability) and imaginatively modifying it.[157] Supposedly one would eventually reach a point at which it was no longer possible to make another variation. There was a 'progressive limitation of possible substitutions'. This invariant would then express the essence or *idea* of that object.

Deleuze's version of this process differs in several important respects from Husserl's. At the most general level, for Husserl, imaginative variation is a supremely rational act. In Deleuze, however, it is still very much an aesthetic act. There is as yet no active consciousness, and there is no active faculty of reason. There is only a newly born faculty of thought which contemplates the dissolved self. The consequences of this general difference can be seen in a more specific difference: in Deleuze there is as yet no object, but only a group of undetermined ideal elements – what Deleuze calls a 'problem'. This is why Deleuze turns to Galois and Abel. They 'elaborated a whole method according to which solvability must follow from the form of the problem' (179–80/233/227). Group theory explains how structure can be abstracted not from the known (Husserl's objects of intuition), but from the unknown (ideal elements). In the language of *Bergsonism*, it applies the test of true and false to problems themselves, not to solutions (BG 15–16). Why does Deleuze attach so much importance to this? It is because, for him, the 'solution' is the 'actual' constituted object, the thing as an assemblage of quality and extensity with which Husserl begins imaginative variation. The entire problem which Deleuze has posed for himself in this chapter is to explain how the Idea of the object, the problem, can be determined without presupposing the already completed object, the solution. The Idea must be 'capable of engendering itself independently of the requirements of representation [. . .]' (274/353/344). Group theory represents a way of determining a problem without reference to potential solutions. How is the problem determined as a problem? Reciprocal determination, or ideal synthesis, is his answer to that question.

Progressive determination is not yet complete determination. Once an invariant is extracted there is still one more moment that needs to appear in the genesis of Ideas. In this last stage of determination, 'singularities' appear. '[C]omplete determination carries out the differentiation of singularities, but it bears only on their existence and distribution [and not on their nature]' (210/271/262). Deleuze often draws this distinction between the 'existence and distribution' of singularities and the 'nature' of singularities. This distinction, like so many others, unfolds along the lines of virtual and actual. By existence and distribution of singularities, he means their coming to be in the Idea (existence) and their placement within the Idea (distribution). By nature, he means the specific, *actual* extensity to which singularities give rise once they are actualized.

For the moment, we are only concerned with singularities in their virtuality, or from the point of view of their existence and distribution. This existence and distribution depends entirely on the state of the differential relations. Deleuze often says that singularities 'correspond' to differential relations: 'The reality of the virtual consists of the differential elements and relations along with the singular point which *correspond* to them' (209/269–70/260).[158] Sometimes he even goes even further and speaks of 'the varieties of relations and [. . .] the singular points *dependent*

upon the values of each variety' (210/270/261; my emphasis).[159]
If singularities 'correspond to' or are 'dependent upon' the differential relations, it is ultimately because they formalize those relations. They bring an end to progressive determination in a *form* which characterizes complete determination. Simon Duffy captures this definition of the singularity as it relates to the prior moments of determination with great clarity:

> according to Deleuze's reading of the infinitesimal calculus, the differential relation is generated by differentials [or ideal elements] and the power series [singularities] are generated in *a process involving the repeated differentiation of the differential relation.* (Duffy 71; my emphasis)

If group theory extracted an invariant by means of free variation or what Duffy calls the 'repeated differentiation of the differential relation', then singularities express that invariant. Singularities, in their virtual form, are nothing other than expressions of the ideal connections created in the ideal synthesis.

We will return to the importance and role of singularities below, but for now we want to ask, what is the systematic function of this odd assemblage of elements, relations and points?

THE OTHER HALF OF THE OBJECT

I suggested above that Deleuze's chapter is divided thematically into two main sections. The first, which we have already covered, deals with a description of Ideas in their virtuality from the point of view of their genesis. The second area of concern is with the actualization of Ideas, the third part of the detective novel or the static genesis. It is the process through which virtual Ideas become actual objects. As we saw above, Deleuze talks about this virtual/actual distinction in many different ways. In the following passage two of the most prominent are clarified: problem/solution and differentiation/differenciation:

> Whereas differentiation determines the virtual content of the Idea as problem, differenciation expresses the actualisation of this virtual and the constitution of solutions [. . .]. Differenciation is like the second part of difference, and in order to designate the integrity or the integrality of

141

the object we require the complex notion of differen*t*/*c*iation. (209/270/261).

Differentiation is the process by which a problem becomes completely determined. Differenciation is the process by which solutions are constituted. However, neither one nor the other, neither differentiation nor differenciation, is by itself capable of determining the 'integrity' of the object. This says two things. First, by itself the virtual is useless. In no way does it contain the totality of the object by itself. It contains only the rules for the production of objects. The object is not at all constituted by the one-directional creativity of the virtual as some commentators have suggested. It is constituted only in differenciation, in the complex interplay between Ideas and intensities. *constitutes* *objects* The second thing this passage tells us is that Ideas are actualized in objects.

Deleuze insists on this relation of actualization to the object. At the beginning of this book we saw one definition of the object: an object is an assemblage of a quality, an extensity and a duration. This definition is a partial definition. It considers the object only from the point of view of its actuality. As we have just seen, by itself, the Idea is also insufficient to define the object: the Idea only considers the object from the point of view of its virtuality.

What the complete determination lacks is the whole set of relations belonging to actual existence. [. . .] *There is thus another part of the object which is determined by actualisation.* (209/270/261; my emphasis)

Therefore, as Deleuze says above, the real definition of the object is contained in the 'complex notion of differen*t*/*c*iation'. One half of the object is virtual. The other half is actual, and the 'integrity' of these two moments is captured by this odd word: different/ciation. Actualization is the process in which the virtual Idea or the 'object in the Idea (*l'objet en Idée*)[160] meets up with the actual object. Differentiation differenciates an object thus determining its quality, extensity and duration.

We will return to this below, but we should be clear that actualization is the actualization only of particular Ideas and not virtuality as a whole. Above we distinguished between events and the Event, particular Ideas and the aleatory point which was the genetic principle and unity of all particular Ideas. Actualization bears only on particular Ideas. Deleuze often describes the aleatory point as the 'non-actualizable part of the event' or the question which persists above and beyond every response. It is the virtual as a whole or the faculty of thought, and it maintains its consistency independently of the process of actualization.

IDEAS AS RULES

When I said above that for Kant the understanding was a faculty of rules and that these rules, the categories, were the rules for the constitution of objects, I was slightly exaggerating their provenance. A category is a rule for the constitution of objects insofar as it gives unity to the synthesis of recognition, but only from a sufficiently broad point of view. They are the rules for any object whatsoever. They are the universal and necessary rules of any possible object, and given the diversity of objects, these concepts have to be extraordinarily broad.

> This notion of 'any object' is bizarre. I say 'the rose is red'. What is that? 'The rose is red' is not complicated, it's a relation between two concepts, the rose and red, and if I say 'what is universal or necessary in that?' I can reply: nothing. Not all objects are roses, not all roses are red. Not all reds are the colour of roses. I would say that there is an experience of the red rose and that this experience is particular, contingent, a posteriori like all experience. (Kant seminar (14 Mar. 1978))

In contrast to particular, empirical concepts, the category is a universal concept to which all objects must conform in order to be constituted as objects.

> When I say 'all objects have a cause', am I not in another domain completely? Evidently I am, I am in a completely different domain because to have a cause is a universal predicate which is applied to all objects of possible experience, to the point that [. . .] if an unknown object emerged in experience before my eyes, this object would not be an object if it

143

didn't have a cause. To have a cause or to be caused is a predicate of a wholly other type than the predicate 'red'. Why? Because the predicate 'to be caused' – to the point where we can wonder, after reflection, is that really a predicate or is it something else? – the predicate 'to be caused' is *predicable of any object of possible experience, to the point where it is not going to define a set or a subset within experience because it is strictly coextensive with the totality of possible experience.* (Kant seminar (14 Mar. 1978); my emphasis)

If the categories are rules, they only bear on objects from the point of view of the very general possibility of their being objects. If the understanding is a faculty of rules, those rules most certainly do not legislate over the particulars of immediate experience. In short, the understanding legislates over phenomena, but it 'never determines *a priori* the *content* of phenomena, the detail of *real* experience or the *particular* laws of this or that object' (KP 62).

If we say, then, that Deleuzian Ideas are precisely rules for the constitution of objects, and that the faculty of thought in Deleuze is also the faculty of rules, we have to distinguish them from the Kantian categories on two points.

First and most simply, in Deleuze Ideas are subject to a genesis. In contrast to the categories which are already given, the Idea is progressively determined in thought by an aleatory point. We can trace this origin back even further thought itself is the product of a progressive development which begins in a field of intensity before passing through the imagination and memory and then coming undone in a failed synthesis of recognition. The faculty of thought and its Ideas therefore have an entirely different birth certificate than the understanding and its categories.

Second whereas a category is the concept of any possible object whatsoever, the Idea is precisely the set of rules which determines the content and the detail of real experience. It contains nothing more than the particular laws of this or that object.[161] Here rules are not the predicates of the object-form or the object = x as they were in Kant. They are the virtual relations of actual experience. In order to fully describe the way in which the Idea is actualized in the object it is necessary to take into account the fifth chapter of *Difference and Repetition*. Deleuze does however make some very important statements regarding the contours of this process in the last pages of the fourth chapter, and in what follows, I will limit myself to these comments.

ACTUALIZATION

How, exactly, do Ideas function as rules for the production of objects? Deleuze never fully answers this question. The first and most basic point that he makes in the second part of this chapter is that there is a simple parallel relationship between Idea and object. This simple parallel relationship will be significantly complicated, but it still goes a long way towards clarifying things. For Deleuze the 'object' is defined as the intersection of quality and extensity (in the biological metaphor quality will be called 'species' and extensity will be called 'parts'). The actualization of Ideas is what determines the actual quality and extensity of the thing, and the two parts of the Idea correspond directly to the two aspects of the object. The differential relations in the Idea determine the qualities in the thing. The singularities in the Idea determine the extensity or external form of the thing.

> How do the dissimilar halves of an object fit together? Qualities and species incarnate the varieties of relation in an actual mode [*sur un mode actuel*]; the organic parts incarnate the corresponding singularities. (210/271/262; translation modified)

Deleuze will continually repeat this simple opposition throughout the book. Virtual relations determine actual qualities. Virtual singularities determine actual extensities.

In what sense could a relation determine quality? This is a very difficult question to answer. Peter Hallward has consistently pointed out that for Deleuze quality is nothing but a contracted quantity.[162] He cites *Bergsonism*. There Deleuze writes, 'What in fact is a sensation? It is the operation of contracting trillions of vibrations onto a receptive surface. Quality emerges from this, quality that is nothing other than contracted quantity' (BG 74).[163] Quality *emerges* from the contraction of trillions of vibrations. We have seen that our transcendental sensibility is populated by intensities. These are the trillions of sensations which affect a passive subject. The crucial word in the quotation however is 'contracted'. Quality is a contracted quantity. It is a synthesis of quantity. We will see in the next chapter that this synthesis which transforms vibrations into quality is no longer a passive synthesis. The passive synthesis of habit which contracted intensity by no means produced a quality. In order for quality to emerge this passive synthesis must be converted into an active synthesis regulated by the Idea. An ideal relation will determine a quality only insofar as it determines a synthesis to organize or contract intensive quantities according to a certain order – and for this reason Deleuze will often say that the intensive quantity itself is what actually creates the quality whereas the Idea simply differenciates that quality. The differential relation in the Idea regulates the synthesis of quantity and causes it to be contracted in such a way that a quality results from the trillions of vibrations submitted to our sensibility. The consequences of this are profound for certain readings of Deleuze. Quality does not issue directly from Ideas as though the virtual were the One-All above being from which all beings emanated. The differential relation is simply a rule which governs a synthesis. It is this synthesis that produces quality by contracting sensations. Quality depends entirely on the organization of intensive quantities, and therefore on the application of Ideas to sensibility.

If relations determine quality by organizing intensive quantities, in what sense do singularities provide an extensive form? Deleuze defines a singularity this way:

> A singularity is the point of departure for a series which extends over all the ordinary points of the system, as far as the neighborhood [*voisinage*] of another singularity which itself gives rise to another series which may either converge or diverge from the first. (278/356–7/348; translation modified)

In his lectures on Leibniz he gives several helpful examples of increasing complexity. We will stay with the simplest: the example of the geometrical figure. A square, Deleuze says, has four singularities – one at each corner. A triangle has three singularities and a cube has eight. These singularities extend themselves across the line of ordinary points all the way to the neighbourhood of the next singularity. From this point of view, as Deleuze puts it, singular points are the 'composition' or 'characterization' of a *form* (175/227–8/223). They determine the form of the object, its extensity or its parts.

We said above that singularities express differential relations. They correspond to and are dependent upon them. Would this suggest that form is nothing more than the organization of quality? It seems that this is exactly what Deleuze means. Deleuze often says that there is no extensity which is not covered over by a quality and that there is no quality that is not distributed in an extensity. 'There is in general no quality which does not refer to a space defined by the singularities corresponding to the differential relations incarnated in that quality' (210/271/26).[164] Quality and extensity are coextensive. Form is quality and quality is form. Where the quality changes, the object changes or encounters a limit. A singularity 'extends over' qualities and thus determines their extension. An object's extension is nothing more than the organization of its quality.

THE SCHEMATISM: SPATIO-TEMPORAL DYNAMISM

Relations determine qualities and singularities determine quantities. Quality is an organization of intensive quantity. Extensity is an organization of quality. These two dimensions of the object do not issue directly from the Idea as though from a creative origin. The virtual half of the object and the actual half are only integrated on the condition that the Idea is *applied* to intensive quantities. In the first half of the genesis, thought had extracted itself from the body. It had expelled the passive self and its impulses and sublimated its affections onto a form of determinability where it could produce Ideas. But Ideas themselves are useless unless they are actualized. Thought must therefore return to the body and organize the field of intensity. The genesis does not proceed directly from thought to representation. Actualization only takes place insofar as thought is folded back onto sensibility.

This process begins with what Deleuze calls 'spatio-temporal dynamisms'. 'These are the actualizing, differenciating agencies [*C'est eux qui sont actualisants, différenciants*]' (214/276/266). They are the actualizers, the differenciators. Deleuze says that these actualizers '*dramatize*' the Idea. They are agents, but they perform a role given to them by the Idea. A spatio-temporal dynamism is not an unorganized movement in space and time. It moves throughout space and time according to the rules given in the Idea.

On the one hand, they create or trace a space corresponding to the differential relations and to the singularities to be actualised. [. . .] On the other hand, the dynamisms are no less temporal than spatial. They constitute a time of actualisation. Not only do these spaces begin to incarnate [*incarner*] differential relations between elements of the reciprocally and completely determined structure, but the times of differenciation incarnate [*incarnent*] the time of the structure, the time of progressive determination. (216/279–80/268–9)[165]

Up to this point there has been a remarkable structural similarity between *Difference and Repetition* and Kant's *Critique of Pure Reason*. Deleuze's three syntheses are modelled after Kant's, and in place of apperception, its object and categories, we get the aleatory point and its Ideas. Given this general structural similarity we have to wonder, to what moment in the *Critique* might this spatio-temporal dynamism correspond. Deleuze makes this an easy question to answer: 'Are not these spatio-temporal dynamisms what Kant called schemata?' (218/281/270).[166]

Deleuze describes the schemata in Kant in this way: 'the schema is a spatio-temporal determination which itself corresponds to the category [. . .]: it does not consist in an image but *in spatio-temporal relations which embody [incarnent] or realize relations which are in fact conceptual*' (KP18/28–92; original emphasis). The differences between the Kantian schematism and the Deleuzian spatio-temporal dynamism are obvious: instead of moving from concept to intuition as in Kant, in Deleuze we move from Idea to sensibility.[167] On the one hand the difference is slight, but the shift from concept to Idea implies a complete reformulation of the entire Kantian edifice which I have continually emphasized. Everything changes its characteristics in Deleuze – the syntheses, the categories, the object, and so forth – even if these concepts follow a similar structural distribution between the two authors.

Despite these differences, we should notice that schematization and dramatization have the same end: to combine conceptual or Ideal determinations with spatio-temporal determinations. They also accomplish this end in the same way: they both 'embody' or 'incarnate' Ideal/conceptual relations. Actualization is the process in which ideal determinations are given intensive determination. It is the process in which the Idea is applied to intensity.

SECTION 6. THE ASYMMETRICAL SYNTHESIS

The act of knowing, judging, or concluding is nothing but the result of a certain behavior of the impulses toward each other. [. . .] a precarious armistice between obscure forces.[168]

The final chapter of *Difference and Repetition* deals primarily with the notion of intensity. This notion appears at two entirely different moments in the system, and Deleuze's chapter is formally divided according to these two appearances. First, it was present at the origin of the genesis. We saw above in both the 1) doctrine of faculties and the passive syntheses that intensity is the given of transcendental sensibility and the ultimate origin of thought. One function of this last chapter of *Difference and Repetition* – roughly the first half of it – will be to further describe this intensive origin and its transmutations throughout the process of passive synthesis. Second, in this chapter Deleuze will also tell us that intensity appears in the process of 2) actualization. It is what takes Ideas out of their virtuality and makes them present (*actuel*) and actual. Intensity is the 'determinant' in the process of actualization. The second half of the chapter describes this process.

Intensity therefore has a dual role which we have to come to terms with. It is not only what begins the entire genesis as the shock given to a transcendental sensibility. It is also what draws this genesis to a close, or to its 'finality', by determining the actualization of Ideas in the particular qualities and extensities

DELEUZE'S *DIFFERENCE AND REPETITION*

which will populate an empirical sensibility. In order to see how intensity fills this dual role we need to take into account three things: first, Deleuze's discussion of the notion of intensity as it appears at the beginning of the chapter; second, the relation between this fuller notion of intensity and doctrine of passive synthesis; third, the role of intensity within actualization.

INTENSITY

Intensity is not virtuality, and it would be a mistake to confuse the two. They can be distinguished from several points of view. Intensity is felt, for example, whereas Ideas are thought. Intensity belongs to the present. It expresses the degree to which a subject is affected by the environment in which it finds itself. Ideas, however, coexist in the future, in the form of determinability. Perhaps most importantly, Ideas and intensities constitute two different types of relations. Ideas are 'made up of relations between differential elements' whereas intensities are 'made up of relations between asymmetrical elements' (244/315/305).[169] It is for this reason that Deleuze's system will encounter a problem analogous to Kant's. In Kant the question was how conceptual determinations could be related to spatio-temporal determinations. In Deleuze the question is how an ideal relation can be related to an intensive relation. In Kant the movement from spatio-temporal determinations to conceptual determinations was accomplished by means of synthesis. For Deleuze too, the movement from intensity to Ideas was accomplished by means of synthesis. In Kant the reverse movement was accomplished by the schematism. In place of the schematism Deleuze will invoke 'dramatization'. We have already seen how synthesis works. What remains is to understand the second process, dramatization. This process is complex, and in order to see the way in which it allows the application of Ideas to intensities it is first necessary to turn to Deleuze's characterization of intensity.

At first this discussion seems to be conducted entirely within the context of the thermodynamics of the nineteenth and early twentieth centuries. Deleuze claims to extract a philosophical principle from the work of Boltzmann, Carnot and Curie. But just as we called into question Deleuze's use of calculus in the last chapter, we again have to wonder, is this excursion into thermodynamics not just another 'metaphor' (to use Badiou's word)?

Deleuze tends to emphasize divisibility when he opposes intensive quantities to extensive quantities. Whereas extensive quantities can be divided into equal parts, intensive quantities cannot (237/306/297). If you had one cup of 30-degree water and divided it into two half-cups, you would then have two half-cups that were still 30 degrees each. A cup of water is an extensive quantity. Extensive quantities can be divided into relative units without changing the nature of what is divided. Water remains water, and one cup is divided equally. There is no such whole-part relationship between intensive quantities. Temperature cannot be divided into constituent parts nor can it be divided without changing the nature of what is divided:

> when I say 'it's 30 degrees', the 30-degree heat is not the sum of three times ten degrees, it's at the level of extensive quantities that thirty is $10 + 10 + 10$, but thirty degrees is not three 10-degree heats. In other words, the rules of addition and subtraction are not valid for intensive quantities.[170]

A temperature is not composed of constituent parts, and it cannot be directly divided without changing the nature of the temperature itself. Deleuze will say that 'In a sense, it is therefore indivisible, *but only because no part exists prior to the division and no part retains the same nature after the division*' (237/306/297; my emphasis). He draws the conclusion that 'each temperature is a difference, and that differences are not composed of differences of the same order but imply a series of heterogeneous terms' (237/306/297). The example of speed makes this point most clearly. Speed is an intensive magnitude which is measured in relation to two 'series of heterogeneous' extensive magnitudes – distance and time ($r = d/t$). Each speed is a 'difference' which 'implies' these two heterogeneous series, movement and time. This point will become important below: intensity is constructed on top of two heterogeneous series.

Deleuze spends most of the first chapter opposing intensity to extensity, but what gradually emerges is not so much their difference from one another, but the degree to which they are intimately related. Intensity is 'cancelled' in quality and extensity. There is a 'tendency on the part of differences in intensity to cancel themselves out in qualified extended systems' (224/289/282). Intensity rushes 'headlong into suicide' (224/289/282). Deleuze usually refers to this process in three ways. Sometimes he calls it 'cancellation', sometimes 'explication', and other times 'individuation'. The important point is that in its cancellation, intensity doesn't simply move towards equilibrium. In cancelling itself it actually *creates* extensity and quality. Whatever word Deleuze uses to express the movement from intensity to extensity, in cancelling itself, intensity creates extensity.

synonyms

Intensity is cancelled insofar as it is drawn outside of itself, *in* extensity and *in* the quality which fills that extensity. However, difference creates both this extensity and this quality. [. . .] Difference of intensity is cancelled or tends to be cancelled in this system, but it creates this system by explicating itself. (228/294/287; original emphasis)

What is at issue in Deleuze's distinction is not the opposition of two types of quantity, but establishing one as the genetic principle of the other. Further, it seems doubtful that Deleuze's project has much to do with nineteenth century physics. Intensity is drawn outside of itself in a quality and an extensity. It is annulled in 'qualified extended systems'. Just like Ideas, intensity ends up covered over in quality and extensity. But as we have already seen, quality and extensity are not the two characteristics of the objects with which physics is concerned. Rather, quality and extensity are the two 'elements of *representation*': as Deleuze puts it in this chapter, 'extensity and quality are the two forms of generality. However, precisely this is sufficient to make them the elements of representation' (235/303/295). In cancelling or explicating itself, intensity becomes represented. Through its explication, difference in intensity becomes confined to the form of identity: 'The formula according to which "to explicate is to identify" is a tautology' (228/294/287). Individuation provides a solution to the problem. It actualizes an Idea. It creates a 'proposition of consciousness'. Intensity is cancelled in 'qualified extensive systems'. Everything points to the fact that intensity is cancelled in representation.

We therefore have to be careful about concentrating too much on the scientific notion of intensity.[171] Deleuze is concerned with founding representation, not thermodynamics. He says of Nietzsche at one point in the chapter that '[i]t is true that Nietzsche was interested in the energetics of his time, but this was not the scientific nostalgia of the philosopher' (243/313/304). The same can be said of Deleuze. In the same way that Deleuze's theory of Ideas was not fundamentally related to mathematics, his theory of intensity is not tied to thermodynamics (and his theory of individuation is not tied to biology). Deleuze is neither a scientist nor a philosopher of science. Science never leaves the realm of fact, but Deleuze is interested in the constitution of facticity itself. What is at issue in these discussions then is not the nature of intensity as it appears in science, or even of founding the scientific notion, but of drawing inspiration from science in order to develop a philosophical concept.[172] 'Intensive quantity is a transcendental principle, not a scientific concept' (241/310/301).

The way in which intensity functions as a transcendental principle is already indicated in the opening sentence of the chapter. Deleuze writes, 'Difference is not diversity' (*La différence n'est pas le divers*) (222/286/280). 'Diversity', *le divers*, is a technical term which Deleuze borrows from the *Critique of Pure Reason*, and which we usually read in English translations of Kant as 'the manifold'. We could therefore rewrite the opening sentences of the chapter this way: 'Difference is not the manifold. The manifold is given. But difference is that by which the given is given'. In saying that difference is that by which the manifold is given, Deleuze seems to be implying that difference is his version of the Kantian 'forms of intuition'. It is what gives objects to be sensed.[173] He makes this implication explicit at the end of the opening paragraph. The form of intuition is no longer space and time as it was for Kant. For Deleuze it is only difference: 'The reason of the sensible, the condition of that which appears, is not space and time but the Unequal in itself [. . .]' (223/287/281).

We have already seen that this was the case in two other places. In the doctrine of the faculties Deleuze spoke of a 'transcendental sensibility which apprehends [intensity] immediately in the encounter' (144/188/181). In the psychoanalytic account of the passive syntheses, Deleuze defined sensibility as a 'field of individuation in which differences in intensity are distributed here and there in the form of excitations' (96/128/119). In the same way that the sensed intensity is passed down the volcanic line of the faculties, so too are the excitations of the field of individuation taken up in the three passive syntheses. Deleuze is saying nothing new then when he tells us that difference is that by which the given is given, or that it is the form (and content) of a transcendental sensibility.

'Intensity has three characteristics' Deleuze says. These three characteristics outline what could be called a simple logic of difference. They express three types of difference and the various relations between them. The first characteristic of intensity is that it 'includes [*comprend*] the unequal in itself. It represents difference in quantity, that which cannot be cancelled [*inannullable*] in difference in quantity or that which is unequalisable in quantity itself' (232/299/291). According to this first characteristic, even if intensity annuls itself in extensity, it remains, like the aleatory point (the non-actualizable part of the event), the uncancelled and uncancellable 'fundamental and original moment present in every [extensive] quantity' (232/299/291). There is a difference which persists beyond every actualization.

Second, intensity 'affirms' difference. 'Affirm' is an odd word to use here. Deleuze seems to be using it in two senses. First, to affirm difference means that intensity is not a negative phenomenon. It is entirely positive (54–5/78/67). In saying this he is returning to his polemic with Hegel that we have already outlined. The second sense follows from the fact that it is not us who affirm difference. 'We *know* intensity only as already developed within an extensity, and as covered over by qualities' (223/287/281; my emphasis). Empirical sensibility, the 'manifest subject' of the introduction, only knows intensity as covered over by quality and extensity. In contrast, difference is what is given to a transcendental sensibility. 'We' cannot therefore affirm difference. Rather, it is intensity which affirms difference.

This does not only mean that intensity affirms itself. Deleuze draws an important distinction between 'intensity', 'difference' and 'distance'. This distinction is the third characteristic of intensity, but it sheds light on the second. 'Within intensity we call that which is really implicating and enveloping *difference*; and we call that which is really implicated and enveloped *distance*' (237/305/287; translation modified). 'Difference' is an enveloping difference. 'Distance' is an enveloped difference. Every difference can become a distance. Intensity, however, differs from the other two in that is constructed upon them. Intensity 'refers to a series of other differences that it affirms by affirming itself' (234/302/294). Intensity, the unequal and uncancellable, is a third kind of difference which affirms both difference and distance, and it does so by affirming itself. You could say that it envelops both enveloped and enveloping difference. It is constructed upon both distance and difference. The verb 'to affirm' therefore takes on a specific sense here. It is a third kind of relationship between differences. Differences can envelop, be enveloped, or they can affirm other differences. 'Difference' then, is not at all a homogenous concept. In fact, there are at least three kinds of difference – and we will see below that this typology is essential to grasping the structure of the genesis of representation as a whole.

Perhaps the most important point is that Deleuze insists on 'a genesis of affirmation as such'. There are 'positive differential elements which determine the genesis of both the affirmation and the difference affirmed' (55/78/67). Affirmation is the third relation between differences in which intensity affirms itself but in so doing also affirms difference and distance. Because there is a genesis of both 'the affirmation and the difference affirmed', it is clear that intensity itself is produced. Intensity as the affirmation of difference *through the affirmation of itself* is constituted on top of the other two series of differences and distances. In fact Deleuze even suggests that this is the 'asymmetrical synthesis of the sensible' itself:

> Constructed on at least two series, one superior and one inferior, with each series referring in turn to other implicated series, intensity affirms even the *lowest*; it make the lowest an object of affirmation. [. . .] Everything goes from high to low, and by that movement affirms the lowest: asymmetrical synthesis. (234/302/294; original emphasis)

Intensity and affirmation explain each other. Intensity is a third type of difference which is constructed upon two other series, distances and differences. It is a difference which is *related to* other differences. 'Affirmation' expresses this relation. Intensity remains related to these differences through the mechanism or relation of 'affirmation'. We saw above that for Deleuze one of the more interesting aspects of the 'determination of species' in Aristotle was that there is a 'transport of difference', a difference of difference, which 'links difference with difference across the successive levels of division until a final difference, that of the *infirma species*, condenses in the chosen direction the entirety of the essence' (31/47/40; translation modified). All the differentia are condensed in the lowest species. It seems that intensity is just such a difference. Intensity links differences to other differences across the successive levels of difference (distance and difference). It is constructed upon the series of distances and differences, and in affirming itself it affirms even the lowest. Even though it is the highest difference, it still affirms and is linked to the lowest difference.

It is essential to see that an intensive quantity is defined as the aggregate of all three characteristics. It is not a difference or a distance. It is intensity which sublimates these other two more basic differences. '[I]ntensive quantities are therefore defined by the enveloping difference, the enveloped distances, and the unequal in itself [. . .]' (238/306/298). How are we to explain this almost hierarchical structure of difference?

PASSIVE SYNTHESIS

At first glance, the first half of the chapter revolves around an overly simple set of relations. On the one hand there is an intensive 'depth' or a '*spatium*' in which differences are organized. On the other hand there is an extensive and qualitative 'system' in which intensity is 'cancelled' or drawn outside of itself. The chapter simply moves back and forth between these two extremes: intensive depths and the system in extensity; difference and its cancellation; intensity and extensity; distance and length; and so on and so on. Things are significantly more complex however. It is not enough to set the intensive *spatium* against extensity in a simple opposition because *intensive depth itself is multilayered.* It comprises three types of difference: intensity, difference and distance.

At the same time that Deleuze outlined the three characteristics of intensity he also established what you could call a logic of difference. He outlined three general relationships between three types of difference. These relationships express the various ways in which depth as a whole can be organized. The lowest kind of difference was called 'distance'. Distance is a first-degree enveloped difference. The second kind of difference was called 'difference'. It is a second-degree difference which envelops distances. The third kind of difference was intensity which was constructed upon the other two series and linked them together by means of 'affirmation'.

Deleuze insists that affirmation is subject to a genesis. What about the other two relationships? Do differences envelop and become enveloped of their own accord, or are these too subject to a genesis? While Deleuze does not make a point of emphasizing it, it becomes clear that *the three passive syntheses of time are what put differences in relation to one another.* From this point of view we cannot take the expression 'depth' to refer to a homogenous field of differences, but to the entire set of relations between synthesis and difference. 'Depth' comprises all three syntheses and the various kinds of difference that result: difference, distance and intensity.

This distribution of depth across the three syntheses might seem surprising. On a first reading, Deleuze's discussion of the passive synthesis plays only a marginal role in the chapter. He mentions them explicitly only two or three times, and then only in an ambiguous way. On a closer reading however one immediately notices that the syntheses are already playing a role from the start, and continue to do so throughout. In the first paragraph Deleuze defines intensity this way:

> Every intensity is differential, by itself a difference. Every intensity is E-E', where E itself refers to an *e-e'*, and *e* to ε-ε' etc.: each intensity is already a *coupling* (in which each element of the couple refers in turn to couples of elements of another order) [. . .]. We call this state of infinitely doubled difference which *resonates* to infinity *disparity.* (222/287/281; my emphasis)

Intensity is a difference which refers to other differences. Now these other differences have specific qualities: each 'intensity' refers to a *resonance* and to a *coupling*. Here Deleuze is clearly repeating themes from the physical account of the passive syntheses. In fact, if we turn to that account, we notice that like 'affirmation' intensity is in fact produced:

> A system[174] must be constituted on the basis of two or more series, each series being defined by the differences between the terms which compose it. If we suppose that the series communicate under the impulse of a force of some kind, then it is apparent that this communication relates difference to other differences, constituting differences between differences within the system. These second-degree differences play the role of 'differenciatior' – in other words, they relate first-degree differences to one another. This state of affairs is adequately expressed by certain physical concepts: *coupling* between the heterogeneous series, from which is derived an *internal resonance* within the system, and from which in turn is derived a *forced movement* the amplitude of which exceeds that of the basic series. (117/154–5/143–4; translation modified)

So far there is nothing new here. The coupling of series represents the first passive synthesis. The resonance which follows under the force of the 'dark precursor' represents the second synthesis. The forced movement which leaves the other two in its wake is the third synthesis. But in the sentence which immediately follows, Deleuze writes,

> The nature of these elements whose value is determined at once both by their difference in the series to which they belong, and by the difference of their difference from one series to another, can be determined: these are intensities, the peculiarity of intensities being to be constituted by a difference which refers to other differences (E-E', where E itself refers to *e-e'*, and *e* to ε-ε' . . .). (117/155/144)

An intensity is a difference which refers to another difference. *Here Deleuze tells us exactly what those other differences which*

intensity refers to are. An intensity refers to two series of differences: on the one hand, it refers to the differences which
the first passive synthesis drew off of the material discontinuity; on the other hand it refers to the difference between
series brought together by the dark precursor. Intensity is
constructed on top of the first two syntheses. It is a transport of difference, or a difference of difference which links
difference to difference across the successive levels of synthesis. 'Refers to' is perhaps not strong enough of a verb
here. Deleuze says that intensities are '*constituted*' by these
differences. Intensity is constituted in the unity of habit and
memory. It is a difference which refers to the drawn-off differences of the first synthesis and the included differences of
the second synthesis.[175]
Once we realize that intensity is *constituted* in the third
synthesis and therefore depends on the first two syntheses,
we cannot avoid noticing the way Deleuze's descriptions of
intensity repeatedly unfold along the lines of the syntheses.
At every turn Deleuze defines intensity as a difference which
refers to other differences where those other differences
are the difference drawn and the resonating difference. For
example, when Deleuze says that 'constituent disparities or
enveloped distances inhabit intensive depth' (235/304/295),
he is not simply multiplying synonyms but is describing the
multilayered structure of depth. Under 'intensive depth' lie
'disparities' or the resonating differences of the second synthesis.[176] And under 'disparities' lie the coupled differences
of the first synthesis, 'distances'. Distances and disparities
belong to depth insofar as intensity, in affirming itself, affirms
even the lowest, thus 'sublimating'[177] distance and difference
and allowing them to inhabit depth in general. All three
syntheses are present in the short statement, 'constituent disparities or enveloped distances inhabit intensive depth'. From
this point of view we can see that the three characteristics of
intensity – the affirmation of unequal, the enveloping difference and the enveloped distance – all refer to the process of
passive synthesis. The uncancellable difference is pure intensity produced in the forced movement of the third synthesis,
but this difference is constructed upon the double series of
differences and distances. The word 'depth' clearly does not

refer to the most fundamental level. There is always a lower depth, or, as Deleuze puts it, it is ultimately

a question of depth and of a lower depth which essentially belongs to it. There is no depth which is not a 'seeker' of a lower depth: it is there that distance develops, but distance understood as the affirmation of that which it distances, difference as a sublimation of the lower. (234–5/302–3/294)

This lower depth to which depth essentially belongs is, of course, difference (resonance) and distance (coupling). Intensity gathers these other two differences together in a transport of difference, and in so doing goes beyond the two basic series.

This seems to raise as many questions as it answers. First and foremost, isn't intensity what was at the beginning? In both the doctrine of the faculties and the psychoanalytic account, isn't intensity what causes the first synthesis to synthesize by raising it to its transcendent exercise? How could it then be constituted in the *third* passive synthesis? With this question we touch on one of the most important themes of *Difference and Repetition*, but one which Deleuze rarely develops. *The passive syntheses represent the progressive extraction or purification of difference.*[178] Intensity was indeed what was originally sensed, but in the first synthesis it was encountered as a difference between. It was *between* discontinuous instants. It was an excitation. It was an intensity in the Freudian sense of the term – an excitation which disrupts the equilibrium of the organism. The first synthesis of habit 'drew off' that difference. The second synthesis gathered those differences together. It related the first-degree differences to one another. It enveloped them. Intensity as such only comes about in the third synthesis. It is only constituted in the forced movement which exceeds the two original series, or in the empty form of time which 'abjures its empirical content' (89/120/111), or in the 'entirely narcissistic ego' which 'abandons all mnemic content' (111/146–7/136). Intensity in the third synthesis is a difference which is no longer caught between matter, or between the different levels of memory. All empirical content, all memory is surpassed in a pure difference which is related only to other differences.

160

This leads to a second problem. I sharply distinguished intensity from virtuality above, but I also argued that, like intensity, virtuality was produced in the third synthesis. It arises in the third time of the series: the eternal return. Deleuze will even say in this chapter that the eternal return 'is said of a world the very ground of which is difference, in which everything rests on disparities, upon differences of differences which reverberate to infinity (the world of intensity)' (241/311/302). Does he not then conflate intensity and virtuality? Not at all. The third synthesis began when the ego became 'entirely narcissistic'. It turned back on itself and contemplated itself. Deleuze never clearly says what causes the subject to turn back on itself. He usually just says that there is a 'violence' which causes the ego to become entirely narcissistic (114/150/139). From where does this violence come?

Each of the first two passive syntheses grounds an active synthesis. The first synthesis goes beyond its sub-representative apprehensions in the direction of a 'real object'. There is a drive to turn a fragmented apprehension into a determinate representation. In the psychoanalytic account, Deleuze names this tendency to go beyond bound excitation to the real object the 'reality principle'. Thanks to the reality principle one goes 'beyond the bound excitations towards the supposition of intentionality of an object' (99/132/123). In its sub-representative aspect, the second synthesis, Mnemosyne, defines pure past or a 'having-been-ness'. As we have already seen, this second synthesis grounds *empirical* association and the reproduction of past presents (a reproduction which was governed by the laws of association). Deleuze called this second aspect of the synthesis 'Eros', the search after memories, or our 'attending-to'.

From the point of view of the first two syntheses, the real object, the representation comprising both a quality and an extensity, is constructed upon a double series: that of apprehensions, and that of reproductions. It is at this point in Kant that recognition would come in to ensure that reproduction appears as reproduction, and not the production of something new. Nothing like this happens in Deleuze. Instead, 'the two references become confused' (109/145/135). The ego gets caught in a chain of confusions: it is unable to distinguish real objects from memories, and transcendental synthesis from empirical synthesis (292/374/364). This confusion is what leads to total narcissism:

> It is by interiorising the difference between the two lines and by experiencing itself as perpetually displaced in the one [i.e. Mnemosyne], perpetually disguised in the other [i.e. real objects], that the libido returns or flows back onto the ego and the passive ego becomes entirely narcissistic. (110/145/135)

The reflux of the libido, or the violence which inaugurates the third synthesis is a direct consequence of the subject's inability to discover a determinate object. Unable to recognize a real object, the ego 'interiorizes' the difference between disguised real objects and displaced virtual objects. Displacement and disguise are two forms of difference. Displacement is the difference which affects the 'dark precursor', the principle of the second synthesis; it is what Deleuze calls 'resonance' in the physical account of the syntheses. Disguise is the difference which affects the series real objects of the first synthesis. When the ego interiorizes or affirms these two differences, a third difference is produced: Intensity. Intensity is a self-affirmation which sublimates and affirms the other two series upon which it is constructed. Intensity is the violence which causes a reflux of the libido onto the ego and thus inaugurates the third synthesis.

The distinction between self and I, intensity and virtuality, sensation and thought, will to power and eternal return, becomes crucial in the third synthesis. How are virtuality and intensity distributed within the structure of the third synthesis? The first moment of the third synthesis, the order of time, still belongs to the passive self or to the 'will to power'. Here an articulation is established within the passive self. The second moment, the totality of time, or the 'caesura', is the advent of a consciousness which will try to bring about a synthesis of the passive self. As Deleuze says in his lectures on Kant, the caesura is the degree zero of intensity from which varying degrees of intensity will arise.[179] These degrees of intensity are precisely the synthesis of the two preceding moments: distance

Handwritten margin notes (top):

1. Formal order / Before / During / After
— Totality / Caesura

2. Series

3. Eternal Return

and difference, coupling and resonance. All of this bears only on the passive subject. We are still within the domain of the will to power, of our own pathos, and intensity is merely the *hohe Stimmung*. Deleuze says that it is the will to power which engenders affirmation (55/78/67).

Both intensity and virtuality are produced in the third synthesis. Even so they are not identical. The two are separated, you could say, by the line of time. The passive subject, the will to power, is gathered in a *hohe Stimmung*, in a violence which goes beyond the initial series and which initiates the genesis of thought in the *order* of time. The caesura expresses the unbalanced unity of thought in the *totality* of time. When the caesura attempts to directly determine the self in the *series* of time, both dissolve and give rise to the *gross Gedanke*, to the eternal return, or to the thinker of Ideas. It is as if there were three syntheses in the third synthesis alone. The first is a failed synthesis with regard to the object (order of time). The second is a failed synthesis with regard to the subject (series of time). The third, the only successful synthesis, is that of the eternal return, or the ideal synthesis of difference.

Handwritten margin notes (right): 1 2 3

As we will see below, once the thinker thinks Ideas, the syntheses no longer fail. Ideas bring unity to both the subject and the object. The processes of individuation and actualization describe the way in which a unified subject thinks a unified object.

ACTIVE SYNTHESIS

There is however still one more difficulty which arises when we conflate depth as a whole with the process of passive synthesis. There are several places in which Deleuze mentions the syntheses which seem to directly contradict the thesis that depth ultimately refers to the sub-representative workings of the passive syntheses. For example, at one point Deleuze writes,

> We should not be surprised that the pure spatial syntheses here repeat the temporal syntheses previously specified: the explication of intensity rests on the first synthesis, that of habit or the present; but the implication of depth rests upon the second synthesis, that of Memory and the past. Furthermore, in depth the proximity and the simmering

of the third synthesis make themselves felt, announcing the universal 'ungrounding'. *It unites a bubbling sensibility and a thought which rumbles in its crater.* (230/296/289; my emphasis)

Deleuze says that we should not be surprised, but it is hard not to be surprised for several reasons. First, the passive syntheses as temporal syntheses had already synthesized intensities, so what would now constitute them as *spatial* syntheses? Second, the first passive synthesis is also a sub-representative synthesis, and in no way does it move towards extensity. True, it does 'bind' excitation, but it does not *cancel* excitation. Third, Deleuze makes it sound as though the third synthesis was the deepest. Memory implicates intensity and habit explicates it, but the third 'complicates it' and maintains the unequal in itself outside of every cancellation. In other words, the third synthesis is the foundation of the other two. But didn't Deleuze just say that the third was in fact constituted on the other two, and that every depth is the affirmation of an even lower depth?

If we take this quotation synthesis by synthesis it becomes clear that Deleuze is referring not to the passive syntheses but to the active. It makes no sense to say that the explication of intensity rests on the first synthesis because the first synthesis doesn't cancel difference. It binds difference, but this binding remains entirely sub-representative whereas the process of explication moves from the sub-representative to qualitative and extensive world of representation. Binding and explication are by no means equivalent processes. There is however a sense in which the first synthesis does leave its sub-representative role and is placed in the service of representation. Founded on the first sub-representative and passive synthesis there was an active synthesis which was directed towards the 'real object', that is, to the object as a synthesis of quality and extensity. In this case, the explication of intensity would indeed rest upon the first passive synthesis, but only insofar as that passive synthesis grounds the active synthesis which intends the real object. Binding grounds explication, but explication is the active synthesis of habit, not the passive.

Deleuze then says that implication rests upon the second synthesis. This proves less problematic because there is a sense in which the second synthesis 'implicates' differences even in its passive and sub-representative function. The second synthesis makes intensities resonate, and thus puts them in relation to one another. We should keep in mind, however, that Deleuze draws a sharp distinction between two 'orders of implication':

> We must therefore distinguish between two orders of impli-
> cation, or degradation: a secondary implication which
> designates the state in which intensities are enveloped by the
> qualities and extensity which explicate them; and a primary
> implication which designates the state in which intensity is
> implicated in itself, at once both enveloping and enveloped.
> (240/309/300)

To which of these two orders is Deleuze referring when he says implication rests on the Memory? By putting intensities in relation to one another, the second passive synthesis undoubtedly brings about 'primary implication'. It turns distance into difference. As the context makes clear through its emphasis on the 'emergence' of the object from depth, however, when Deleuze says that implication rests on the second synthesis in the above quotation, he is referring to 'secondary implication'. Secondary implication describes the way in which intensities remain implicated in extensity or the way in which the intensive depth still maintains a presence in its cancelled state.

This is precisely the role of the active synthesis founded on top of memory. Earlier, in the discussion of the second passive syntheses above, I had intentionally overlooked the paradoxes of the pure past because, I argued, they referred only to the relation between a pure past and a represented present. This is exactly what is at issue in 'secondary implication'. Each paradox expresses the way in which a pure, sub-representative past insists or is implicated in the represented present. Even if the pure past is not represented in the empirical present, it is contemporaneous with that present, coexists with that present and pre-exists that present. It is continually implicated in the representation which it founds. Further, this secondary implication adds a new dimension to the active synthesis. Whereas the first passive synthesis could only be extended towards the identity of an object, by joining with memory it is able to 'reflect' and 'recognize' that object. Now

> an active synthesis is established upon the foundation of the passive syntheses: this consists in relating the bound excitation to an object supposed to be both real and the end of our actions (synthesis of recognition, supported by the passive synthesis of reproduction [or habit which reproduces the object it contemplates: the eye that binds light is itself a bound light]). (98/130–1/120)[180]

Instead of resonating difference, the second active synthesis leads to 'recognition' and 'reproduction'.

This turn to active synthesis is not at all a marginal and passing moment in Deleuze's chapter which pertains only to the passage I quoted above. Instead of speaking of active syntheses in this chapter, Deleuze far more frequently speaks of 'good' and 'common sense', but this is just another way of talking about the active syntheses. The two active syntheses redistribute between themselves the roles of good sense and common sense. Deleuze explained the relation between these two concepts in relation to the cancellation of difference in great detail at the beginning of the chapter. Good sense, which 'is *based upon* a synthesis of time, in particular the one we have determined as the first synthesis', has the function of cancelling difference (225/290/284). It 'essentially distributes or repartitions [. . .]. A distribution is in conformity with good sense when it tends to banish difference from the distributed' (224/289/282–3). Common sense, on the other hand rests on the second synthesis of time. It provides the 'unity and ground' of both the subject and the object (226/291/284–5). Further, unlike the passive syntheses which were incapable of functioning in harmony with one another, good sense and common sense are mutually implicated in one another. The one cannot function without the other. Common sense points

> beyond itself towards another, dynamic instance, capable of determining the indeterminate object as this or that, and of

individualizing the self situated in this ensemble of objects. This other instance is good sense, which takes its point of departure from a difference at the origin of individuation. However, precisely because it ensures the distribution of that difference in such a manner that it tends to be cancelled in the object, and because it provides a rule according to which the different objects tend to equalize themselves and the different Selves tend to become uniform, good sense in turn points toward the instance of common sense which provides it with both the form of a universal self and an indeterminate object. (226/291/285)

Good sense cancels difference in the direction of an object (quality + extensity), but common sense provides the object-form to which this diversity is related. There is a tendency for readers of Deleuze to dismiss good and common sense because Deleuze continually criticizes these notions. It often seems as though he invents elaborate descriptions of the two only in order to point beyond them. However, if actualization is the process through which we move from virtuality to an actuality defined by a quality and an extensity, and if individuation is the process through which intensity is cancelled, how can we deny that these two concepts must be constitutive moments of the static genesis? They are what cancels difference. They constitute the dual process of individuation and actualization. It is true the paradox is primary in the order of concepts and that 'good sense is always secondary' (227/292/285), but it *is* secondary.

Deleuze said above that the 'pure spatial syntheses' 'repeat' the temporal syntheses or that they 'rest on' the temporal syntheses. The 'pure spatial syntheses' 'rest on' the passive syntheses in the sense that they are the active syntheses founded upon them. We can now understand why they are called *'spatial'* syntheses. Intensity is defined as an 'intensive *spatium'*, but this intensive space lacks the spatial dimensions with which the manifest subject is familiar in empirical intuition:

No doubt the high and the low, the right and the left, the figure and ground are individuating factors which trace rises and falls, currents and descents in extensity. However, since they take place within an already developed extensity, their value is only relative. They therefore flow from a deeper instance – depth itself, which is not an extension, but a pure *implex*. (229/295/288; original emphasis)[181]

Up/down, right/left, front/back are spatial determinations that apply only to the developed world of extensity. Depth however is not space. It is the primordial experience from which space springs forth. The 'pure spatial syntheses' do not therefore refer to the pure temporal syntheses which put difference in commu-nication with itself. They refer to the way in which an 'object' is made to 'emerge' from the shadow of depth (230/296/289). They represent the movement from intensity to extensity, and, therefore, *they represent the active syntheses which 'rest upon' the passive syntheses.*[182]

What about the third synthesis? Does the third synthesis also have an active form? In fact, the third synthesis changes its character here as well. If we look closely at Deleuze's words regarding the third synthesis in the above quote we will notice that the third synthesis is no longer a failed synthesis. Now it coordinates two faculties:

Furthermore, in depth the proximity and the simmering of the third synthesis make themselves felt, announcing the universal 'ungrounding'. *It unites a bubbling sensibility and a thought which rumbles in its crater.* (230/296/289; my emphasis)

In the repeated failure of synthesis, the third synthesis only separated the self from the I, and ultimately led to their dissol-ution. Now, however, the third synthesis *unites* two faculties: a sensibility 'bubbling' with intensities and a thought, 'rumbling' with Ideas. At this point, and only at this point, do intensities begin to *express* Ideas. We will see that Ideas are then able to regulate synthesis and the discordant use of the faculties becomes harmonious. From now on good sense and common sense, imagination and memory, work together in the produc-tion of a common object and a common subject.

INDIVIDUATION AND ACTUALIZATION

Individuation and actualization are two different processes which end up at the same destination: a represented object comprising an extensity and a quality. Intensity is cancelled in quality and extensity and Ideas are actualized in that same quality and extensity. Deleuze is very clear however that the two *are* different processes, and further, that it would be a mistake to confuse the virtual with intensity. It is true that they share important characteristics and that the ideal connections and singularities of the Idea could hardly be described as 'extensive', but Ideas and intensities belong to two separate faculties, with two separate processes, with two kinds of relation (intensive and ideal), and both relate to different dimensions of time. Ideas belong to the future whereas intensity expresses the immediate present of affection. *Individuation is the process in which these two faculties are brought together.*

At a very general level we can make several important points regarding the process of individuation. First, individuation, not actualization, is the 'act of solving a problem' (246/317/307). The movement from the problem to the solution, from Idea to representation, is not made from within the virtual, but takes place only insofar as intensities *select* Ideas and actualize their relations and singularities. Intensities pull Ideas outside of their virtuality. They bring the future into the present.

> [Intensity] introduces into these [differential] relations, and between Ideas themselves, a new type of distinction. Henceforward, the Ideas, the relations, the variations in those relations and distinctive points are in a sense separated: instead of coexisting, they enter into states of simultaneity or succession. (252/325/314; translation modified)[183]

An intensity selects an Idea and draws it out of its coexistence into a present in which it passes. It is not only the Idea that undergoes a significant transformation however.

This is the second general point, Ideas give form to intensity. The relation between Ideas is somewhat like the relation between matter and form. Intensities are the matter of sensation, trillions of uncontracted sensations, but through 'dramatiza-tion', Ideas give form to this matter. They 'differenciate' it. Deleuze will avoid this hylomorphic explanation for several reasons. The most important is that Ideas are not pregiven forms which are imposed from without on a static matter. Ideas are rules of production which govern the synthesis of sensibil-ity. This why he prefers the biological *metaphor.* Ideas are the DNA. Intensity is the cytoplasm (251/323/313; cf. 216/279/269). Ideas are rules for production which regulate the organization of an 'intensive environment', but the nature of that environ-ment determines the way in which Ideas are actualized. When intensity selects an Idea, then, it too undergoes a transform-ation. Ideas are actualized according to present circumstance, but in expressing an Idea, circumstance becomes organized or differenciated.

Even though intensity undergoes a significant transform-ation, it is still the active element in actualization. It 'is because of the action of the field of individuation that such and such [Ideas] are actualised – in other words, organized within intu-ition' (247/318/308). Intensity always has the upper hand in individuation. It is what selects a particular Idea to be actu-alized. It is the 'determinant' in the process of actualization (245/316/307). 'Individuation always governs actualization' (251/323/313). Ideas are selected according to the requirements of an 'intensive environment' (251/323/313). It would clearly be a mistake to privilege the virtual then. Thought is at the service of sensibility for Deleuze. Ideas, the conditions of real experience, are both produced (dynamic genesis) and selected (static genesis) according to the immediate circumstance and the requirements of the environment. They are there to deter-mine what was first sensed.

If we want to leave this general level and get into the specif-ics of actualization and individuation, however, we find that it is actually quite difficult. Deleuze is not at all clear as to how individuation is actually carried out. In fact for the most part he only emphasizes the very *first* moment of actualiza-tion: dramatization. Dramatization we saw is Deleuze's version of the schematism. (In this chapter, he calls the schematism 'extension (*extensio*)' or the act by which extensity (*exstensum*) is produced (231/298/291).) Deleuze defined the schematism in

Kant as the process through which spatio-temporal relations *incarnate* conceptual determinations.

[T]he schema is a spatio-temporal determination which itself corresponds to the category [. . .]: it does not consist in an image but *in spatio-temporal relations which embody [incarnent] or realize relations which are in fact conceptual.* (KP18/28–92; my emphasis)

This is where the process of individuation begins in Deleuze: intensities 'incarnate' or 'express' Ideal relations (Cf. 252/325/314–15). Intensities 'focus on' the relations and singularities of Ideas. What happens once Ideas are expressed? How or why does this lead to either actualization or individuation?

In order to grasp the process of individuation, we have to emphasize that dramatization is not something that takes place out in the open. Dramatization is the process in which thought is folded back onto sensibility. When the third synthesis in its active form unites these two faculties, Ideas become expressed by intensities, but the intensities which express Ideas are contained and organized within what Deleuze calls here the 'individual in intensity'.[184] The individual in *extensity* is the individual object, the product, the determinate representation of a thing comprising a quality and an extensity. It is the solution to a problem (246/316/308). The 'individual in *intensity*' is a 'field of individuation'. It is the set of undeveloped, undifferenciated intensities. It is these that express Ideas. In the following quotation Deleuze is describing the individual in intensity.

Individuals are signal-sign systems. All individuality is intensive, and therefore serial, stepped and communicating, comprising and affirming in itself the differences in intensities by which it is constituted. (246/317/307)

The individual is not, then, a homogenous field. *The individual in intensity is a system* – a serial, stepped and communicating system. Deleuze often calls this ensemble of intensities and individuating factors the 'system of the dissolved self' (254/333/322). We know what this means: just like the notion of 'depth', the intensive individual spans the set of passive syntheses. These syntheses constitute the systematicity of the dissolved self. Each synthesis is one step in this communicating system. In fact these two expressions, 'depth' and the 'individual in intensity', refer to one and the same concept. Deleuze had already described this system of the dissolved self in the physical account of the syntheses. 'The system is populated by subjects, both larval subjects and passive selves: passive selves because they are indistinguishable from the contemplation of couplings and resonances; larval subjects because they are the supports or patients of the dynamisms' (118/155/144).[185] The passive selves refer to the egos of the first two syntheses. The larval subject refers to the ego of the third synthesis which supports spatio-temporal dynamisms or dramatizations.[186] The system of the dissolved self, or the individual in intensity is the entire set of syntheses.

This point could not be overemphasized: when Ideas are expressed by intensities, *they are incorporated back into the entire system of the dissolved self*. Deleuze sometimes draws a distinction between the thinker and the thought. The thinker is the passive self, the larval subject or the 'embryo' which experiences 'forced movements'. Ideas are the thoughts. The more technical version of this statement says that Ideas are 'expressed in individuating factors, in the implicated world of intensive quantities which constitute the universal concrete individuality of the thinker or the system of the dissolved self' (259/333/322). Ideas, which 'swarm' around the fractured I, are expressed (thought) by the *system* of the dissolved self (the thinker).

The most interesting aspect of this statement is the simple fact that the thinker is able to think Ideas. This is new. In the third synthesis both the thinker and the thought dissolved. The thinker did not think Ideas. It tried to think the object, and it tried to think itself. It failed in both endeavours, and this failure led to the production of Ideas in the eternal return. Now however, the thinker thinks Ideas. Self and I are no longer separated from one another. Now a dissolved self is set in relation to a fractured I. The two are 'correlated' (259/332/322) in the active synthesis which unites a rumbling thought with a bubbling sensibility. The consequences of this are enormous and determine the entire process of individuation.

172

When the thinker thinks Ideas, Ideas are expressed by the dissolved self as a whole. They are inevitably taken up into the syntheses. In the following quotation the word 'disparateness' stands for the Idea, or the problem. 'The act of individuation consists not in suppressing the problem, but in integrating the elements of the disparateness into a state of coupling which ensures its internal resonance' (246/317/307). The act of individuation, instead of suppressing the problem integrates the elements of the problem *into the first two syntheses*: coupling and resonance. This marks a second stage of individuation. The first stage can be expressed in several ways: thought is folded back onto sensibility, intensities express Ideas, or self and I are correlated. It is the active synthesis of thought. In the second stage, *Ideas are incorporated into the syntheses of the dissolved self*. The problem is integrated into coupling and resonance.

Even if Deleuze never explains why it is the case, he makes it clear that each synthesis, coupling and resonance, incorporates a specific moment of the Idea. The singularities of an Idea are incorporated by the first synthesis whereas the relations are incorporated by the second: 'the intensive series of individuating factors envelop ideal singularities [. . .]; the resonances between series put the ideal relations into play' (279/357/349). This is crucial. Intensive *series* incorporate singularities. The *resonance* of these series brings ideal relations into play. Imagination contemplates the singularities of the Idea. Memory contemplates the ideal relations of the Idea.

The first time the subject ran through the genesis, there was not yet a faculty of thought containing virtual Ideas. The virtual was produced and Ideas were determined in 'the third time of the series'. This means that the intensities of sensibility did not – indeed, could not – express differential relations. Now, however, thanks to dramatization and its correlation of the self and I, intensities express or incarnate differential relations and singularities. This completely changes the nature of synthesis. It transforms passive syntheses into active syntheses.

What is an active synthesis? In Kant, a passive synthesis was one that took place in the imagination outside of the jurisdiction of the understanding. As Deleuze puts it, it took place in the mind but not by the mind. It was an unconscious synthesis. Kant's third synthesis, however did take place under the jurisdiction of the understanding, and further, it was subject to the categories which functioned as rules for synthesis. An active synthesis is a rule-governed synthesis.

When intensity expresses Ideas and incorporates their relations and singularities into the system of the dissolved self, the syntheses which constitute that system become active syntheses. Deleuze says that intensive *series* express singularities whereas resonance brings relations into play. The imagination now apprehends intensities which express singularities. When the imagination couples that intensity, it now comes under the influence of a singularity. It becomes an active synthesis. When resonance gathers together differences which express ideal relations, it too becomes an active synthesis.

The active synthesis of the imagination points beyond itself towards the intentionality of the object whereas the active synthesis of memory gives this synthesis unity in the form of the object and the form of the subject. We would seem to be finally approaching the unity of the object in representation. The odd thing is that despite the importance of this part of the genesis, Deleuze never develops it in *Difference and Repetition*. He tells us that Ideas are incorporated into the entire system of the dissolved self. He tells us that by virtue of this incorporation 'series' envelop singularities while 'resonance' expresses relations. And we can guess that imagination will therefore go on to determine extensity and that memory will go on to determine quality, but Deleuze will never explain how. We can get a slightly better sense for how this happens if we turn to his discussion of good and common sense.

'Good sense' is the expression Deleuze uses in this chapter to describe the active synthesis founded upon habit. Good sense points beyond intensity towards the intentionality of an object. 'Common sense' is Deleuze's expression for the active synthesis founded upon memory. It grounds recognition or the resemblance of objects according to their qualities. Deleuze will reaffirm that good sense, under the influence of ideal singularities, determines extensity and that common sense, under the influence of ideal relations, determines quality. Good sense, he says, 'involves the *quantitative* synthesis of difference' whereas common sense 'involves the *qualitative* synthesis of diversity related to an object supposed the same for all the faculties of a single subject' (226/292/285; my emphases). Good sense is a quantitative synthesis. Common sense is a qualitative synthesis. Good sense is founded on the first passive synthesis which operates on the series. These series express singularities, and when singularities are actualized they determine extensity. This is why good sense is a quantitative synthesis. Common sense, however, is founded on the second synthesis of memory which brings about a resonance across series. This resonance puts ideal relations into play. When ideal relations are actualized, they determine qualities. That is why common sense is called a qualitative synthesis.

How, though, does this result in representation? It is obvious at a general level. We saw that good sense 'essentially distributes or repartitions [. . .]' and that 'A distribution is in conformity with good sense when it tends to banish difference from the distributed' (224/289/282–3). Good sense turns intensity into extensity. It cancels difference and thus gives rise to a world in which parts are external to one another. Common sense provides a unity for the synthesis in the direction of a subject and object. The two syntheses are also now underwritten by the third synthesis so they now function harmoniously. The first bringing the trillions of sensations to the form of the object and the second contracting them into determinate qualities. Even if Deleuze's text is consistent on these points they are quite difficult to grasp. This is because Deleuze's work on the theory of active synthesis is not yet completely developed in *Difference and Repetition*, nor is it in the next work, *The Logic of Sense*, where he will devote only two very short chapters to the static genesis.

It won't be until *Anti-Oedipus* (1972) that the active syntheses get their first real theorization under the heading 'social-production', and even there Deleuze's account is not as thorough as we might like. While this aspect of Deleuze's thought will require much more research we can at least indicate two significant differences between *Anti-Oedipus* and *Difference and Repetition* with regard to the question of active synthesis. First, in *Anti-Oedipus* good sense (territorialism) and common sense (despotism) are no longer referred to just one synthesis. Instead, each moment operates all three of the formerly passive syntheses. In *Difference and Repetition*, for example, imagination, under the constraint of incarnated singularities, determines the form or extensity of the actual object. In *Anti-Oedipus* however, all *three* syntheses come into play in each moment.[187] The second difference is that Deleuze says nothing in *Anti-Oedipus* of Ideas or their singularities and relations. This doesn't mean that they are not there. In fact, if there are active syntheses, then we have to assume that they are governed by the Idea. Deleuze is not explicit on this point, however, and for that reason *Anti-Oedipus*, despite its development of the theme of active synthesis, still can't answer the question as to how Ideas determine syntheses. The striking absence of the virtual from *Anti-Oedipus* is no doubt the reason why the second volume of *Capitalism and Schizophrenia* begins with 'The Rhizome', an introduction which takes up precisely the theme of the relation between the passive self and the fractured I. Of course, between *Difference and Repetition* and *Capitalism and Schizophrenia* all the words have changed, but we have already seen that *Difference and Repetition, by itself*, traverses over ten different technical vocabularies. It is not the words that count in Deleuze, but, as in Fichte, it is the relations between them.

How, then, do individuation and actualization unfold in *Difference and Repetition*? While I admit it is unsatisfying to simply point towards research that has not yet been widely undertaken, we can still draw a few important conclusions. It is clear that there is no direct and parallel movement from the virtual to the actual as Deleuze suggested in chapter four. Singularities do not immediately determine extensities. Ideal relations do not immediately determine qualities. Individuation begins when the third synthesis in its active form unites a bubbling sensibility with a rumbling thought, when it brings about a correlation between self and I, or when it dramatizes the Idea. Not only does it unite thought and sensibility but it regulates and ensures the harmonious exercise of the other two faculties that will come into play: imagination and memory, good sense and common sense. When the Idea is applied to sensibility it is divided. Singularities are incarnated in distances whereas relations are incarnated in differences. The synthesis that couples distances – habit – now couples under the influence of the singularity incarnated in the series it contemplates. It becomes an active synthesis which partitions and cancels. It becomes the good sense that turns intensity into extensity. The second synthesis, resonance, 'puts ideal relations into play'. Memory becomes an active, qualitative synthesis, which determines the quality that will cover each extensity. At the end of the process we are left with an empirical sensibility contemplating the quality and extensity of a determinate object.

SECTION 7. REPRESENTATION AND REPETITION

THE OTHER-STRUCTURE

For the most part, the conclusion to *Difference and Repetition* simply summarizes what Deleuze had said in the earlier chapters. He spends much of the chapter tying up loose ends and recapitulating the main themes. There are a few exceptions to this, but I have worked most of those comments into my discussion of the main body of the text above.

Perhaps the most important innovation Deleuze makes in the conclusion is his elaboration of the Other-structure. In my second chapter I described the way in which the Other-structure brought the genesis to an end. Deleuze mentions the Other for the first time only briefly in the last pages of the last chapter. He presents it there as a 'centre of envelopment' which causes each representation to express its origins. He returns to this in slightly more detail in the conclusion. In the conclusion he makes two points. First, he repeats his point that that the Other is neither another person nor even a 'particular structure of the perceptual world in general'. Rather, 'it is a structure which grounds and ensures the overall functioning of this world as a whole' (281/360/352). This is easy to understand if we keep in mind that Deleuze uses the word 'Other' to describe the potentialities which swarm around any representation. What is potential for me is actual for the Other. The potentialities pertain solely to the actualized object. They refer only to the aggregate of quality and extensity which has just been actualized. This is why it is not a structure in the world of perception. It is the structure which first gives rise to this world. It encloses 'individuating factors and pre-individual singularities within the limits of objects and subjects which are then offered to representation as perceivers or perceived' (281–2/360/352). Perception begins with potentiality. The potentialities of the Other complete the genesis of representation. Second Deleuze reaffirms that the Other-structure functions as a centre of envelopment. It maintains our connection to the world of individuating factors at the level of representation.

> The Other is not reducible to the individuating factors [. . .], but it 'represents' or stands for them in a certain sense. In effect, among the developed qualities and extensities of the perceptual world, it envelops and expresses possible worlds which do not exist outside of their expression. (281/360/351)

I suggested in my second chapter that here Deleuze is reviving the Husserlian notion of the 'world' or the 'idea in the Kantian sense'. This is true, but it is clear now that the Other plays a crucial *epistemological* role as well. We saw above that for Deleuze any representation was true only insofar as it was produced, or only insofar as it was the limit of a genetic series which began in the Idea. Further, representations only possess a 'derived' truth in relation to the 'originary' truth of the Idea. The Other is what maintains the connection between the originary and the derived truth.

SUMMARY OF THE GENESIS

Looking back over *Difference and Repetition* from the point of view of its conceptual structure, three aspects of the work tend to stand out. The first is that the entire book unfolds between the two coordinates laid out in the introduction: the latent subject and the manifest subject, transcendental sensibility and empirical sensibility. *Difference and Repetition* is Deleuze's transcendental aesthetic. An elementary consciousness contemplates singularities. It takes them up into a series of three syntheses, but is unable to recognize either itself or an object. This causes consciousness to dissolve and open up onto a field of determinability in which it is able to produce Ideas. With Ideas in hand, consciousness can return to sensibility and turn what was only a flux of material impressions into determinate representations. The conceptual structure tells a story which begins with the dissolved and its indeterminate object and which concludes with the determinate object of perception enclosed within a swarm of potentialities.

The second aspect is the Kantian structure of the whole work. There are important differences between Deleuze and Kant. There is no form of intuition or unity of apperception in Deleuze, and the Deleuzian subject is not distributed across a static formalism. It is riveted to real experience and to the conditions of its emergence. However, even if Deleuze rewrites Kant from the point of view of genesis and completely removes the formalism, much of the Kantian framework remains intact. The form of intuition might have become a field of intensity, and the unity of apperception an aleatory point. Even so, the movement from intensity to Idea is still accomplished by the three syntheses (the third of which fails), and the movement from Idea back to sensibility is still accomplished by means of the schematism. Even the 'Idea in the Kantian sense' reappears at the end of the genesis in the form of the Other-structure.

Finally, I have suggested throughout this work, and defended this claim elsewhere, that all of Deleuze's books develop the same conceptual structure. What sets *Difference and Repetition* apart from all of the others is its emphasis on temporality. This is for me the most striking aspect of the work. *The Logic of Sense, Cinema 1 and 2, Capitalism and Schizophrenia* and *What is Philosophy?*, to name only those in which it is most apparent, all elaborate the genesis of representation. They all repeat the conceptual structure of *Difference and Repetition* in their own way, but none of them shows in such great detail the way in which the entire transcendental life of the subject is temporally structured.

The first synthesis produces the present in general. The second produces the past. The virtual as a form of determinability is the future. As Ideas are actualized they leave the future and become present or actual. The form of the represented object is produced in the first active synthesis. Unlike the living present constituted by the trillions of vibrations that habit tired itself out in trying to grasp, this representation is well-defined. It has concrete borders, *partes extra partes*. It is the empirical present which passes. The 'now' that passes in time. It does not pass into oblivion however. It is taken up in the active synthesis of memory. The second active synthesis

179

2nd synth: gives this representation a quality, making it amenable to the 'law of resemblance' and submitting it to the 'variable relations of resemblance and contiguity known as forms of association'. 3rd The Other-structure cushions every object within a horizon of potentialities. We could therefore indicate the entire genesis by the temporality of each moment, and since each moment also belongs to a synthesis, it is clear that all synthesis even active, is temporal.

CHAPTER 4

RECEPTION AND INFLUENCE

The reception and influence of *Difference and Repetition* in France is difficult to trace at this point. It had an immediate impact on some of the most important thinkers in France directly following its publication. Michel Foucault,[1] Maurice Blanchot,[2] Pierre Klossowski,[3] Jean-François Lyotard,[4] and later, Alain Badiou, to name only a few all incorporated themes from the text into their works. Even Jacques Lacan, who had been thoroughly impressed with Deleuze's 1967 *Coldness and Cruelty*[5] and who had attempted to recruit Deleuze into his following,[6] had read the work but seems to have given far more attention to the recurrence of his name than to the conceptual apparatus developed there.[7] Whether or not this exchange between Deleuze and his contemporaries went beyond the level of thematic appropriation is difficult to tell however. All of these writers were original thinkers in their own right, and their comments on *Difference and Repetition*, with the exception of Badiou's and Lacan's, often remain at the level of excessive praise coupled with the characteristic silent twisting of the text so that it meets the agenda of the philosopher in question (this technique was by no means specific to Deleuze).[8] This makes it remarkably difficult to determine the quality and extent of relations between each philosopher without taking each writer in question as a whole. Laudatory sentences and oblique references are not enough to indicate anything other than the incestuous nature of French philosophy.

The reception of *Difference and Repetition* in the English speaking world is just as complicated as the immediate French reception of the text. The work itself was not translated until 1994, and it was primarily Deleuze's work with Guattari that had attracted, and continues to attract, the most attention. For the most part *Difference and Repetition* remained in the background, almost as a legitimizing anchor for these more popular

181

works. It was widely acknowledged as Deleuze's masterwork and considered the book which any serious Deleuzian would ultimately have to engage with, but more often than not it simply stood as that unknown source which explained everything without ever being explained itself. What is becoming? The virtual. What is a rhizome? The virtual. And if one was pressed to explain the virtual, one simply said 'Bergson's ontological memory'.[9] Few scholars attempted – with the exception of John Marks, Keith Ansell-Pearson and Dan Smith – to engage with the structure of the work as such. In fact as recently as 2001 Todd May was able to say with some accuracy that *Difference and Repetition* was a neglected text.[10] It is only in recent years that it has begun to be appreciated by critics, and for that reason even though it was written in 1968, it still has the air of something new and contemporary about it. To date the critics have tended to read the text in two directions.

The first has been an interesting and perhaps symptomatic tendency to overemphasize Deleuze's use of mathematical and scientific metaphors. This is true of both the critical and apologetic accounts. Perhaps the most infamous moment of the text's reception came in the form of Alan Sokal and Jean Bricmont critique of Deleuze's use of science and mathematics in *Fashionable Nonsense*, an unfortunate text that exemplifies better than any other what Nietzsche meant by *ressentiment* and the priestly caste.[11] They claimed that Deleuze misunderstood what he said about the calculus, and further, that he revived false problems that had already been solved with the notion of the limit (as if Deleuze's return to a pre-formal calculus was unintentional!).

What makes Sokal and Bricmont's text interesting – and I don't mean this critically – is that they regularly point out that they don't understand anything. In fact there is relatively little commentary on their part. They simply quote Deleuze and/or Guattari, and then assert that the passage is meaningless. This is the real importance of their study (if it has any). They are in no way able to conclude that there has been an abuse of science and mathematics, but only an alternative use. Deleuze's style does not conform to the rules of the game that they set out at the beginning of their book.[12] What they discover is that French philosophy is written in an entirely different discursive field in which the direct discourse upon which Sokal and Bricmont insist is itself considered to be inherently deceptive.

However, we shouldn't pretend that, unlike Sokal and Bricmont, we possess a point of view from which Deleuze's text becomes clear. The extreme difficulty of the text plays an important role in both its critical and apologetic reception. Much of the best work on Deleuze over the past 50 years is characterized simply by a persistent attempt to make sense of Deleuze. One of the most notable events in the reception of *Difference and Repetition* from this point of view was Manuel DeLanda's 2002 *Intensive Science and Virtual Philosophy*, a monumental work which set off an entirely new line of research in Deleuze studies. DeLanda's work is still one of the best and most clear studies of *Difference and Repetition* as a whole, mostly because nobody has done a better job of not only clarifying and explaining Deleuze's forays into biology, mathematics and science in general, but also of showing the way in which these excursions help Deleuze realize a non-essentialist metaphysics.

If there is a shortcoming in DeLanda's text it is that he 'reconstructs' Deleuze entirely within the language of science and mathematics, and tends to ignore the fact that the whole of *Difference and Repetition* is a theory of subjectivity. For example, when DeLanda discusses the first synthesis of time he writes, 'It is true that Deleuze sometimes presents his theory of synthesis of the present by contraction of immediate past and future, as a psychological theory, but this is simply a matter of convenience of presentation and not fundamental to his account.'[13] It obviously isn't a simple matter of convenience because Deleuze never talks of 'oscillators' or, for that matter, of a synthesis of past and future (it is rather a synthesis of discontinuous matter which produces a present; it is this produced present that has a temporal structure comprising a past and a future). DeLanda is no longer simply reconstructing at this point. He is using his reconstruction to dismiss a more consistent interpretation of Deleuze's texts. Synthesis makes no sense if it takes place outside of a passive and transcendental ego. As a result, DeLanda's insistence on translating Deleuze into the legitimating discourses of science and mathematics causes him to not only overlook the most fundamental dimension of Deleuze's thought but to recast Deleuze's ontology as a 'realist ontology' thus dragging Deleuze back into the false alternative – mind or matter – that French philosophy had just overcome (4–5).

The second tendency in the reception of the text has been to emphasize a more traditionally philosophical and often ontological dimension. As I suggested above, the majority of this work remains an attempt to simply make sense of the text. In the early days this was split between Leonard Lawlor and Jeff Bell's work on the phenomenological dimensions of Deleuze' thought on the one hand and the tendency to emphasize Deleuze's vitalism in John Marks's and Keith Ansell-Pearson's work on the other. Dan Smith is unique in that he leaves nothing untouched from phenomenology to vitalism to biology and mathematics to ontology. If there is something that is particularly confusing in *Difference and Repetition* chances are good that he has not only written on it, but has done so clearly and with authority. More recently Levi Bryant has published an excellent study of *Difference and Repetition* which clarifies many of the more difficult aspects of the work.[14]

One of the most interesting and more recent tendencies has been to situate Deleuze in relation to German Idealism. In this book I emphasized Deleuze's Kantianism, but Deleuze's reading of Kant is strongly coloured by his readings of Novalis, Maïmon, Schelling and Hegel.[15] From Fichte, Deleuze takes two of his most characteristic notions – the notion of system as the process through which a genetic point or principle comes to know itself, and the conception of a philosophical style which maintains the structure of the system but continually undermines and changes the technical vocabulary through which the system is communicated. This tendency to emphasize Deleuze's idealist roots will no doubt mark some of the most useful criticism of Deleuze's thought to come.

There have been two important and strongly critical moments in the reception of Deleuze's text, both of which have caused Deleuze's more sympathetic readers to go back and revise some of the most well-established commonplaces of Deleuze studies. Alain Badiou and Peter Hallward have both levelled almost identical criticisms at *Difference and Repetition*. Badiou famously argued that Deleuze's philosophy constitutes a renewed metaphysics of the One, and he centres his reading of Deleuze around three points: '1. This philosophy is organized around a metaphysics of the One. 2. It proposes an ethics of thought that requires dispossession and asceticism. 3. It is systematic and abstract'.[16] Perhaps the most important point, however, is a fourth which is not listed here: for Badiou the virtual is also transcendent to the world, not immanent.[17] Peter Hallward has made the same arguments. He argued in great detail that the virtual is a resurrection of an old theology, and that it remains transcendent to the beings that it univocally creates.

Hallward and Badiou are clearly not writing within the context of the attempt to make sense of Deleuze. Each has a separate agenda which, in their eyes, Deleuze is unable to meet. Peter Hallward is in the process of developing a practical philosophy which engages with and transforms the world, and on his reading Deleuze's project is one that allows us to only continually escape the world. Badiou on the other hand is creating one of the most interesting and challenging ontologies of the century, and he never hides the fact that he engages with Deleuze's work from the point of view of his own project. Thus he rightly points out to his critics that,

> Even if [they] intended to show – and they should in conformity with the doctrine of free indirect discourse that they've inherited – that my claims about Deleuze conformed to the theses of my book *Being and Event*, it would still be necessary, as Deleuze himself at least attempted, to encapsulate the singularity of that work.[18]

A real engagement with either Hallward or Badiou's reading must take place on the level of their separate projects.

Even though their readings, in the final analysis, must be understood in relation to these projects, both Hallward and Badiou have posed their works as readings of Deleuze, and to a certain degree they can still be evaluated from this point of view. I simply want to highlight two points in relation to their work that my reading of *Difference and Repetition* might allow us to make. Both Hallward and Badiou are able to develop their interpretations of Deleuze only on the condition that they overlook two things. First, both of them actively conflate the virtual with intensity whereas Deleuze very clearly and deliberately distinguishes the two. Second, neither notices that the virtual is produced by the three passive syntheses. Hallward points out that Deleuze repeatedly claims that the virtual is produced, but instead of following Deleuze through to his detailed description of the role of the three syntheses in this production, Hallward mysteriously claims that Deleuze does every thing he can to *obscure* this process and instead discovers the genesis of the virtual somewhere in *Anti-Oedipus*.[19] Because these two oversights cut to the heart of Deleuze's ontology and Deleuze's politics it is tempting to wonder whether Hallward and Badiou have actually been able to get past Deleuze or whether they need to in the first place.

While no one has yet gotten to the heart of Deleuze's ontology, the notion that *Difference and Repetition* develops a line of philosophical thought which precludes political engagement from the start has been convincingly argued by against by a number of Deleuze's readers, from Hardt and Negri,[20] to Paul Patton,[21] and in particular, by Ian Buchanan who has constantly emphasized from his very first work that Deleuze's thought has a profound utopian dimension to it. What he says of *Anti-Oedipus* might be said of *Difference and Repetition* as well. It is 'a utopian book in the strictest sense: it offers a blueprint for a different world, not by describing that world in fantastic terms, but by showing the way out of this one. And that remains a worthwhile but *incomplete* project'.[22]

The reception of *Difference and Repetition* on all fronts, political, critical and ontological, is defined by the difficulty of the text. In a review of Hélène Cixous's *Neutre*, Deleuze wrote, after characterizing her as an 'exceedingly difficult author', that in order to discover Cixious's real originality we have to 'position ourselves within the point of view she herself has invented and from which the work becomes easy to read, leading the reader by the hand' (DI 230). We are still very much on the lookout for this point of view, and perhaps slightly sceptical that Deleuze will ever be easy to read.

NOTES

1: CONTEXT: KANT MEETS HUSSERL

1. DI 96. Paul Patton has more or less consistently translated '*qualification*' and '*spécification*' as 'determination of quality' and 'determination of species'.
2. See DI 98, 99 and 102.
3. NP 89. The ominous expression 'nothing can escape it' is Kant's. See CPR Axx.
4. See NP 86–94.
5. NP 88.
6. DI 61.
7. DI 61.
8. Kant seminar (4 Apr. 1978).
9. For my summary of Deleuze's summary of Kant see chapter 3, section 4 below.
10. E&J 26; original emphasis.
11. This is Donn Welton's characterization. Welton gives a lucid account of this shift from static to genetic phenomenology in chapter five of *The Origin of Meaning*.
12. Jean Wahl's exchange with Ludwig Landgrebe is also fascinating from this point of view. It has been translated and collected in *Apriori and World*.
13. Ricoeur, *An Analysis*, p. 205.
14. Ibid. p. 12.
15. This commentary has been translated and published separately from Husserl's text as *A Key to Edmund Husserl's Ideas I*.
16. See, for example, Bataille, pp. 15–16 and 113. It is again Ricoeur who is the most clear on this point. In *Freud and Philosophy* he argued that psychoanalysis went beyond the Husserl of *Ideas I* by bracketing consciousness itself: 'what we are confronted with is not a reduction *to* consciousness, but a reduction *of* consciousness' (Ricoeur, *Freud*, p. 424; original emphases). Freud went beyond Husserl in his metapsychology and was able to found the genesis of the object in the body and its drives: 'The notion of instinctual vicissitudes is thus substituted for the laws of representation of the old psychology of consciousness. In the context of this instinctual economy one can attempt to work out a true genesis of the notion of object, in accordance with the economic distributions of the libido' (Ricoeur, *Freud*, p. 425). In an interesting twist however Ricoeur suggests that perhaps Husserl had in fact gone as far as Freud and that the project of passive genesis has the potential, if adequately developed, to provide

the phenomenological equivalent of the psychoanalytic theory of drives (Ricoeur, p. 425). Deleuze takes up this suggestion in *Difference and Repetition* when he recasts the passive syntheses in the language of psychoanalysis and attributes each synthesis to a particular drive.

17. Bergson, *Matter and Memory*, p. 34. Perception is 'impersonal' because it does not belong to a self-conscious subject. The subject here is completely and utterly absorbed in its *object to the degree that it becomes the object itself*. As Bergson puts it, the subject 'coincides with the object perceived and which is, in fact, exteriority itself' (MM 66). Cf. Sartre's *Transcendence of the Ego* and Merleau-Ponty's *The Phenomenology of Perception*, pp. 69–71. Following Sartre and Merleau-Ponty Deleuze too will describe the virtual as an impersonal transcendental field in *The Logic of Sense*, but his notion, as we will see below, has nothing at all to do with sensation. It is rather thought's freedom from sensation.

2: OVERVIEW OF THEMES

1. Ricoeur puts it this way: each present cogitatio 'implies something virtual or potential. Every situation of thought, be it perceived, imagined, willed, etc., implies a possibility of continuing to perceive, to imagine to will, in certain motivational directions. Every situation calls for an investigation where the potentialities involved prescribe the style of their own actualization' (*An Analysis* 97).
2. CTM §19–22 and 28. On all of these points see Ricoeur, *An Analysis*, pp. 90–105.
3. See Levinas TI 19.
4. And it is not hard to see the roots of Leibniz's theory of petites perceptions in Descartes. Cf. §201 of the *Principles of Philosophy*. For Leibniz and Descartes however, these imperceptible perceptions were actual, not potential.
5. 'The part of the object that I do not see I posit as visible to Others, so that when I will have walked around to reach this hidden part, I will have joined the Others behind the object, and I will have totalized it in the way that I had already anticipated' (LS 305).
6. CTM §19–22 and 28; cf. Ricoeur on this point, *An Analysis*, pp. 90–105.
7. In *The Logic of Sense* Deleuze will call these three moments 'primary order' (matter), 'secondary organization' (Idea) and 'tertiary order' (representation). See 239–49.
8. Genette, *Narrative Discourse*, p. 172. See chapter six of Claire Colebrook's *Gilles Deleuze* for an excellent discussion of the role of free indirect discourse in Deleuze.
9. For an excellent discussion of the role of free indirect discourse in Deleuze's study of cinema, see Patricia Pisters' *The Matrix of Visual Culture*, p. 92.
10. Leibniz (15 Apr. 1980).

11. Leibniz (15 Apr. 1980).
12. Spinoza (24 Jan. 1978).
13. Kant (04 Apr. 1978).
14. Kant (28 Mar. 1978).
15. See LS xiv and DR xx/3/xix.
16. This adds a whole new level of difficulty, because now we have to weave between not only Deleuze's voice and Nietzsche's, for example, but also Deleuze and Deleuze's interpretations of Nietzsche which are sometimes reflections of Deleuze's own thought, but other times old-fashioned attempts at a faithful representation.
17. (xv/NA/xiii).
18. What follows is an extension of Claire Colebrook's arguments in *Philosophy and Post-Structuralist Theory*, pp. 228–33. Cf. Merleau-Ponty on the need to construct a new logic of sensation or of 'immanence' in opposition to classical logic in PP 57; cf. 42–5.
19. Deleuze makes this point in his *Anti-Oedipus* seminar (14 Jan. 1974).
20. See *History of the Concept of Time*, p. 122.
21. Colebrook, *Philosophy and Post-Structuralist Theory*, p. 228; original emphasis.
22. Ibid. 233.
23. Klossowski, *Vicious Circle*, p. 30.
24. Ibid. p. 33; original emphasis.
25. Ibid. p. 38; original emphasis.
26. Ibid. p. 33; original emphasis.
27. Blanchot, *Friendship*, p. 175.
28. Cf. C1 59: 'This in-itself of the image is matter: not something hidden behind the image, but on the contrary, the absolute identity of the image and movement'.
29. See also (127/166–7/155).
30. It is perhaps at this level of style – and not that of concepts – that we can best articulate the distance between Badiou and Deleuze. For Badiou, it is not enough to go from direct discourse to free indirect discourse. One has to abandon natural language altogether. See *Theoretical Writings*, p. 80; cf. 16–20 and chapter three of *Being and Event*.

3: READING THE TEXT

Section 1. The Introduction: Repetition and Difference

1. It is worth pointing out that the words 'difference' and 'repetition', even in their technical use, do not have one meaning. Neither 'difference' nor 'repetition' is used univocally.
2. It is true that Deleuze says 'our conduct'. All this means is that he is in the process of revising the notion of subjectivity. We are the manifest subject which is constituted by an unconscious latent subject.

3. Hegel, *Phenomenology*, p. 58.
4. Ibid. p. 59.
5. Hyppolite, *Genesis and Structure*, p. 84.
6. Hyppolite, LE, p. 15.
7. Kant puts it this way: 'There are therefore certain laws, and indeed *a priori*, which first make a nature possible; the empirical laws can only obtain and be found by means of experience, and indeed in accord with original laws, in accordance with which experience first becomes possible' (CPR A216/B263).
8. If we say that the movement in question pertains to 'thought', we have to be careful because it is precisely the nature of thought that is in question. Kierkegaard, for example, will insist that the only true repetition does not occur in nature and in its astronomical cycles but pertains to 'individuals in their freedom', the 'finite spirit' and in particular to the process by which 'the finite spirit contemplatively abandons itself in sympathy with its repetitive movement' (Kierkegaard, 288, 292). But Deleuze will go further and ask, 'is the movement in the sphere of the mind, or in the entrails of the earth which knows neither God nor self' (11/29/12)? We could formulate his question this way: is it the movement of the manifest subject or of the latent subject?
9. For a very readable account of the nature of repetition in Kierkegaard and the way in which it is opposed to both Hegelian mediation and Platonic recollection, see the first chapter of John Caputo's *Radical Hermeneutics*. The first three chapters of that work provide an excellent introduction to the theme of repetition in general.
10. See Kierkegaard, *Repetition*, p. 149.
11. For an excellent description of the Leibnizian aspects, see Dan Smith's essays, 'Deleuze on Leibniz' and 'Knowledge of Pure Events'.
12. Leibniz seminar (6 May 1980).
13. What is true of a drop of water is true of Alexander the Great: 'There are in the soul [i.e. concept] of Alexander, from all time, traces of all that has happened to him, and marks of everything that will happen to him – and even traces of everything that happens in the universe – though no one but God can know them all' (Leibniz, *Discourse on Metaphysics*, §8).
14. In both *Difference and Repetition* and the Leibniz seminars Deleuze reaches this conclusion to which we will return below: 'There is only conceptual difference. In other words, if you assign a difference between two things, there is necessarily a difference in the concept' (Leibniz seminar (6 May 1980)).
15. Deleuze, however, will deny this in both his seminars and in *The Fold*.
16. *Principles of Nature and Grace*, §13; my emphasis.
17. Cf. *Discourse on Metaphysics*, §15: 'Thus a substance which is of an infinite extent, insofar as it expresses everything, becomes limited by the more or less perfect manner of if its expression'.

18. Deleuze frequently alludes to this passage in Leibniz throughout his discussion of the blocked concept in *Difference and Repetition* – especially in his comments on the various faculties (memory and recognition).
19. Cf. *Principles of Nature and Grace*, §13.
20. NE 57.
21. For an excellent description of this relation in Leibniz, see Deleuze's Leibniz seminar (29 Apr. 1980).
22. See (220/284/273) and (289/369/360).
23. '[M]ediation is a chimera, which in Hegel is supposed to explain everything and which is also the only thing he never tried to explain' (Kierkegaard, *Fear and Trembling*, p. 42; cf. *Repetition*, p. 149).

Section 2. Difference in Itself

24. *Science of Logic*, p. 417; original emphases. Cf. Hyppolite's comments on this notion of difference in LE p. 118.
25. Deleuze's own interpretation of Aristotle is heavily indebted to Porphyry's (which is why he mixes Greek and Latin terms). For more nuanced reading with more fidelity to Aristotle, see chapter four of Jeff Bell's *Philosophy at the Edge of Chaos*.
26. Deleuze is alluding here to the *Metaphysics* 1038a where Aristotle explains that the form of an individual is given through the 'differentia of differentia'. The last differentia in the series will, as Deleuze puts it, 'condense' the first genus and the series of differences, into the form of the object.
27. See Bell, *Philosophy at the Edge of Chaos*, p. 122. Cf. Aristotle's *Metaphysics* 1054b.
28. Leibniz, *Discourse on Metaphysics*, §8.
29. Ibid. §8.
30. Leibniz seminar (6 May 1980).
31. Leibniz, *New Essays*, p. 290.
32. See *Principles of Nature and Grace* §2.
33. *New Essays*, p. 55.
34. Ibid.
35. See (47–8/67–9/58–9); LS 110 and 171; and the seminars on Leibniz (6 May 1980).
36. See, for example, his seminar on Leibniz (29 Apr. 1980).
37. Cf. LS 171–6.
38. Both Catherine Malabou ('Who's Afraid of Hegelian Wolves') and Bruce Baugh (*The French Hegel*) have written extensively on Deleuze's relation to Hegel. In a fascinating work Simon Duffy has suggested that the distance between Hegel and Deleuze begins with their respective readings of Spinoza. See *The Logic of Expression*. The best study however is still Juliette Simont's *Essai sur la quantite, la qualite, la relation chez Kant, Hegel, Deleuze*.
39. In fact he even described *The Logic of Sense* in these terms: 'This book is an attempt to develop a logical and psychological novel'

(LS xiv). As Leonard Lawlor points out, the expression 'logic of sense' is used twice by Hyppolite to describe Hegel's thought (LE xiii). (Although it is tempting to take this as the best candidate for the title, one would also have to consider the influence of Merleau-Ponty's repeated claims to develop a 'logic of sense' or a 'logic of immanence' on Deleuze's title as well.)

40. *Anti-Oedipus* Seminar (14 Jan. 1974).
41. 'Hegelian dialectic will push this alterity up to contradiction' (LE 113).
42. Cf. (49–50/70 1/60–1).
43. See (29/45/38) and (262/337/330).
44. Ricoeur says that phenomenology begins with a 'genuine metaphysical decision concerning the status of [. . .] phenomena' (*An Analysis* 9). He explains that 'phenomenology carries out a frontal attack on a conviction belonging to all Galileans. The first truth of the world is not the truth of mathematical physics but the truth of perception; or rather the truth of science is erected as a superstructure upon a first foundation of presence and existence, that of the world lived through perceptually' (9). Levinas elaborates this decision in great detail throughout the opening chapters of *The Theory of Intuition*.
45. Foucault is particularly clear on this point. See 'Theatrum Philosophicum', p. 186.
46. Cf. Nietzsche's famous complaint that the notion of God or Being should come last, not first. Philosophers mistake 'the last for the first. They put that which comes at the end – unfortunately! for it ought not to come at all! – the "highest concepts", that is to say the most general, the emptiest concepts, the last fumes of evaporating reality, at the beginning *as* the beginning' (*Twilight* 47; original emphasis).
47. Cf. LS 70, 72, 81, 86 and 95.
48. See Mary Louise Gill's 'Individuation and Individuals in Aristotle' for a particularly clear description of these questions. See also, Alberto Toscano's introduction to *The Theatre of Production*.
49. The need for such a theory of individuation can be found in at least two directions. On the one hand, it is a rejection of Kantian idealism (and indeed, it is not hard to hear the phenomenological overtones in Deleuze's criticism of analogical individuation from the point of view of constitution). The forms of thought cannot be pregiven, but must be constituted in real experience. On the other hand (and I hesitate to claim its relevance for Deleuze because I do not think that he is a philosopher of science or concerned with biology as such but simply found in it an inspirational metaphor), is the 'Copernican Revolution of Darwinism' in which individuation is primary to specification (249/320/310). Manuel DeLanda is excellent on this point. See *Intensive Science*, pp. 58–9. For science as a source of *inspiration* for philosophy see Deleuze's review of Simondon (DI 89).

50. For another lucid account of the notion of univocity as it relates to traditional ontology see Dan Smith's essay 'The Doctrine of Univocity'.
51. *History of the Concept of Time*, pp. 173–4; original emphases. Like so many others, this passage found its way into *Being and Time* with very little modification. See §20, p. 93.
52. Deleuze emphasizes this as well as many of the themes which follow in the following definition of univocal being: 'pure immanence requires as a principle the equality of being, or of the positing of equal being: not only is being equal in itself, but it is seen to be equally present in all beings. And the Cause appears as everywhere equally close: there is no remote causation. *Beings are not defined by their rank in a hierarchy, are not more or less remote from the One, but each depends directly on God*, participating in the equality of being, receiving immediately all that it is by its essence fitted to receive, irrespective of any proximity or remoteness. Furthermore, pure immanence requires a Being that is univocal and constitutes a Nature, and that consists in positive forms common to producer and product to cause and effect. We know that immanence does not do away with the distinction of essences; but there must be common forms that constitute the essence of substance as cause, while they contain the essences of modes as effects' (EP 173; my emphasis).
53. *Anti-Oedipus* Seminar (14 Jan. 1974).
54. Whenever Leibniz defines monads as ultimately simple elements he then asks what could act as a means of distinguishing between them. His answer is that it is a monad's *affections*. 'Therefore one monad, in itself and at a particular moment, can only be distinguished from another by internal qualities and activities, which can be nothing else but its *perceptions* [. . .] and its *appetitions* [. . .], which are the principles of change' (*Principles of Nature and Grace* §2). See *Monadology* § 7–14; cf. the critique of atomism in NE 231.
55. Deleuze, of course, will do everything he can to overcome or mitigate this (Cf. EP 180–1) but in the end, even he will admit that the attributes still mediate between substance and the modes.
56. Cf. WP 60.
57. Although it is a difficult read, chapter eleven of *Expressionism in Philosophy* gives a remarkably detailed history of the concept of immanence and univocal being as it developed from Plato to Spinoza.
58. Deleuze elaborates on this point in one of his lectures. For Duns Scotus, Being was metaphysically univocal, but physically analogical: 'Then what: you treat God as matter? Are a dog and a man in the same sense? Quite tricky, that. And nevertheless there is a man, the greatest thinker of the Middle Ages, who says yes, being is univocal, that is Duns Scotus. This story of Duns Scotus' univocal being turns out rather badly – but happily he took precautions, he said yes but be careful: being is univocal insofar as it is being. That is to say that it's metaphysically univocal. He said: sure it's analogical, which is to

say that it's said in several senses physically. This is what interests me: he was at the border of heresy, had he not specified metaphysically univocal and physically analogical, he would have been done for. But for Duns Scotus' disciples, less prudent than he was, it turned out badly. Because I say: being is univocal, this means: there is no categorical difference between the assumed senses of the word "being" and being is said in one and the same sense of everything which is. In a certain manner this means that the tick is God; there is no difference of category, there is no difference of substance, there is no difference of form. It becomes a mad thought.' (*Anti-Oedipus* seminar (14 Jan. 1974)). Cf. EP 177–8.

59. Cf.: 'Substance and modes, cause and effects, only have being and are only known though the common forms [i.e. the attributes] that *actually constitute* the essence of the one [God], and actually contain the essence of the others' (EP 181; my emphasis).

60. Cf.: 'Univocity of being, in so far as it is immediately related to difference, demands that we show how individuating difference *precedes* generic, specific, and even individual differences within being; how a prior field of individuation within being conditions at once the determination of species and forms [. . .]. If individuation does not take place either by form or by matter, neither qualitatively nor extensionally, this is not only because it differs in kind but *because it is already presupposed by the forms, matters, and extensive parts*' (38/56–7/48; my emphases).

61. Klossowski, *Such a Deathly Desire*, p. 108. Cf. Heidegger, *History of the Concept of Time*, p. 77 for a similar account of the traditional account of consciousness.

62. See Heidegger, *The Eternal Recurrence of the Same*, p. 156. Blanchot will also emphasize this: Blanchot puts it this way: 'the Will to Power is the ultimate fact; the Eternal Return is the thought of thoughts'. Blanchot, *Infinite Conversation*, p. 273.

63. Cf. (125/163–4/153).

64. Cf. NP 189.

65. Admittedly, this interpretation seems to break down in *one* place (199–201/258–60/250–2).

66. See pg 150 below for more on the distinction between virtuality and intensity.

67. Cf. Klossowski, *Nietzsche and the Vicious Circle*, p. 50.

68. Deleuze emphasizes this in a lecture on Leibniz in a short discussion of Merleau-Ponty's essay 'Everywhere and Nowhere'. The rationalists 'innocently begin with the infinite'. But this is no longer possible. As Merleau-Ponty puts it, 'today we no longer believe in the infinite'. But neither Merleau-Ponty nor Deleuze shy away from the infinite. Merleau-Ponty goes on to claim that 'the only reason why passing to the infinite infinite does not seem to us to be the answer is that we are taking up again in a more radical way the task which that intrepid century had believed itself rid of forever' (*Signs* 152). Instead of rejecting the infinite, the infinite will have

to emerge from within the finite. See Deleuze's Leibniz seminar (22 Apr. 1980).

Section 3. Critical and Dogmatic Images of Thought

69. It is worth pointing out again that the word 'singularity' in this context refers to the immediate object of intuition – not to a mathematical point.
70. The adjectives 'dynamic' and 'static' characterize the starting points of each genesis. The first begins in moving (dynamic) matter. The second begins after thought has escaped from matter and become pure time – the 'pure and empty form of time' in which there is no longer movement, that is, it is now static.
71. Deleuze's characterization of the dogmatic image has been well documented in the secondary literature. See in particular Paola Marrati's essay 'Against the Doxa' and the first chapter of Paul Patton's *Deleuze and the Political*. James Williams has also described the dogmatic image of thought in great detail in his critical introduction.
72. '. . . we do not speak of this or that image of thought, variable according to the philosophy in question, but of a single Image in general which constitutes the subjective presupposition of philosophy as a whole' (132/172/167).
73. See APS 269.
74. These levels are all clearly described in the introduction to *Experience and Judgment*.
75. See Lyotard, *Phenomenology*, p. 33.
76. For an excellent analysis of these themes, see Eugen Fink's essay 'The Phenomenological Philosophy of Edmund Husserl and Contemporary Criticism'. Deleuze would take up Merleau-Ponty's version of the reduction in critique of 'objectivism' and 'subjectivism' in *Proust and Signs*.
77. See Husserl's *Ideas I* §62. Merleau-Ponty also follows Husserl's adoption of Kantian terminology to describe the reduction when he refers to the 'natural or dogmatic attitude' (PP 45). Ricoeur emphasized this distinction throughout his commentary on *Ideas I*.
78. For a lucid and thorough discussion of Deleuze's doctrine of the faculties which differs slightly from the one I am going to present, see Levi Bryant's *Difference and Giveness*.
79. Deleuze seems to be referring to Leibniz's own critique of faculty psychology here. Leibniz wrote in the *New Essays*, 'But inactive faculties – in short, the pure powers of the Schoolmen [Scholastic philosophers] – are mere fictions, unknown to nature and obtainable only by abstraction. For where will one ever find in the world a faculty consisting in sheer power without performing any act?' (*New Essays* 110). Perhaps in response to this Deleuze writes in *Pericles and Verdi*, 'by what act does one proceed from potential to actual? Reason is the act. But by reason we understand not a faculty but

a process which consists precisely in actualizing a potential [. . .]'.
In other words, a faculty cannot be considered a sheer power independent of its actualization, but is inseparable from the act itself.
Thought is not a natural possibility but the act of thinking itself.

80. As we have already seen the expression 'transcendental empiricism' was the name Husserl gave to his genetic phenomenology. We have also already seen that Deleuze's method is a general formulation of the phenomenological reduction: do not trace the transcendental from the empirical. What remains then, is to describe this genesis – a task which is also a deeply Husserlian undertaking.

81. This isn't to admit a Proustian influence on *Difference and Repetition*. It is simply to notice Deleuze's malice, the way he attributes his own ideas in one book to Proust, in another to Nietzsche and in yet a third to Artaud.

82. This a second sense in which Deleuze's philosophy can be described as a transcendental empiricism. In the first, Husserlian sense, it is called a transcendental empiricism because it involves an experience of the transcendental. But in this second, more traditional sense, it is an empiricism because everything comes back to sensibility.

83. See Dan Smith's excellent commentary on these pages in 'Deleuze's Theory of Sensation', pp. 30–4.

84. See (191/247–8/240–4).

85. Despite the fact that almost everything written on Deleuze to date has been concerned with the static genesis alone, Deleuze's epistemology has gotten relatively little attention. Elie During's article 'A History of Problems' is a fascinating and readable account of the historical situation in which Deleuze was writing, as is Todd May's *Between Genealogy and Epistemology* (esp. chapter six). Dan Smith's 'Axiomatics and Problematics' contains a short account of Deleuze's relationship to French epistemology. Manuel DeLanda has also written clearly and extensively on aspects of Deleuze's epistemology throughout *Intensive Science*.

86. Deleuze cites several historical examples of transcendental error which help clarify what he means: superstition in both Lucretius (*De Rerum Natura*) and Spinoza (*Theologico-Politcal Treatise*), illusion in Kant's *Critique of Pure Reason*, and alienation in Hegel are some of the more well-known of his examples. Superstition, illusion and alienation are not instances where thought accidentally gets something wrong. They constitute the fundamental and unavoidable misadventure of thought. In Spinoza thought begins with superstition and works its way out with the help of philosophy, for example. In Kant, critique frees us from the natural illusions of reason.

87. In his discussion of the image of thought in *Nietzsche and Philosophy*, Deleuze reaches the same conclusion: 'According to this image [i.e. the dogmatic] everything in fact opposed to thought has only one effect on thought as such: leading it into error. [. . .] Mature, considered thought has other enemies; negative states which are profound in entirely different ways. Stupidity is a structure of thought as

such: it is not a means of self-deception, it expresses the non-sense in thought by right' (NP 105).

88. For this reason Deleuze will liken this synthesis to the schematism in Kant, a process in which the imagination gave spatio-temporal coordinates to concepts. It introduced the concept of the understanding to the forms of intuition, space and time.

89. See Frege's 'Function and Concept', p. 138. Frege also uses this example in 'On Sense and Reference', p. 156.

90. See the introduction to *Experience and Judgment* for Husserl's version of this scenario.

91. In *Nietzsche and Philosophy*, Deleuze described such a condition as a condition that is 'no wider than what it conditions, that changes itself with the conditioned and determines itself in each case along with what it determines' (NP 50).

92. Cf. E&J 21.

93. In *Proust and Signs*, Deleuze had already developed this account of an apprenticeship which is structured by the progressive development of the faculties.

Section 4. The Three Passive Syntheses

94. Deleuze consistently stresses that each of the three passive syntheses 'is essentially asymmetrical' (71/97/91). For the second synthesis see (81/110/103); for the third see (89/120/111).

95. Deleuze is clearly thinking of Husserl when he makes the same claim in his lectures on Kant. See esp. (28 Mar. 1978): 'it's from this level of the analysis of the synthesis of perception that Kant can be considered as the founder of phenomenology.'

96. As Béatrice Longuenesse points, the word Kant is using for 'imagination' here is *Einbildung* and not *Einbildungskraft*. She draws the conclusion that these section headings refer not to the *faculty* of synthesis but only to the representations ' "in" which there is an act of synthesis' (Longuenesse 35). However, Kant is often quite clear that these representations depend on their respective faculties as their source.

97. Kant provides similar accounts which divide the three syntheses into three faculties at A79, A97 and A115.

98. For a clear and more detailed discussion of this, see Rudolph Makkreel's *Imagination and Interpretation in Kant*, pp. 27–8.

99. In order to give the reader a concrete sense of passive synthesis, Merleau-Ponty uses the following example. If you hold your index finger a short distance in front of your face and focus on it, there is only one finger. If you look past it into the distance, it becomes two fingers. When you refocus your attention it becomes one finger again without you ever doing anything. That is a passive synthesis. If you were drunk, however, and still saw two fingers, you could tell yourself, 'even though I see two, I know there is only one'. Such purely intellectual act would constitute an active synthesis.

100. Deleuze often cites this example. Kant asks us two imagine two bodies – his famous example is two hands or gloves – that are exactly identical. Each would have the same concept; which means that each would have the exact same set of determinations. Each subject would contain identical predicates. Even so, he argues, one could not superimpose a right hand over a left hand. There must therefore be determinations which are not in the concept and are not reducible to conceptual determinations – in this case spatial determinations. See Deleuze's Kant Seminar (14 Mar. 1978) and §13 of Kant's *Prolegomena*.

101. Heidegger too will not only emphasize this point, but he will also show how synthesis founds logic in Kant in the same that I suggested Deleuze was trying to do in contrast to Frege and his successors. See *The Phenomenological Interpretation of Kant's Critique of Pure Reason*, pp. 181–4.

102. It is important to remember that where English speakers read 'manifold', French speakers read *'le divers'* or *'diversité'*.

103. If the mind were to continually reproduce appearances without recognizing them it would be left with 'unruly heaps of them' (CPR A121).

104. This is important in light of the theme of passive synthesis. Despite Husserl's reading of the A deduction, there are several passages in the A deduction in which we can see Kant suggesting that even in 1781 that all combination is in fact the result of the understanding. Deleuze is clearly avoiding such a reading. In fact Deleuze will stress in the following quotation that 'the synthesis of the imagination, taken in itself, is not at all self-conscious'. It is passive.

105. Cf. Kant seminar (28 Mar. 1978). In order to transition from the first two syntheses Deleuze writes, 'In order to perceive we still need for this space and this time, determined by the synthesis, or what comes to the same thing, that which contains this space and this time, must be related to a form, to a form of what? Not to a form of space or time since we have the form of space and time. What other form? You can see the progression. We started from the form of space and time in general, as the form of intuition, then the act of imagination determines a space, a given space and a given time, through the two aspects of the synthesis. In this case it's a form – not the form of space and time – but a spatio-temporal form, the form of a house or the form of a lion for example, but we need yet another form in order for there to be perception. It is necessary for this space and time, or what contains this determined space and time, to be related to the form of an object.'

106. See *The Phenomenological Interpretation*, p. 187.

107. 'For this unity of consciousness would be impossible if in the cognition of the manifold [i.e. in the thought of the object = X] the mind could not become conscious of the identity of the function [or rule] by means of which this manifold is synthetically combined into one cognition' (CPR A108).

108. See *The Phenomenological Interpretation*, p. 179.
109. Deleuze never quotes Heidegger in this chapter (and he rarely mentions Kant for that matter). He does, however quote *Kant and the Problem of Metaphysics* later in *Difference and Repetition* (201/260/252); and Heidegger's text played an enormous role in Deleuze's 1956–1957 seminar, *Qu'est-ce que fonder?* I wouldn't want to suggest, however, that this lack of citation matters – in fact it's part of the game: 'The philosophical learning of an author is not assessed by numbers of quotations, nor by the always fanciful and conjectural checklists of libraries, but by the apologetic and polemical directions of his work itself' (NP 162).
110. Heidegger hints towards this in KPM (122), but he develops it in great detail in the lectures from which KPM was drawn. See *Phenomenological Interpretation*, pp. 170–80.
111. *Phenomenological Interpretation*, p. 180.
112. The table of contents in the French edition makes this division particularly clear. Both English editions make this structure difficult to grasp. The Continuum Impacts edition of the text omits both the analytic table of contents and the section breaks within the body of the text. While the Columbia edition maintains, for the most part, Deleuze's section breaks within the text, it makes them uniform, omits the higher-level section breaks within the text and within the analytic table of contents, and frequently breaks Deleuze's paragraphs in half.
113. See (70–6/96–103/90–7).
114. Merleau-Ponty's discussion of temporal synthesis also began with the problem of discontinuity (PP 479).
115. Perhaps the most infamous name that he has given this first synthesis is 'body without organs'. It is easy to make the connection between the two concepts if we notice that in both *The Logic of Sense* and *Anti-Oedipus* the body without organs is what brings about a synthesis of discontinuous matter.
116. Deleuze's comments here are deeply indebted to Bergson's arguments in the third chapter of *Duration and Simultaneity*.
117. Deleuze, of course, takes this notion of the living present from Husserl.
118. See (103/136/127). Deleuze will call this the 'object = X', the 'dark precursor' and the 'phallus' at various points. It would be a mistake to confuse this principle of the second synthesis with the principle of the third synthesis, the 'aleatory point', or what Deleuze called in *The Logic of Sense*, the 'castrated phallus' (as opposed to the 'still intact phallus' of the second synthesis).
119. See (85/115/107) and (274/351/344).
120. It is true that Deleuze speaks of the passing of the living present in this passage, but this is an exception. When Deleuze says 'the present which passes' he almost always means the present of representation, and not the sub-representative present in general.

Keeping this distinction in mind while reading the second chapter will greatly clarify a number of difficult passages.

121. In the opening chapters of *Kant and the Problem of Metaphysics* where Heidegger raises the problem of finitude, he first defines finitude in a negative way by opposing human intuition to divine intuition. He suggests that for a positive definition 'The finitude of human knowledge must first of all be sought in the finitude of its own intuition' (KPM 17). Deleuze's notion of a 'contractile range' provides just such a definition.

122. The original translation reads: the second synthesis is 'that to which habit and present belong' (79/108/101). Levi Bryant is particularly good on these points. See *Difference and Giveness*, pp. 108–11.

123. See chapter three of *Bergsonism* and chapter five of *Proust and Signs* (esp. p. 58).

124. See chapter three of *The Structure of Behavior*.

125. Vincent Descombes describes this aspect of Merleau-Ponty's thought well: 'A behaviour pattern is not the *reaction* to a *stimulus*, but rather the *response elicited* by a situation. The faculty of apprehending the situation as a question to which it will reply must thus be ascribed to the organism whose behaviour is under consideration' (Descombes 58; original emphases).

126. Cf.: 'The unity of the object is based on the foreshadowing of an imminent order which is about to spring upon us a reply to questions merely latent in the landscape. It solves a problem set only in the form of a vague feeling of uneasiness, it organizes elements which up to that moment did not belong to the same universe [. . .]' (PP 20). See also PP 370, 372 and note 156 below.

127. Cf. *Creative Evolution*, p. 262.

128. 'Faced with this extremely difficult texts, the task of the commentator is to multiply the distinctions, even and above all when these texts confine themselves to suggesting the distinctions, rather than establishing them strictly' (BG 63).

129. There is an important omission from the English translation immediately following a quotation of Heidegger in which Deleuze affirms the relation of thought to the empty form of time: ' "Man can think in the sense that he has the possibility to do so. This possibility alone, however, is no guarantee to us that we are capable of thinking;" thought only thinks when it is constrained and forced in the presence of that which "gives thinking" or of that which is to be thought – and that which is to be thought is really the unthinkable or the non-thought, that is to say, the perpetual *fact* that "we are not yet thinking" (according to (*suivant*) the pure form of time)' (144/188/181–2; original emphasis). Thinking follows from or is in accordance with the pure form of time.

130. 'In effect, this pure form or straight line is defined by an order which distributes a *before*, a *during*, and an *after*; by a totality which incorporates all three in the simultaneity of it's *a priori* synthesis;

NOTES

and by a series which makes a type of repetition correspond to each' (294/376/366).

131. Deleuze's language throughout his discussion of the third synthesis directly adopts that of the French translation of this passage: 'Les schêmes ne sont donc que des *déterminations de temps à priori* d'après des règles, qui suivant l'ordre des catégories, ont pour objet la *série du temps*, *la matière du temps*, *l'ordre du temps*, et enfin *l'ensemble du temps* par rapport à toutes les choses possibles' (CPR fr. 223; original emphases).

132. For example, the *series* of time results from the application of the category of quantity to the form of time in sensibility. Quantity partitions time into extensive magnitudes, thus producing determinate instants, external to one another which can then pass in time. Time then becomes serial. The *content* of time is determined by the application of the category quality. This results in a synthesis which fills out each extensive magnitude with a particular quality in the form of an intensive magnitude. The instants thus take on a content (Deleuze leaves this one out, because for him, empty time, as the name suggests, has no content). Together, the categories of quality and quantity determine the quality and extent of the instant. The application of the category relation determines the various relations between these instants (are the instants successive or simultaneous?). It determines the *order* of time. Finally, the application of the category of modality determines the relation of instants to *time as a whole* insofar as it determines whether such an instant is actual, necessary, or even possible. This is what the expressions 'order', 'totality' and 'series' mean in Kant.

133. Deleuze summarizes the process in this way: '(1) all phenomena are in space and time; (2) the *a priori* synthesis of the imagination bears *a priori* on space and time themselves; (3) phenomena are therefore necessarily subject to the transcendental unity of this synthesis and to the categories which represent it *a priori*' (KP 17).

134. Deleuze captures the strange situation in which such a subject would find itself: 'The activity of thought applies to a receptive being, to a passive subject which represents that activity to itself rather than enacts it, which experiences its effect rather than initiates it, and which lives it like an Other within itself' (86/116/108).

135. See (87/117–18/109) where Deleuze claims that the first synthesis replaces Kantian receptivity.

136. This is not at all true of *The Logic of Sense*, however. What he calls the 'empty form of time' in *Difference and Repetition* is called the Oedipus complex in *The Logic of Sense*. What he calls the future in *Difference and Repetition* is called 'the empty form of time' or 'Aion' in *The Logic of Sense*.

137. Deleuze is clearly following the course of the apprenticeship he outlined in *Proust and Signs*. First the apprentice tried to find truth in objects or worldly signs (objectivism). Not finding it there, the apprentice turned inward a searched for truth in subjective signs

201

(subjectivism). But truth is neither objective nor subjective. It can only be found in 'essence' or 'sense', in the signs of art which are interpreted by the faculty of thought.

138. Deleuze elaborates on Hölderlin's reading in great detail in his Kant seminar (21 Mar. 1978). Ronald Bogue has described Beaufret's reading and its relation to Deleuze in great detail in 'The Betrayal of God'.

139. Cf. 'Hamlet is not a man of skepticism or doubt, but the man of Critique. I am separated from myself by the form of time and yet I am one, because the I necessarily affects this form by bringing about its synthesis [. . .]' (EC 30).

140. This is why he calls this stage of the genesis the 'Oedipal stage' rather than the 'empty form of time' in *The Logic of Sense*. Deleuze rewrites the Oedipus complex from the point of view of the paradox of inner sense filtered though Hölderlin.

141. Deleuze is alluding to Blanchot here. For Blanchot, 'the work' was a space which could be approached only though death. He described it as a 'throw of the dice', a space of a murmuring 'anonymous, impersonal being', in which a 'living point' or a 'sign which designates only itself', makes 'mobile connections' and 'relationships of comprehension' between meaningless elements. In short, it is the space of sense. See *The Space of Literature*, pp. 198–207 and *The Book to Come* pp. 233–6.

Section 5. The Ideal Synthesis of Difference

142. Kant seminar (04 Apr. 1978).

143. In *The Logic of Sense*, Deleuze speaks of a 'counter-actualization' which makes the return to unindividuated materiality impossible. Counter-actualization ensures the mind's independence from the unindividuated matter of 'corporeal depth' (LS 168).

144. 'There is as yet nothing mathematical in these definitions [of the Idea as an assemblage of elements, relations and singular points]. Mathematics appears with the fields of solution in which dialectical Ideas of the last order are incarnated [. . .]' (181/234–5/229). In short, mathematics is an example taken from the actual (or from the field of solutions), and cannot therefore describe by itself the *mathesis universalis* of the virtual.

145. That said, Dan Smith has given an admirably clear account of the relation between Ideas and the calculus in his essay 'Axiomatics and Problematics'. Simon Duffy has provided a more technical version in *The Logic of Expression*. Levi Bryant has developed the Kantian aspect of Ideas in *Difference and Giveness*, pp. 159–74. Dan Smith has helpfully described Deleuze's theory of Ideas in relation to historical notions from Plato to Kant to Hegel. See 'Deleuze, Kant, and the Theory of Immanent Ideas'.

146. For example, 'it is the solution that counts, but the problem always has the solution it deserves, in terms of the way in which it is

posed (*le pose*)' (BG 16/5; translation modified). The problem is 'better resolved the more *it is* determined' (179/232/226; original emphasis).

147. Merleau-Ponty exerts a profound influence on this chapter that I cannot develop here. In the *Phenomenology of Perception* the muddled problem appeared as a 'positive indeterminacy', and the process of determining a solution was what he called 'thought': 'This passage from the indeterminate to the determinate, this recasting at every moment of its own history in the unity of a new meaning, is thought itself' (PP 36). This passage has several important characteristics in common with Deleuze's. First, constitution unfolds in the absence of a model. It spontaneously creates meaning '*without any ideal model* of a significant grouping' (PP 61). Second, for Merleau-Ponty, the problem must therefore possess its own form of spontaneous self organization. 'The unity of the object is based on the foreshadowing of an imminent order which is about to spring upon us a reply to questions merely latent in the landscape. It solves a problem set only in the form of a vague feeling of uneasiness, it organizes elements which up to that moment did not belong to the same universe [. . .]' (PP 20). 'Now here, the data of the problem are not prior to its solution, and perception is just that act which creates at a stroke, along with the cluster of data, the meaning which unites them' (PP 42; cf. 35). See note 125.

148. I have inserted phrases from the French translation into Hollingdale's English translation in order to show the degree to which Deleuze drew from this passage. In English, the phrase 'divine game of creation' is nowhere to be found, nor is the word 'affirmation'.

149. Poulet's essay is also an excellent account of the importance of transcendental empiricism for Blanchot.

150. Deleuze is likely alluding to Blanchot's essay on Artaud in *The Book to Come* (see esp. p. 36); but this notion, as Poulet suggests, appears throughout Blanchot's work of this period. See in particular Blanchot's *The Space of Literature* (esp. pp. 44–6) and the closing pages of his essay 'The Book to Come' (which develops the theme of the dice throw in relation to the genesis of sense) in *The Book to Come*.

151. Deleuze discusses the various way in which particular Ideas can be distinguished from one another in their coexistence on (186–7/241–2/235–6).

152. Cf. LS: 'Each throw emits singular points [. . .]. But the set of throws is included in the aleatory point, a unique cast which is endlessly displaced throughout all series' (LS 59).

153. Deleuze will express this by saying that the movement between 'A and B and B and A' in a reciprocal synthesis represents 'the progressive tour or description of the whole of a problematic field' (210/272/262). Reciprocal synthesis is tied to the state of the entire problematic field.

154. Peter Hallward has provided a very readable and introductory account of the differential relation in *Out of This World*, p. 171n5.
155. Deleuze's description of this in his Leibniz seminar (22 Apr. 1980) is particularly clear: '[W]e will say that dx or dy is the infinitely small quantity assumed to be added or subtracted from x or from y. Now there is an invention! The infinitely small quantity . . . that is, it's the smallest variation of the quantity considered. It is unassignable by convention. Thus $dx = 0$ in [relation to] x [because it] is the smallest quantity by which x can vary, so it equals zero. [For the same reason] $dy = 0$ in relation to y. The notion of evanescent difference is beginning to take shape. It's a variation or a difference, dx or dy; it is smaller than any given or givable quantity. It's a mathematical symbol. In a sense, it's crazy, in a sense it's operational. For what? Here is what is formidable in the symbolism of differential calculus: $dx = 0$ in relation to x, the smallest difference, the smallest increase of which the quantity x or the unassignable quantity y might be capable, it's infinitely small. The miracle [is that] dy/dx is not equal to zero, and furthermore: dy/dx has a perfectly expressible finite quantity. These are relative, uniquely relative. dx is nothing in relation to y, dy is nothing in relation to y, but then dy/dx is something. A stupefying, admirable, and great mathematical discovery.' Dan Smith gives a particularly clear description of these ideas in his essay 'Axiomatics'. For a much more technical version, see chapter two of Simon Duffy's *The Logic of Expression*.
156. See Manuel DeLanda's description of this process in *Intensive Science*: 'The importance of groups of transformations is that they can be used to classify geometric figures by their *invariants* [. . .]' (17; original emphasis).
157. See §87 of *Experience and Judgment*. For a clear description of this process with particular resonance for Deleuze's interpretation, see Lyotard's *Phenomenology*, pp. 37–42.
158. See also (187/242/235).
159. Cf. 'Complete determination must not be confused with reciprocal determination. The latter concerned the differential relations and their degrees or varieties [. . .]. The former concerns the values of a relation – in other words, the composition of a form or the distribution of singular points which characterize it [i.e. the form]' (175/227–8/223).
160. The English translation reads, the 'object as it exists in the Idea' (169/220/215). See also DI 100.
161. Deleuze claims inspiration on this point from Maïmon: 'A particular object is the result of the particular rule of its production or the mode of its differential [. . .]' (174/225–6/221), but often reformulates it in his own way: '[D]ifferentials certainly do not correspond to any engendered quantity, but rather constitute an unconditioned rule for the production of knowledge of quantity' (175/227/222).

162. See *Out of This World*, p. 19 and *Absolutely Postcolonial*, p. 12.
163. John Protevi is one of the few to try to take this claim into the details. In his review of Hallward's *Out of This World*, Protevi writes, 'If an Idea is a set of differential relations, that is, linked rates of change, then the Idea of color is the linkage of rates of change of electromagnetic vibrations, and colors are actualized by eyes/brains/bodies which express certain of those relations.'
164. At one point Deleuze says that differenciation is 'at once composition and qualification, organization and specification' (214/ 277/266; translation modified).
165. This is an aspect that I have underplayed for reasons of length. The time of progressive determination also determines a time of actualization and the duration of the object. 'By virtue of its progressivity, every structure has a purely logical, ideal, or dialectical time. However, this virtual time itself determines a time of differenciation, or rather rhythms or different times of actualisation which correspond to the relations and singularities of the structure and, for their part, measure the passage from virtual to actual' (210–11/272/262). Deleuze calls this time of actualization the 'differential rhythm'.
166. Deleuze develops this relation between schemata and spatiotemporal dynamism in his fourth lecture on Kant (4 Apr. 1978).
167. At several points Deleuze describes actualization as 'organization in intuition' (247/318/308; cf. 231/298/290).

Section 6. The Asymmetrical Synthesis

168. Klossowski, 'Nietzsche, Polytheism, and Parody', p. 108.
169. Deleuze never says what these asymmetrical elements are, but it is clear from chapter two that they are the discontinuous instants of a fragmented materiality.
170. Kant seminar (21 Mar. 1978).
171. But we also do not want to jump to the conclusion that Deleuze is taking up the Kantian notion of intensity because Deleuze inverts the relation between intensity and the real. In Kant quality was a degree of intensity which was produced in relation to the empty form of time as intensity = 0. But in Deleuze quality is produced not through the production of intensity or the movement from 0 to 1, but through its cancellation. Cf. Deleuze's Kant seminar (21 Mar. 1978).
172. Cf. DI 89.
173. See CPR A19/B33.
174. The English translation is slightly misleading on this point insofar as it suggests that these systems are 'constituted by (*affectés par*) the eternal return' (116/153/142). To say that these systems are constituted by the eternal return implies that they come after the eternal return and are produced by it. Deleuze does not say that these systems are *constituted* by the eternal return, he only

says they are *affected* by it. It is something that happens to these systems.

175. Deleuze describes the *constitution* of intensity in much greater detail in *Anti-Oedipus* (cf. AO 19–21). 'Where do these pure intensities come from? They come from the two preceding forces, repulsion and attraction, and from the opposition of these two forces. [. . .] In a word, the opposition of the forces of attraction and repulsion produces an open series of intensive elements, all of them positive, that are never an expression of the final equilibrium of a system, but consist, rather, of an unlimited number of stationary, metastable states through which a subject passes' (AO 19). Intensity *comes from* 'the two preceding forces of repulsion and attraction'. These two forces refer to the first two passive syntheses. In the fatigue of habit the first synthesis repels 'partial objects' or discontinuous matter. In the second synthesis memory 'attracts' or 'records' partial objects. The third synthesis measures repulsion against attraction and derives intensity, which expresses the quantity of affection, or the degree to which the subject is affected by matter.

176. 'We call this state of infinitely doubled difference which resonates to infinity *disparity*' (222/287/281; original emphasis).

177. See (235/303/294).

178. The opening chapters of *Cinema 1* develop this Hegelian theme most directly. There, 'movement-images', or the discontinuous material instants, are defined by the relative relations between them. These relations ultimately relate to a 'whole', but consciousness must attain this whole through the progressive synthesis of relations. It reaches the whole only after the failure of the third synthesis (or the 'crisis in the action-image') has given rise to a new consciousness: the 'time-image'. Here consciousness realizes that the relations between movement-images were actually temporal relations all along. This theme of the gradual extraction of essence also plays a fundamental role in *Proust and Signs*, where the apprentice fails to find truth in either the worldly signs ('objectivism') or within himself ('subjectivism'). He finally discovers the signs of art, or essence which were already there from the beginning, but only in an impure state. The apprenticeship is the gradual uncovering of essence which was there from the start.

179. Kant seminar (21 Mar. 1978).

180. See also (82/112/104).

181. Merleau-Ponty also argued that 'More directly than the other dimensions of space, depth forces us to reject the preconceived notion of the world and rediscover the primordial experience from which it springs' (PP 298).

182. Deleuze further emphasizes this point immediately following his remarks on the syntheses when he writes this:

We know that sensation or perception has an ontological aspect: precisely the syntheses which are peculiar to it, confronted by that which can only be sensed or that which can only be perceived. Now it appears that depth is essentially *implicated* in the perception of extensity. (230/296/289; original emphasis)

In his lectures on Kant, Deleuze consistently describes the three syntheses as Kant's theory of perception. It seems that in this context, 'perception' again means the aggregate of three passive syntheses. This aggregate has an 'ontological' aspect. This aspect is the one we have already encountered: the syntheses as free, passive and sub-representative. But there is a second aspect to perception in which it is no longer ontological, but epiphenomenal: the perception of quality and extensity. It is this second aspect that defines the 'pure spatial syntheses'.

183. Cf. 'with actualization a new type of specific and partitive distinction takes the place of the fluent ideal distinction' (206–7/267/258).
184. Deleuze consistently says that whereas Ideas are pre-individual, intensities, while they may anticipate the self and the I, are still individual (258/332/321).
185. Cf. 'However, the self in the form of a passive self is only an event which takes place in pre-existing fields of individuation: it contemplates and contracts the individuating factors of such fields, and constitutes itself at the points of resonance of their series' (276/354/346).
186. Deleuze calls it a 'larval' subject in order to oppose it to 'a substantial, completed, and well-constituted subject such as the Cartesian Cogito' (118/156/145).
187. Deleuze will call this segmentation of intensity into extensive parts 'territorialization' in *Anti-Oedipus*. This expression is easily traced back to *Difference and Repetition*. In *Difference and Repetition*, Deleuze suggests that 'good sense' might have its foundation in 'the agrarian question': 'A distribution of this type proceeds by fixed and proportional determinations which may be assimilated to "properties" or limited territories within representation. The agrarian question may well have been very important for this organization of judgment as the faculty which distinguishes parts [. . .]' (36/54/45).

4: RECEPTION AND INFLUENCE

1. See John Marks's *Vitalism and Multiplicity* for a detailed account of the relationship between Deleuze and Foucault.
2. Whereas Deleuze' presence is undetectable in Blanchot's earlier works, he is clearly visible already in *The Infinite Conversation* (1969) (pp. 162, 214 and 274), and more clearly in *The Step Not Beyond* (1973) (see pp. 16, 42–3). Of course, the real influence goes in the other direction, from Blanchot to Deleuze.
3. See chapter five of Eleanor Kaufman's *The Delirium of Praise*.
4. Lyotard develops in his own way the notion of intensity in *Libidinal Economy*. For an interesting comparison of Lyotard and Deleuze

from the point of view of the event, see Lisa Otty's 'Avant-garde Aesthetics: Kitsch, Intensity and the Work of Art'.

5. Deleuze's work clearly altered the way in which Lacan thought about sadism and masochism, and Lacan frequently referred to *Coldness and Cruelty* with great praise, at one point describing it as counterweight to 'trembling imbecility that reigns in the field of psychoanalysis'. See Seminar XVI (22 Jan. 1969) p. 217.

6. See Dan Smith's review 'The Inverse Side of the Structure'.

7. For example, Lacan wrote, 'It happens, for example, that a Mr. Gilles Deleuze, continuing his work, has brought out his theses in the form of two monumental (*capitaux*) books, the first of which interests us greatly. I think that from its title alone, *Difference and Repetition*, you can see that it must have some relation to my discourse, and of course he would be the first to know that' (Seminar XVI (12 Mar. 1969) p. 367). Lacan notes that he is mentioned several times in both *Difference and Repetition* and *The Logic of Sense*, and that of the multiple times that he is 'invoked' only on one point does Deleuze break away from Lacan's teaching (LS 360n5). Lacan asks Jacques Nassif to explain what exactly Deleuze thought was flawed. Predictably and understandably Nassif's commentary, after many apologies, ends up siding with Lacan. Deleuze is not mentioned again in Lacan's seminars.

8. Eleanor Kaufman has described this new genera of the 'laudatory essay' in great detail in *The Delirium of Praise*.

9. The image painted of Deleuze by those working in what was once called 'theory' has received a lot of negative criticism. But it was not all bad. Claire Colebrook, Ian Buchanan and Jean-Jacques Lecercle are only three of the several important exceptions to this.

10. See Todd May, 'The Ontology and Politics of Gilles Deleuze'.

11. Gary Gutting gives a fair appraisal of Bricmont and Sokal in his introduction to *Continental Science and Philosophy*. See esp. p. 15.

12. See Alan and Bricmont, *Fashionable Nonsense*, pp. 9–10.

13. DeLanda, *Intensive Science and Virtual Philosophy*, p. 110.

14. Bryant's *Difference and Giveness* is an extended study of the doctrine of the faculties, which concludes with an excellent chapter on the Other-structure.

15. See Juliette Simont', Simon Duffy, Iain Hamilton Grant and Alberto Toscano.

16. Badiou, *Deleuze*, p. 17.

17. See Badiou, *Deleuze*, chapter four.

18. Badiou, *Theoretical Writings*, p. 68.

19. Peter Hallward, *Out of this World*, pp. 43–4.

20. See Michael Hardt and Antonio Negri, *Empire*, pp. 206.

21. See Paul Patton, *Deleuze and the Political*.

22. Buchanan, *Deleuze and Guattari's* Anti-Oedipus, p. 139; my emphasis.

BIBLIOGRAPHY

Ansell-Pearson. *Germinal Life: The Difference and Repetition of Deleuze*. New York: Routledge, 1999.

Badiou, Alain. *Being and Event*. Trans. Oliver Feltham. New York: Continuum, 2006.

—. *Deleuze: The Clamor of Being*. Trans. Louise Burchill. Minneapolis, MN: University of Minnesota Press, 1999.

—. *Theoretical Writings*. Trans. and ed. Ray Brassier and Alberto Toscano. New York: Continuum, 2004.

Bataille, Georges. *Visions of Excess: Selected Writings, 1927–1939*. Trans. Allan Stoekl. Minneapolis, MN: University of Minnesota Press, 1985.

Baugh, Bruce. *French Hegel: From Surrealism to Postmodernism*. New York: Routledge, 2003.

Beistegui, Miguel de. *Truth and Genesis*. Bloomington, IN: Indiana University Press, 2004.

Bell, Jeffery A. *Philosophy at the Edge of Chaos: Gilles Deleuze and the Philosophy of Difference*. Toronto: University of Toronto Press, 2006.

—. *The Problem of Difference: Phenomenology and Poststructuralism*. Toronto: University of Toronto Press, 1998.

Bergson, Henri. *Creative Evolution*. Trans. Arthur Mitchell. Mineola, NY: Dover Publications, 1998.

—. *Matter and Memory*. Trans. N. M. Paul and W. S. Palmer. New York: Zone Books, 1991.

Blanchot, Maurice. *The Book to Come*. Trans. Charlotte Mandell. Stanford, CA: Stanford University Press, 2003.

—. *Friendship*. Trans. Elizabeth Rottenberg. Stanford, CA: Stanford University Press.

—. *The Infinite Conversation*. Trans. Susan Hanson. Minneapolis, MN: University of Minnesota Press, 1993.

—. *The Space of Literature*. Trans. Ann Smock. Lincoln, NE: University of Nebraska Press, 1982.

—. *The Step Not Beyond*. Trans. Lycette Nelson. Albany, NY: SUNY Press, 1992.

Bogue, Ronald. 'The Betrayal of God'. In *Deleuze and Religion*. Ed. Mary Bryden. London: Routledge, 2001.

Bryant, Levi. *Difference and Giveness: Deleuze's Transcendental Empiricism and the Ontology of Immanence*. Evanston, IL: Northwestern University Press, 2008.

Buchanan, Ian. *Deleuze and Guattari's* Anti-Oedipus*: A Reader's Guide*. London: Continuum, 2008.

—. *Deleuzism: A Metacommentary*. Edinburgh: Edinburgh University Press, 2000.

Caputo, John. *Radical Hermeneutics: Repetition, Deconstruction, and the Hermeneutic Project*. Bloomington, IN: Indiana University Press, 1987.

Colebrook, Claire. *Gilles Deleuze*. New York: Routledge, 2002.

—. *Philosophy and Post-Structuralist Theory: From Kant to Deleuze*. Edinburgh: Edinburgh University Press, 2005.

DeLanda, Manuel. *Intensive Science and Virtual Philosophy*. London: Continuum, 2002.

Deleuze, Gilles. *Bergsonism*. Trans. Hugh Tomlinson and Barbara Habberjam. New York: Zone Books, 1991. (*Le Bergsonisme*. Paris: PUF, 1966).

—. *Cinema 1: The Movement-Image*. Trans. Hugh Tomlinson and Barbara Habberjam. Minneapolis, MN: University of Minnesota Press, 1986 [1983].

—. *Cinema 2: The Time-Image*. Trans. Hugh Tomlinson and Robert Galeta. Minneapolis, MN: University of Minnesota Press, 1989 [1985].

—. *Desert Islands and Other Texts 1953–1974*. Trans. Michael Taormina. Ed. David Lapoujade. New York: Semiotext(e), 2004 [2002].

—. *Difference and Repetition*. Trans. Paul Patton. New York: Columbia University Press, 1994. (*Différence et repetition*. Paris: PUF, 2003) [1968].

—. *Empiricism and Subjectivity: An Essay on Hume's Theory of Human Nature*. Tans. Constantin Boundas. New York: Columbia University Press, 1991 [1953].

—. *Essays Critical and Clinical*. Trans. Daniel W. Smith and Michael A. Greco. London: Verso, 1998 [1993].

—. *Expressionism in Philosophy: Spinoza*. Trans. Martin Joughin. New York: Zone Books, 1990 [1968].

—. *The Fold: Leibniz and the Baroque*. Trans. Tom Conley. Minneapolis, MN: University of Minnesota Press, 1993 [1988].

—. *Foucault*. Trans. Seán Hand. Minneapolis, MN: University of Minnesota Press, 2000 [1986].

—. *Kant's Critical Philosophy: The Doctrine of the Faculties*. Trans. Hugh Tomlinson and Barbara Habberjam. Minneapolis, MN: University of Minnesota Press, 1984 [1963].

—. *The Logic of Sense*. Trans. Mark Lester with Charles Stivale. Ed. Constantin V. Boundas. New York: Columbia University Press, 1990 [1969].

—. *Masochism: Coldness and Cruelty*. Tans. Jean McNeil. New York: Zone Books, 1991 [1967].

—. *Nietzsche and Philosophy*. Trans. Hugh Tomlinson. New York: Columbia University Press, 1986 [1962].

—. 'Pericles and Verdi: The Philosophy of François Châtelet'. In *Dialogues II*. Trans. Joe Hughes. New York: Columbia University Press, 2007.

Deleuze, Gilles. *Proust and Signs*. Trans. Richard Howard. Minneapolis, MN: University of Minnesota Press, 2000 [1964].
—. *Seminars*. www.webdeleuze.com/php/sommaire.html [last accessed on 10 Sept. 2008].
Descartes, René. *Mediations*. In *Selected Philosophical Writings*. Trans. John Cottingham and Robert Stoothoff. New York: Cambridge University Press, 1988.
—. *Objections and Replies*. In *Selected Philosophical Writings*. Trans. John Cottingham and Robert Stoothoff. New York: Cambridge University Press, 1988.
—. *Principles of Philosophy*. In *Selected Philosophical Writings*. Trans. John Cottingham and Robert Stoothoff. New York: Cambridge University Press, 1988.
Duffy, Simon. *The Logic of Expression: Quality, Quantity and Intensity in Spinoza, Hegel and Deleuze*. Burlington, VT: Ashgate, 2006.
During, Elie. ' "A History of Problems": Bergson and the French Epistemological Tradition'. *Journal of the British Society for Phenomenology* 35.1(2004).
Fink, Eugen. 'The Phenomenological Philosophy of Edmund Husserl and Contemporary Criticism'. In *The Phenomenology of Husserl: Selected Critical Readings*. Trans. R. O. Elveton. Ed. R. O. Elveton. Chicago: Quadrangle Books, 1970.
Foucault, Michel. 'Theatrum Philosophicum'. Trans. Donald F. Bouchard and Sherry Simon. *Language, Counter-Memory, Practice: Selected Essays and Interviews*. Ed. Donald F. Bouchard. Ithaca, NY: Cornell University Press, 1977.
Frege, G. *The Frege Reader*. Ed. Michael Beaney. Malden, MA: Blackwell Publishing, 1997.
Genette, Gérard. *Narrative Discourse: An Essay in Method*. Trans. Jane E. Lewin. Ithaca, NY: Cornell University Press, 1980.
Gill, Mary Louise. 'Individuals and Individuation in Aristotle'. In *Unity, Identity, and Explanation in Aristotle's Metaphysics*. Ed. Scaltsas et al. New York: Oxford University Press, 2001.
Grant, Iain Hamilton. *Philosophies of Nature After Schelling*. London: Continuum, 2006.
—. ' "Philosophy Become Genetic:" The Physics of the World Soul'. In *The New Schelling*. Ed. Judith Norman and Alistair Welchman. New York: Continuum, 2004.
Gutting, Gary. 'Introduction'. *The Continental Philosophy of Science*. Oxford: Blackwell Publishing, 2005.
Hallward, Peter. *Absolutely Postcolonial: Writing between the Singular and the Specific*. New York: Palgrave, 2001.
—. *Out of this World: Deleuze and the Philosophy of Creation*. New York: Verso, 2006.
Hansen, Mark. 'Becoming as Creative Involution?: Contextualizing Deleuze and Guattari's Biophilosophy'. *Postmodern Culture* 11.1 (2000).

Hardt, Michael and Antonio Negri. *Empire*. Cambridge, MA: Harvard University Press, 2000.

Hegel. G. W. F. *Hegel's Science of Logic*. Trans. A. V. Miller. New York: Humanity Books, 1969.

Heidegger, Martin. *Being and Time*. Trans. Joan Stambaugh. Albany, NY: SUNY Press, 1996.

—. *History of the Concept of Time: Prolegomena*. Trans. Theodore Kisiel. Bloomington, IN: Indiana University Press, 1985.

—. *Kant and the Problem of Metaphysics*. Trans. Richard Taft. Bloomington, IN: Indiana University Press, 1997.

—. *Phenomenological Interpretation of Kant's* Critique of Pure Reason. Trans. Parvis Emad and Kenneth Maly. Bloomington, IN: Indiana University Press, 1997.

—. *What is Called Thinking?* Trans. J. Glenn Gray and Fred Wieck. New York: Perennial, 2004.

Hölderlin, Friedrich. *Essays and Letters on Theory*. Trans. Thomas Pfau. Albany, NY: SUNY Press, 1988.

Husserl, Edmund. *Analyses Concerning Passive and Active Syntheses: Lectures on Transcendental Logic*. Trans. Anthony Steinbock. Dordrecht: Kluwer Academic Publishers, 2001.

—. *Cartesian Meditations: An Introduction to Phenomenology*. Trans. Dorion Cairns. The Hague: Martinus Nijhoff, 1977.

—. *Experience and Judgment: Investigations in a Genealogy of Logic*. Ed. Ludwig Landgrebe. Trans. James E. Churchill and Karl Ameriks. Evanston, IL: Northwestern University Press, 1973.

—. *The Idea of Phenomenology*. Trans. William P. Alston and George Nakhnikian. The Hague: Martinus Nijhoff, 1964.

—. *Ideas I*. Trans. F. Kersten. Dordrecht: Kluwer Academic Publishers, 1998.

Hyppolite, Jean. *Genesis and Structure of Hegel's Phenomenology of Spirit*. Trans. Samuel Cherniak and John Heckman. Evanston, IL: Northwestern University Press, 1974.

—. *Logic and Existence*. Trans. Leonard Lawlor and Amit Sen. Albany, NY: SUNY Press, 1997.

Joyce, James. *Ulysses*. New York: Oxford University Press, 1998.

Kant, Immanuel. *Critique of Pure Reason*. Trans. Guyer and Wood. New York: Cambridge University Press, 1998.

—. *Prolegomena to Any Future Metaphysics*. Trans. Peter G. Lucas and Günter Zöller. Oxford: Oxford University Press, 2004.

Kaufman, Eleanor. *The Delirium of Praise: Bataille, Blanchot, Deleuze, Foucault, Klossowski*. Baltimore, MD: Johns Hopkins University Press, 2001.

Kierkegaard, Soren. *Fear and Trembling and Repetition*. Trans. Howard V. Hong and Edna H. Hong. Princeton, NJ: Princeton University Press, 1983.

Klossowski, Pierre. *Nietzsche and the Vicious Circle*. Trans. Daniel W. Smith. London: Continuum, 2005.

Klossowski, Pierre. 'Nietzsche, Polytheism, and Parody'. In *Such a Deathly Desire*. Trans. Russell Ford. Albany, NY: SUNY Press, 2007.

Lacan, Jacques. *Séminaires de Lacan*. http://gaogoa.free.fr/ SeminaireS.htm [last accessed on 10 Sept. 2008].

Lawlor, Leonard. *Thinking through French Philosophy: The Being of the Question*. Bloomington, IN: Indiana University Press, 2003.

Lecercle, J. J. *Deleuze and Language*. Basingstoke: Palgrave Macmillan, 2002.

Leibniz, Gottfried Wilhelm. *Discourse on Metaphysics*. In *Philosophical Papers and Letters*. Trans. and ed. Leroy E. Loemker. Dordrecht, Holland: D. Reidel Publishing Company, 1969.

—. *New Essays Concerning Human Understanding*. Trans. Peter Remnant and Jonathan Bennett. New York: Cambridge University Press, 1996.

—. *Philosophical Papers and Letters*. Trans. and ed. Leroy E. Loemker. Dordrecht, Holland: D. Reidel Publishing Company, 1969.

—. *Philosophical Writings*. Trans. Mary Morris and G. H. R. Parkinson. London: Everyman, 1995.

—. *Principles of Nature and Grace*. In *Philosophical Writings*. Trans. Mary Morris and G. H. R. Parkinson. London: Everyman, 1995.

Levinas, Emmanuel. *The Theory of Intuition in Husserl's Phenomenology*. Trans. André Orianne. Evanston, IL: Northwestern University Press, 1995.

Longuenesse, Béatrice. *Kant and the Capacity to Judge: Sensibility and Discursivity in the Transcendental Analytic of the Critique of Pure Reason*. Trans. Charles T. Wolff. Princeton, NJ: Princeton University Press, 1998.

Lyotard, Jean François. *Libidinal Economy*. Trans. Iain Hamilton Grant. Bloomington, IN: Indiana University Press, 1993.

—. *Phenomenology*. Trans. Brian Beakley. Albany, NY: SUNY Press, 1991.

Makkreel, Rudolph A. *Imagination and Interpretation in Kant: The Hermeneutic Import of the Critique of Judgment*. Chicago, IL: University of Chicago Press, 1990.

Malabou, Catherine. 'Who's Afraid of Hegelian Wolves?' In *Deleuze: A Critical Reader*. Ed. Paul Patton. Oxford: Blackwell Publishing, 1996.

Marks, John. *Gilles Deleuze: Vitalism and Multiplicity*. London: Pluto Press, 1998.

Marrati, Paola. 'Against the Doxa: Politics of Immanence and Becoming-Minoritarian'. In *Micropolitics of Media Culture: Reading the Rhizomes of Deleuze and Guattari*. Ed. Patricia Pisters. Amsterdam: Amsterdam University Press, 2001.

May, Todd. *Between Genealogy and Epistemology: Psychology, Politics, and Knowledge in the Thought of Michel Foucault*. University Park, PA: Pennsylvania State University Press, 1993.

—. 'The Ontology and Politics of Gilles Deleuze' *Theory and Event* 5.3 (2001).

Merleau-Ponty, Maurice. 'Everywhere and Nowhere'. In *Signs*. Trans. Richard McCleary. Evanston, IL: Northwestern University Press, 1964.

—. *Phenomenology of Perception*. Trans. Colin Smith. London: Routledge, 2005.

—. *The Structure of Behavior*. Trans. Alden L. Fisher. Pittsburgh, PA: Duquesne University Press, 2006.

Nietzsche, Friedrich. *Thus Spoke Zarathustra*. Trans. R. J. Hollingdale. New York: Penguin Books, 1969.

—. *Twilight of the Idols and the Anti-Christ*. Trans. R. J. Hollingdale. New York: Penguin, 1990.

Otty, Lisa. 'Avant-garde Aesthetics: Kitsch, Intensity and the Work of Art'. *Litteraria Pragensia* 16.32 (2006), 36–58.

Patton, Paul. *Deleuze and the Political*. New York: Routledge, 2000.

Pisters, Patricia. *The Matrix of Visual Culture: Working with Deleuze in Film Theory*. Stanford, CA: Stanford University Press, 2003.

Porphyry. *Introduction*. Trans. Jonathan Barnes. Oxford: Oxford University Press, 2003.

Poulet, Georges. 'Maurice Blanchot as Novelist'. *Yale French Studies*, No. 8, What's Novel in the Novel (1951), 77–81.

Protevi, John. Hallward Review.

Ricoeur, Paul. *Freud and Philosophy: An Essay on Interpretation*. Trans. Denis Savage. New Haven, CT: Yale University Press, 1970.

—. *Husserl: An Analysis of His Phenomenology*. Trans. Edward G. Ballard and Lester E. Embree. Evanston, IL: Northwestern University Press, 1967.

—. *A Key to Edmund Husserl's Ideas I*. Trans. Bond Harris and J. B. Spurlock. Milwaukee, WI: Marquette University Press, 1996.

Sartre, Jean-Paul. *The Transcendence of the Ego: An Existentialist Theory of Consciousness*. Trans. Forrest Williams and Robert Kirkpatrick. New York: Hill and Wang, 1960.

Simont, Juliette. *Essai sur la quantité, la qualité, la relation chez Kant, Hegel, Deleuze: Les 'fleurs noires' de la logique philosophique*. Paris, L'Harmattan, 1997.

Smith, Daniel W. 'Axiomatics and Problematics as Two Modes of Formalization: Deleuze's Epistemology of Mathematics'. *Virtual Mathematics*. Ed. Simon Duffy. Manchester: Clinamen Press, 2006.

—. 'Deleuze, Kant, and the Theory of Immanent Ideas'. *Deleuze and Philosophy*. Ed. Constantin V. Boundas. Edinburgh: Edinburgh University Press, 2006.

—. 'Deleuze on Leibniz: Difference, Continuity, and the Calculus'. In *Current Continental Theory and Modern Philosophy*. Ed. Stephen H. Daniel. Evanston, IL: Northwestern University Press, 2005.

—. 'Deleuze's Theory of Sensation: Overcoming the Kantian Duality'. In *Deleuze: A Critical Reader*. Ed. Paul Patton. Oxford: Blackwell Publishing, 1996.

——. 'The Doctrine of Univocity: Deleuze's Ontology of Immanence'. In *Deleuze and Religion*. Ed. Mary Bryden. London: Routledge, 2001.

——. 'The Inverse Side of the Structure: Žižek on Deleuze on Lacan'. *Criticism* 46.4 (2004), 635–650.

——. 'Knowledge of Pure Events: A Note on Deleuze's Analytic of Concepts'. *Ereignis auf Französisch: von Bergson bis Deleuze*. Ed. Marc Rölli. Munich: Wilhelm Fink Verlag, 2004.

Sokal, Alan and Jean Bricmont. *Fashionable Nonsense: Postmodern Intellectuals' Abuse of Science*. New York: Picador, 1998.

Toscano, Alberto. 'Philosophy and the Experience of Construction'. In *The New Schelling*. Ed. Judith Norman and Alistair Welchman. New York: Continuum, 2004.

——. *The Theatre of Production: Philosophy and Individuation between Kant and Deleuze*. New York: Palgrave Macmillan, 2006.

Wahl, Jean. 'Notes on Some Empiricist Aspects in the Thought of Husserl'. In *Apriori and World: European Contributions to Husserlian Phenomenology*. The Hague: Martinus Nijhoff, 1981.

Welton, Donn. *The Origins of Meaning: A Critical Study of the Thresholds of Husserlian Phenomenology*. The Hague: Martinus Nijhoff, 1983.

INDEX

Made in the USA
San Bernardino, CA
11 March 2013